Literature in Translation

TRANSLATION STUDIES
BRIAN J. BAER, EDITOR
Albrecht Neubert, Gert Jäger, and Gregory M. Shreve, Founding Editors

Literature in Translation

Teaching Issues and Reading Practices

———

Edited by
CAROL MAIER
and
FRANÇOISE MASSARDIER-KENNEY

———

The Kent State University Press
KENT, OHIO

To Greg Shreve, for his unwavering support of so many
in translation studies.

© 2010 by The Kent State University Press, Kent, Ohio 44242
All rights reserved
Library of Congress Catalog Card Number 2010023663
ISBN 978-1-60635-108-6 (paper)
Manufactured in the United States of America

Library of Congress Cataloging-in-Publication Data
Literature in translation : teaching issues and reading practices / edited by Carol Maier
and Françoise Massardier-Kenney.
    p.   cm. — (Translation studies; 8)
Includes bibliographical references and index.
ISBN 978-1-60635-049-2 (alk. paper) ∞
1. Translating and interpreting. 2. Literature—Study and teaching. I. Maier, Carol, 1943–
II. Massardier-Kenney, Françoise.
P306.2.L59 2010
418'.02—dc22   2010023663

British Library Cataloging-in-Publication data are available.

14 13 12 11 10   5 4 3 2 1

Contents

POWER STRUGGLES

BELIEFS AND VALUES

Acknowledgments

A truly collaborative endeavor, *Literature in Translation* has benefited from numerous contributions during its conceptualization and preparation. We are grateful to several anonymous readers whose helpful comments and suggestions we considered carefully and heeded to the best of our ability. We also want to express our gratitude to Brent Winter for his meticulous copyediting. In addition, we want to offer our thanks to the chapter authors, not only for their essays but also for their continued support of our project; to Julianna Watson and Marlène Nativelle, for their work with formatting; and to the MFA students in the first Reading in Translation class, for their enthusiastic response to our pedagogical experiments with the translation-related issues and reading practices discussed in this volume.

Finally, we acknowledge a particular debt of gratitude to Susan C. Brantly for her help with the last revisions of the essay by Niels Ingwerson, of whose passing we learned as our manuscript was nearing completion. Although we never had the opportunity to meet Niels in person, we came to know and admire him through our many exchanges.

Introduction

Carol Maier and Françoise Massardier-Kenney

The last several decades have seen college and university students across the United States reading a wide variety of literary works from around the world, as literature in English translation has made its way onto the reading lists of courses in such disciplines and interdisciplines as anthropology, creative writing, ethnic studies, gender studies, philosophy, world literature, and sociology. On the one hand, this is cause for rejoicing. Students in this mostly monolingual society, which often forgets its own plurilingual origins and development, are still not learning foreign languages in sufficient numbers; but through translation, they are at least becoming acquainted with the multilingual world in which they live and in which they will work. Moreover, many world literature courses have expanded their reach. Starting from a conception of world literature as the teaching of "great books" culled from the literary canon of Europe and America, world literature is slowly becoming what David Damrosch has referred to as "a mode of reading" (281) that will allow students to engage with worlds that are beyond their own time and place. This expansion, which enables readers to become aware of other cultures and to connect them with their own, cannot but lead to an appreciation of "linguistic diversity and alterity" (Pizer 7).

However, the positive impact of reading books from other countries is not always maximized, because literature in English translation is often taught as if it had been originally written in English. This means that students may not be familiarized with the context in which that literature was produced and thus not made aware of the cultural, linguistic, and literary effects that translation involves. Although students may read foreign works, they submit them to their own cultural norms. If, as Roland Greene has suggested, we must "learn 'to live with translation strategically,'" it is crucial that instructors and students understand both the context of the original work and the principal issues of literary translation (Feal 5). Without such an understanding, students read translated material, but they do not read *in* translation, and the benefits of intercultural communication may be jeopardized. It is not enough for books from other languages and countries to be available in translation; the positive contact that literature in translation can offer must be fully exploited if readers are not, in the words of William Deresiewicz, to impose their own image on the world (23).

Here a true challenge arises for an instructor. All too frequently, books in translation contain no introductory information about the mediation that translation invariably implies or about the stakes involved in the transfer of another culture into English. Nor can one count on finding suggestions for further reading about the author or the culture of the source text. Instructors are often left on their own; lacking the appropriate pedagogical tools, they may find themselves unable to provide information about either the original work or about translation itself. They may also feel uneasy about teaching material for which they lack adequate preparation; in fact, they may believe that it is neither professional nor ethical to do so (see Arrojo, Rose, and Maier). Consequently, they may restrict themselves to teaching well-known works in translation with which they are already familiar, or work originally written in English, when available (as in the case of literature from Africa or India).

The purpose of *Literature in Translation: Teaching Issues and Reading Practices* is to address this pedagogical lack, which is seldom addressed in discussions about comparative literature, world literature, or translation pedagogy. The isolated treatments of this subject that do exist are found in collections of essays (Dingwaney and Maier; Venuti, "Teaching in Translation"; White), journals (Maier, "Teaching Monolingual Students"), book chapters (Venuti, "The Pedagogy of Translation"), or essays about teaching specific works (Maier, "Teaching the Literature"). In addition, most current instruction-related research in the area of translation is devoted to translator training. (See, for example, Sonia Colina's *Translation Teaching: From Research to the Classroom*). Our volume is not intended for instructors who train translators but for both undergraduate and graduate instructors across the curriculum who use in their classrooms literary material that has been translated into English. It is our hope that this collection of essays will provide a substantial introduction to the varied and complex issues involved in reading and teaching a work in translation. We have chosen contributors who reflect the wide range of scholars, practicing translators, and translation theorists currently working in the field; all of them are actively engaged in translation and have experience teaching literature in translation. They were asked to draw upon examples of both well-known works currently taught in English translations and works that, although available in translation, are rarely taught in American classrooms. In addition, contributors were each assigned a particular topic and were asked to assist instructors in reading and presenting translations *as* translations by providing them with background information, sources, and practical suggestions (methodology).

The chapters in part 1, "General Principles," introduce general guiding principles for instructors who teach texts in translation and should be considered as a whole. In "Choosing and Introducing a Translation," Carol Maier offers recommendations for assessing translations and selecting a version or versions that can be used confidently in the classroom. She also suggests resources that teachers and students can use to evaluate translations. Her discussion is followed by Françoise Massardier-Kenney's discussion of the four hierarchical relations that have shaped discussions of translation throughout history. As Massardier-Kenney explains, readers of translations do not have to be well-versed in translation scholarship to be informed readers; but their responses to translations are enhanced if they are familiar with the major theoretical issues that inform the production and evaluation of literary translations. She refers to select essays that are written in a way that makes them accessible to both instructors and students.

The two opening chapters are followed by Isabel Garayta's "'Toto, I've a Feeling We Aren't in Kansas Anymore': Reading and Presenting Texts in Translation from 'Familiar' Cultures." One of the major issues in teaching texts in translation is presenting the cultural, historical, and literary conditions that give a work a specific place in the literary landscape of the country in which it originates. Reading in translation without having an awareness of those foreign conditions can give rise to the rejection of a work or to the misleading assumption that one has understood it fully. This chapter outlines specific strategies for identifying and presenting unfamiliar contexts of cultures with which American readers may assume they are familiar. Yunte Huang's essay deals with the same issues as those Garayta addresses, but within the context of more distant cultures and the specific problems they may present to a student. Huang focuses on Chinese concepts of self, time, and the relation of subject to object that differ considerably from their counterparts in Western culture. Like the preceding chapter, this one offers strategies and suggestions for research and teaching. It includes a bibliography of resources for analyzing major linguistic and cultural differences between pertinent language pairs.

Another informative way to explore the act of translation is to look at translators themselves, both living translators and fictional representations. In this context, Rosemary Arrojo turns to works of fiction ranging from Borges's "Pierre Menard, Author of the *Quixote*" to the recent novels of Brazilian author Moacyr Scliar in the mid-1990s and Portuguese author José Saramago. She examines the subversive nature of translation and its undermining of traditional beliefs in the stability of meaning, in order to explore the role of the translator as it relates to some of the key issues of translation theory and practice. In particular, she endeavors to make more explicit the apprehension and distrust that translation often seems to trigger. By using such texts in the classroom, instructors can prompt students to consider and discuss translation from a critical perspective and encourage them to reflect on the relation between originals and their interpretations, and between authors and interpreters. Sergio Waisman, on the other hand, is a living translator who works from his personal experience as a translator from Spanish to discuss the presence of the translator in the text. Showing readers how they can detect such a presence, Waisman discusses the mediation of the translator and questions the notion of fidelity that many critics take for granted.

Ronald Christ's essay, "Translation Transvalued," which closes part 1 of our volume, provides a rarely seen view of the material context surrounding publication of translations in the United States. Christ, a publisher, editor, and translator, helps instructors understand the commercial concerns that bear heavily upon the publication of translated material by candidly discussing such issues as the market for literary translations in the United States, the status of translators and translation, and the hierarchies that exist between languages.

Part 2, "Issues and Contexts," presents a series of essays that examine the production of works in several literary traditions, with a focus on three major themes—identity and relationships, power struggles, and beliefs and values— that are particularly relevant to specific geographical areas or linguistic and cultural communities. This grouping around different sets of issues and a simultaneous emphasis on different geographical areas work together to foreground the discomfort that can result from reading in translation—in this case, the discomfort that might be caused by the unsettling of familiar categories and the consequent need to assume altered points of view. For instance, our definition of "region" includes various geographical points of view, ranging from one relatively small area with a single dominant linguistic and literary system (Japan or Israel), to large areas that exceed the borders of individual countries but are unified by the dominance of one or two languages (Latin America), to areas with multiple cultures (Eastern Europe), to whole continents (Africa). These diverse visions stimulate the complex process of reading in translation: readers are encouraged to ask what the geographical grids they use to configure other languages and cultures reveal about their own postures.

The grouping of essays in part 2 also foregrounds the range of perspectives suggested by multilingualism (South Asia, Africa) and monolingualism, echoing the discussions in part 1 about the integral relation between translation practices and the uneven positions of languages and literatures in the "World Republic of Letters." For instance, using literary texts as anthropological, rather than literary, data means one thing in the context of Latin America, which has reached a position of power since the triumph of magical realism; it means quite another in the context of Africa, a continent not yet constituted as a central force in the literary field.

The essays in part 2, whether they address translation practices in specific national contexts or translating difficulties, benefit from being read side by side with (or against) the more general essays in part 1, rather than in isolation. Similarly, an issue discussed in the context of one language may be usefully applied to another, such as the region with which the reader is most familiar. In the first cluster of chapters, the authors use the issues of identity and relationships to consider texts from three different contexts: Asia, Latin America, and Scandinavia. Tomoko Aoyama and Judy Wakabayashi explore the connections between self, identity, and language, and they discuss the challenges that the Japanese concepts of the self and interactions present to translators into Western languages, and indirectly to readers of the English versions. Their examples range from a traditional novel like *The Tale of Genji* to the works of the major modern writer Sōseki. Similarly, Michelle Yeh's consideration of Chinese traditions shows how translation and pluralist readings (i.e., use of multiple translations) can be used to gain insight into Chinese cultural practices. Her comparative readings range from the *Book of Songs* to the great Chinese novel *Dream of the Red Chamber,* providing essential contexts for a tradition little known in the West.

In her essay, Kathleen Ross addresses these same themes of identity and relationships through a consideration of Latin American texts from three genres—novel, poetry, and the *testimonio*—drawing on examples from Gabriel García Márquez, Pablo Neruda, and Rigoberta Menchú, as well as less-known contemporary authors. These examples both confirm national myths about national identity and reflect cultural differences throughout Latin America. She provides a nuanced discussion of identity from both dominant and marginal perspectives, and her methodology, which considers literary works in terms of their cultural content, can be usefully applied by instructors of other translated works. Scandinavia, the last region included in this section, is often less studied than others in the West, but it is an integral part of the Western tradition. Niels Ingwerson and his colleagues discuss the major linguistic, literary, and cultural features of Nordic languages through detailed analysis of key concepts in works ranging from the Finnish *Kalevala* to those by such well-known authors as Strindberg, Ibsen, Dinesen, and Andersen.

The next cluster of essays focuses on power struggles. In her examination of power struggles in South Asia, Christi Merrill encourages instructors to reconsider Western assumptions about literature and translation. She convincingly argues that the multilingual nature of South Asian countries has led to a "translating consciousness" that values translated works as able "to transform, to translate, to restate, to revitalize the original." She shows that "such an approach promotes a flexible heterogeneity that might serve as a model for challenging us to rethink the ways we demarcate difference in the rhetoric of nationalist-minded or even globalized identitarian politics."

This issue of power struggles is also addressed by Paul Bandia, in the different context of the African continent. Bandia discusses the key role of translation in shaping the literature of many African countries and examines translation practices in representing African sociocultural realities and worldviews. He describes the complex situation of African literature and calls for reading and teaching strategies that bring to light "both the writing-as-translation strategies used by creative writers and the interlingual translation processes involved in the translating of intercultural writing from non-Western societies." Bandia's focus on specifically literary questions and on European languages in Africa indirectly forces us to confront the legacy of colonialism in our speaking of "Africa." This discussion of translation in Africa is paralleled by Kelly Washbourne's analysis of Latin American "transnational writers." Washbourne also describes the effects of translation on the hierarchical relations that exist between languages—in this case, between Spanish and English. He focuses his discussion of these linguistic power struggles on two contemporary generations of Latin American writers (the "McOndo" and "Crack" groups) who rebel against their magical realist forebears and embrace North American values.

The essays in the last section of this volume feature translation issues as seen through the prism of beliefs and values, first in the context of Eastern Europe and second in the Middle East (both in Arabic-speaking countries and in Israel). Brian Baer shows the West's tendency to perceive Eastern Europe as the less-developed other, and he analyzes how the choices of texts translated and the approaches chosen to translate these texts have contributed to the formation of a problematic view of this complex configuration of cultures. He traces the different translation moments that have shaped our ideas about "Eastern Europe" and forces readers to reconsider their homogenizing images of these literatures.

Allen Hibbard also outlines the tendencies that have marked translation, here in the case of Arabic. He focuses in particular on exoticization and domestication, and he discusses the specific linguistic and cultural differences that make translating from Arabic a particular challenge to Westerners. His analysis of linguistic characteristics such as cumulative patterns, diglossic styles, and code-mixing, as well as his recommendations for approaches and readings, provide the reader with an entry into a literature that embodies some of the tensions that exist between the West and the Arab world. Current cultural and political conflicts are less present in Chana Bloch's discussion of the translation issues presented by Hebrew literature, but the centrality of the Bible to the Western canon makes the discussion of the impact of its translation essential reading. Bloch shows how intertextuality and the multiplicity of meanings caused by Hebrew's particular lexical root formation has had a significant impact on the Bible, which has been disseminated through translation. She then turns to the work of contemporary Israeli poet Yehuda Amichai, explaining that what characterizes his work is precisely an intertextuality that resists translation and presents challenges to translators.

In short, then, through a consideration of general translation principles as well as an attention to specific but complex regional, cultural, and linguistic patterns, the editors of this volume and their contributors hope to provide instructors with a range of resources that will both encourage and enable them to create a hospitable space for the foreign in their various classes.

WORKS CITED

Arrojo, Rosemary, Marilyn Gaddis Rose, and Carol Maier. "Teaching Literature in Translation." *ATA Chronicle* February 2005: 19–20, 35.

Colina, Sonia. *Translation Teaching: From Research to the Classroom.* New York: McGraw-Hill, 2003.

Damrosch, David. "Reading in Translation." In *How to Read World Literature,* 65–85. Chichester, UK: Wiley-Blackwell, 2009.

———. *What is World Literature?* Princeton, NJ: Princeton University Press, 2003.

Deresiewicz, William. "The Literary World System." Review of *The World Republic of Letters,* by Pascale Casanova, trans. M. B. DeBevoise. *The Nation,* January 3, 2005, 21–23.

Dingwaney, Anuradha, and Carol Maier. "Between Languages and Cultures: Translation as a Method for Cross-Cultural Teaching." In *Between Languages and Cultures: Translation and Cross-Cultural Texts,* edited by Anuradha Dingwaney and Carol Maier, 303–19. Pittsburgh: University of Pittsburgh Press, 1995.

Feal, Rosemary. "English, Foreign Languages and Interdisciplinarity: Encounter on Mount Baldy." *MLA Newsletter* Fall 2003: 5–6.

Maier, Carol. "Teaching the Literature of the Spanish Civil War in Translation." In *Teaching Representations of the Spanish Civil War,* edited by Nöel Valis, 248–57. New York: Modern Language Association of America, 2007.

———. "Teaching Monolingual Students to Read in Translation (as Translators)." *ADFL Bulletin* 33, no. 1 (2001): 44–46.

Pizer, David. *The Idea of World Literature.* Baton Rouge: Louisiana State University Press, 2006.

Venuti, Lawrence. "The Pedagogy of Literature." In *The Scandals of Translation: Toward an Ethics of Difference,* 88–105. London and New York: Routledge, 2000.

———. "Teaching in Translation." In *Teaching World Literature,* edited by David Damrosch, 86–96. New York: Modern Language Association of America, 2009.

White, Steven. "Translation and Teaching: The Dangers of Representing Latin America for Students in the United States." In *Voice-Overs: Translation and Latin American Literature,* edited by Daniel Balderston and Marc E. Schwartz, 235–44. Albany, NY: SUNY Press, 2002.

PART ONE

—

General Principles

Choosing and Introducing a Translation

Carol Maier

> We sleep in language, if language does not
> come to wake us with its strangeness.
> Robert Kelly, "On Translation"

A promise of exposure to the unfamiliar—and the perception of its allure! What better way to preface an essay about choosing a translation? The question is not merely rhetorical, because writing this chapter presented a challenge that can be summed up nicely as the absence of "a consensus among translators, readers, and critics as to what a translation should do" (Stanton 620). At the same time, however, as a reader of two translations of the same poem will no doubt sense instinctively, some translations are better than others. Consequently, the goal of this essay, despite the lack of established, reliable guidelines, is to provide a set of recommendations that will enable an instructor to select an appropriate translation for a given course and to introduce it to a class. There may not be much help available in the way of specific criteria, but the task of choosing a translation (whether there is one option or many) offers the opportunity to think about both literature and language from an altered—or what Robert Kelly might call *awakened*—perspective. The following recommendations should encourage an instructor to entertain the unfamiliar and make informed choices.

Be aware of expectations. Even before beginning to read the available versions of a particular text, it is important to review one's thoughts about translation. Instructors who teach literary works, be they canonical or not, often find themselves faced with a variety of options. Availability, price, and the extent of ancillary information are no doubt considered automatically;

and those are important considerations. It is also important, however, for instructors—both as readers and as scholars—to be aware of their own assumptions about translation and their criteria for evaluating a work in translation. Those assumptions and requirements are often unacknowledged, but they affect the way a reader approaches literature in translation. This is not to suggest that one's preferences be set aside, but it is to suggest that they be held in abeyance as options are reviewed.

For instance, an instructor might be tempted to forgo a reading of Keith Waldrop's prose translation of *The Flowers of Evil* because of a conviction shared with many who, like Walter Martin, another of Baudelaire's translators, find the preservation of "rhymes and regular strophes" essential in the translation of poetry (441). But not to read Waldrop's versions because of his use of the verset ("a measured prose that allows the sentence to dominate . . . checked by a sense of line that restricts it" [xxiv]) would deprive that instructor of the opportunity to engage with Baudelaire in the words of an accomplished contemporary poet and translator. Whether or not instructors decide to use Waldrop's versions or other prose versions because they cannot be considered poetry per se, they will find their acquaintance with Baudelaire enriched by a reading of those versions. After all, readers guided solely by their expectations and preferences jeopardize their chances of experiencing the risky readings that can put one unexpectedly in touch with language used in unanticipated ways. Again using Waldrop's *Flowers* as an example, Lucas Klein has suggested that, while the lines are indeed not lines of poetry, the English "constantly points to the forms of the original" (34).

Read well. In other words, read, or at least consult, as many versions of the original as possible, and read with awareness that the work being read is a work in translation. The first of those suggestions is a question of research, persistence, and the openness called for above. As Nicholas Lezard comments in a review of Robin Kirkpatrick's translation of Dante's *Inferno,* even if one has read multiple versions of a work, it is useful to read yet another: "You could entomb yourself . . . with the huge number of available translations, [but] you should still have a look at this [new] one" (18).[1] The second suggestion involves reading with an eye to translation, to the ways in which translations, no matter how imperceptible the translator's work, will bear signs that they were written in a language other than English. Here, fortunately, it *is* possible to point to a reliable guide, two in fact: David Damrosch's wide-ranging discussion in *How to Read World Literature* of "the fascinating problems raised when

we read in translation" (4) and Lawrence Venuti's "How to Read a Translation," which offers five "rules" for reading translations. Advising readers to
(1) attend to the formal features of a work rather than read primarily for the
meaning, Venuti also urges them (2) to accept unfamiliar usage, such as terms
and forms of address; (3) to recognize and investigate, whenever possible, the
cultural milieu of the original; (4) to read any accompanying material provided by the translator, as a way of learning not only about the original but
also about the approach that guided the translator; and (5) to bear in mind
that all literary works, no matter how singular, belong to a complex web of
traditions and that in order to understand those traditions it is necessary to
read more than one translation. Venuti's rules have been summarized here
very briefly, but both his essay and Damrosch's bear reading in full; they are
replete with commentary and examples that will sensitize one to the issues
that translation involves and will lead to a reading both more pleasurable and
more knowledgeable.[2]

Consider the purpose. Given that multiple translations exist for many canonical works, an instructor will need to bear in mind the purpose and context
for the work's inclusion in a course. While the instructor of a class in world
literature, for example, might prefer Edith Grossman's recent translation of
Don Quixote, the instructor of a course in the history of the European novel
or the novel of the eighteenth century might choose Tobias Smolett's version, made in 1755. Similarly, for a course focused exclusively on poetry, an
instructor might make a point of using translations of Pablo Neruda's work
by North American poets such as Robert Bly or Nathaniel Tarn, who were
his close contemporaries. Different considerations, however, might lead an
instructor to choose John Felstiner's versions in *Translating Neruda* or Steven
Kessler's versions in Barry Brukoff's *Machu Picchu.*

For drama courses, purpose, audience, and venue assume particular importance. Absent gross errors of meaning, as Michael Ewans has explained,
the crucial requirement here is that a translation be "actable—that it be
composed of words which actors can easily speak" (123). Ewans's comments are based on his work with Greek tragedy, but they apply to work
with drama in general. Of course, the extent to which "actability" (as opposed, for example, to a desire for annotations or a definite preference for
rhyme and meter) is a factor in an instructor's selection and the context in
which performance is to be considered will be determinant. One thinks of
the contrasts between recent translations of Aeschylus's *Oresteia* by David

Grene and Wendy Doninger O'Flaherty, Tony Harrison, Ted Hughes, and Alan Shapiro and Peter Burian, to cite just one example of translations that would be acceptable in some situations but not in others.

Remember that no translation occurs in a vacuum. All translations have histories; they are all, to use Jerome McGann's term, "social acts" or "specific deeds of critical reflection made in a concert of related moves and frames of reference . . . that constitute the present as an interpreted inheritance from a past that has been long fashioned by other interpreting agents" (137). As such, all translations are "coded and scored with human activity" (136), and in order to make an informed choice of one rather than another, an instructor will want to know as much as possible about the circumstances in which that activity took place. This is true even if, like McGann, one considers translation not "scholarly" but "performative" interpretation—that is, forms of interpretation such as translation and parody that involve the "direct commentary" described by Dante Gabriel Rosetti, in which many questions of interpretation are addressed and resolved "without discussion" (from the preface to Rosetti's *Early Italian Poets,* qtd. in McGann 130). For, like the discussion-laden scholarly interpretations discussed by McGann, translations also have authors: the translators whose work both reflects and responds to the conventions of the time in which they work. In addition, like scholarly interpreters, translators often deal with texts that have long histories of editions and variants that make them less than definitive; and like scholarly interpreters (perhaps even more so), translators too negotiate the publication of their work with editors, publishers, and sometimes even authors.

Recent work in translation studies (carried out by scholarly interpreters who scrutinize translators' performative interpretations) has begun to document the coding and scoring that marks translations and to prove the points of interpretation on which translators have not often commented. In this context, instructors will benefit from reading, for example, Alberto Mira's fictitious dialogue between a translator and an editor about the translator's authority, or Isabelle Vanderschelden's essay on retranslation, or Yopie Prins's discussion of translations of Sappho's poetry in Victorian England, or Jean-Marc Gouvanic's use of Pierre Bourdieu's work to explore the contributions of three twentieth-century French translators. Information about the translators and the situations in which translations were produced is often difficult, if not impossible, to locate, particularly for noncanonical texts. However, instructors will want to read any additional translations by the translators whose work they consider and to read whatever they can find about those translators themselves. (Gregory Rabassa's *If This Be Treason,* Donald Keene's *On Familiar Terms,* and Denys Johnson-Davies's *Memories in Translation,* for example, contain information about the work of those translators from Spanish and Portuguese, Greek, and Arabic, respectively.)

Instructors will also want to read any comments made by the translators and pay close attention to the edition(s) they used, the people whom they consulted, and the conditions of publication. Translators' comments are often quite substantive, even though they can also serve as self-justifications, and they can shed light on the ways in which one translation differs from another. For example, Tom Lathrop's lengthy introduction to his translation of *Don Quixote* will be of interest to instructors who work with Cervantes's novel, no matter which translation they select. The same could be said with respect to William Gass's *Reading Rilke* if one is teaching the *Duino Elegies* or E. H. and A. M. Blackmore's introduction to their volume if one is teaching Victor Hugo's poetry.

Consult reviews, review essays, and criticism. Reviewers of literary works in translation are notorious for either neglecting to note that the work was not originally written in English or for describing a translation or its translator with a single adjective. What is more, reviewers who explicitly state their evaluative criteria are the exception rather than the rule. At the same time, however, reviews can be very helpful, because they often contain information about the original work or its author; about the inclusion (or lack) of commentary, notes, or glossary; or about the reception of other English-language translations of works by a book's author. This is particularly true if a reviewer also explains or at least alludes to the criteria that served as a basis for judgment. For example, the comment with which Thomas F. Dillingham closes his review of Waldrop's *Flowers* makes clear a preference that has underlain his discussion, despite his praise for passages in which he finds "strength and beauty" (20): "this reader longs for the effort to recreate the prosodic energy as well as the thought of the great poet"(20). William Logan's comment that Christopher Logue "has the significant advantage, for a radical translator, of knowing no Greek" (178) is similarly telling, alerting the reader that for Logan, a thorough knowledge of the language of the original is not a requirement.

Fortunately, substantive, thoughtful reviews of translations are appearing with increasing regularity in a number of literary magazines and journals (although one could not go so far as to consider it a trend).[3] This is especially true in the case of retranslations, which often give rise to relatively long reviews or review essays, affording a reviewer the space necessary not only to describe a translation but also to evaluate it, frequently in the context of previous versions. Almost invariably, and no matter how opinionated the reviewer, these reviews will prove useful to an instructor. For example, instructors of *Anna Karenina* have the advantage of the reviews published when the latest translation of the novel appeared (that of Richard Pevear and Larissa Volokhonsky, in 2001) in addition to Liza Knapp's discussion of all the versions available, as well as extensive commentary in magazines and newspapers about Tolstoy in translation (for instance, David Remnick's "The Translator Wars").

Journals in translation studies also publish reviews, and those reviews usually include a discussion of the issues involved in evaluation itself, in addition to comments about the title or titles under review. Anthony Pym, in his discussion of two translations of *Don Quixote* (those of Tobias Smollett and Edith Grossman), for example, refers to many other translations and offers an overview of Cervantes translations across the centuries. Even when translation scholars focus on a single translation, their reviews tend to place the work in a cultural and historical context, in addition to (or even instead of) comparing the translation and the original or the translation and other translations of the same work. A good example here is Maria Tymoczko's essay on the variety of ways that she would evaluate Seamus Heaney's *Sweeney Astray* (*Buile Suibhne*).

Choose one, use many (if not all). Arguably (as most things are when one discusses value and quality in literary translation), this is the most important of the recommendations. As Jorge Luis Borges has explained eloquently (in the words of translator Eliot Weinberger), "the concept of the 'definitive' text corresponds only to religion or exhaustion" (69). Consequently, to limit oneself to one version when more than one version is available is to deprive oneself (or one's students) of the pleasure of awakening to the strangeness of language that is often revealed strikingly by variations, even small ones, among multiple versions of a given text. Asking students to purchase more than one version would in most cases be inappropriate, but instructors can explain their reasons for choosing the translation they did and provide students with information about or access to additional versions; they can also use those versions in class. Even if neither the instructor nor the students can read the original, variations such as a small difference in titles can give rise to a provocative discussion. Think, for example, of Gabriela Mistral's "La extranjera" as "The Foreigner" (Doris Dana, Ursula K. Le Guin), "The Alien" (Kate Flores), and "The Stranger" (Langston Hughes), or of Victor Hugo's "Mes deux filles" as "My Two Daughters" (Blackmore) and "My Two Girls" (Brooks Haxton). In both cases, an instructor would certainly want students to read each version. No choice should be considered final, however. Instructors need to stay alert to new translations, new editions of existing translations, and translations of work by authors of whom we have yet to learn.

Present provocatively. A student's first step toward a knowledgeable reading of a work in translation is "an overt recognition" that translation has occurred, as Isabel Garayta explains in her essay in this volume. The importance of this recognition cannot be overemphasized, and once a translation is chosen, an instructor's first task is to prompt it. To a large extent, this involves setting the students on the path the instructor followed in selecting the translated work they are reading. Consequently, even before students are asked to read the text, they should be encouraged to consider their expectations of both a translated work in general and of this translated work in particular. One of the best ways to initiate such a consideration is to ask students to reflect on any previous experiences they might have had with translations and translated literature. For example, have they done any translation or interpreting themselves? Have they read translations before? Do they have preconceived notions about the role that translation might play in the transmission of a work, perhaps by compromising its credibility? What might they know about the author, the author's language and culture, or the period in which the original work was written, and how might that knowledge—or its lack— affect their responsiveness to the work?[4]

With respect to the work itself, preliminary questions for discussion can focus on the translator's status in the literary market as evidenced by the publisher's presentation of the translation and the degree of prominence granted to the translator. Does the translator's name appear on the cover, for instance, and does the book's cover copy include a mention of translation? Does the publisher hold the copyright for the translation instead of the translator? Until quite recently this was routinely the case, and in some quarters it still is, even in a large publishing house like Farrar, Straus and Giroux, which holds the copyright for Krishna Winston's translation of Peter Handke's *Crossing the Sierra de Gredos*. When the translator does hold the copyright, as Sarah Adams does for her translation of Faïza Guène's *Kiffe Kiffe Tomorrow*, the ramifications of a comment such as the following can be discussed: "This translation is an edited version of Sarah Adams's translation." If there is an introduction, was it written by the translator, or by someone else, such as a scholar or English-language author whose attention and praise the publisher (and perhaps the author and translator as well) hope will lend credibility to the work? Each of these questions will encourage students to read with translation in mind and will lead to further attentiveness to the presence of translation—or its apparent absence.

Once the translation has been presented as a translation, students can be asked to note the use of foreign words, names, and references as they read, and to consider whether such usages contribute to or detract from the reader's understanding of the text. A similar question can be asked if there are translator's notes or a glossary. If there is a translator's preface or afterword, students can consider whether the translator seems to have interpreted the work appropriately and to have presented his or her own work reliably. Further discussions will probe the role of translation further, but those discussions will be most fruitful if translation has been in the minds of the both the instructor and the students from the very start.

NOTES

1. This is not to say that all versions are equally accomplished. On the contrary, as indicated at the beginning of this essay, some translations are superior to others. Disparate versions, however, are often likely to result from divergent readings rather than from inaccuracy, and readings in translation will be enriched by exposure to those plural readings. It is also worth bearing in mind here Jeffrey R. Di Leo's comment that "there is just as much to say to say about bad books as there is to say about good ones" (3) and R. M. Berry's admission that "no book has ever made a difference to me that someone whose judgment I respected didn't find execrable" (3).

2. For an extended discussion of reading and evaluating translations, see Antoine Berman, *Toward a Translation Criticism: John Dunne* (trans. Françoise Massardier-Kenney; Kent, OH: Kent State University Press, 2009). The method of "productive criticism" that Berman proposes requires a knowledge of the original text, but his comments about the different forms of translation analysis, his detailed examples, and his insistence that the reading of translations is a skill in itself will enrich the understanding of any teacher.

3. One thinks, for example, of the *New York Review of Books* or the *Times Literary Supplement,* but thoughtful reviews of translations are also found in such publications as the *American Book Review, Bloomsbury Review, Bookforum, Rain Taxi,* and numerous others.

4. For further reading about presenting literary works in translation, see Damrosch, Lefevere, Maier, and Venuti ("The Pedagogy of Literature" and "Teaching in Translation").

WORKS CITED

Baudelaire, Charles. *Complete Poems.* Translated by Walter Martin. Manchester, UK: Carcanet, 1997.

———. *The Flowers of Evil.* Translated by Keith Waldrop. Middletown, CT: Wesleyan University Press, 2006.

Berry, R. M. "Bad Books." *American Book Review* (January–February 2010): 3–4.

Borges, Jorge Luis. "The Homeric Versions." Translated by Eliot Weinberger. In *Selected Non-fictions,* edited by Eliot Weinberger, 67–74. New York: Norton, 2000.

Cervantes, Miguel de. *Don Quixote.* Translated by Tobias Smollett. New York: Farrar, Straus and Giroux, 1986.

———. *Don Quixote.* Translated by Edith Grossman. New York: Ecco, 2003.

———. *Don Quixote.* Translated by Tom Lathrop. Newark, DE: European Masterpieces, 2005.

Damrosch, David. "Reading in Translation." In *How to Read World Literature,* 65–85. Chichester, UK: Wiley-Blackwell, 2009.

Di Leo, Jeffrey R. "Introduction to Focus: Top 40 Bad Books." *American Book Review* (January–February 2010): 3.

Dillingham, Thomas F. Review of *The Flowers of Evil,* by Charles Baudelaire, translated by Keith Waldrop. *American Book Review* (May–June 2007): 19–20.

Ewans, Michael. "Aischylos: For Actors, in the Round." In *The Art of Translation: Voices from the Field,* edited by Rosanna Warren, 120–39. Boston: Northeastern University Press, 1989.

Gass, William H. *Reading Rilke: Reflections on the Problems of Translation.* New York: Knopf, 1999.

Gouvanic, Jean-Marc. "A Bourdieusian Theory of Translation, or the Coincidence of Practical Instances." *The Translator* 11, no. 2 (2005): 147–66.

Guène, Faïza. *Kiffe Kiffe Tomorrow.* Translated by Sara Adams. Orlando, FL: Harcourt Books, 2006.

Handke, Peter. *Crossing the Sierra de Gredos.* Translated by Krishna Winston. New York: Farrar, Straus and Giroux, 2007.

Hugo, Victor. "My Two Daughters" [Mes deux filles]. In *Selected Poems of Victor Hugo: A Bilingual Edition,* translated by E. H. Blackmore and A. M. Blackmore, 162–63. Chicago: University of Chicago Press, 2001.

———. "My Two Girls" [Mes deux filles]. In *Selected Poems,* translated by Brooks Haxton, 18–19. New York: Penguin, 2001.

Johnson-Davies, Denys. *Memories in Translation: A Life between the Lines of Arabic Literature.* Cairo: American University in Cairo Press, 2006.

Keene, Donald. *On Familiar Terms: To Japan and Back, a Lifetime Across Cultures.* New York: Kodansha International, 1996.

Kelly, Robert. "On Translation." PEN. May 22, 2010. http://www.pen.org/viewmedia. php/prmMID/108.

Klein, Lucas. Review of *The Flowers of Evil,* by Charles Baudelaire, translated by Keith Waldrop. *Rain Taxi* 11, no. 4 (Winter 2006/2007): 34.

Knapp, Lisa. "Russian Editions and English Translations." In *Approaches to Teaching "Anna Karenina,"* edited by Lisa Knapp and Amy Mandelker, 37–46. New York: Modern Language Association of America, 2003.

Lefevere, André. *Translating Literature: Practice and Theory in a Comparative Literature Context.* New York: Modern Language Association of America, 1992.

Lezard, Nicholas. Review of *The Divine Comedy I: Inferno,* by Dante Alighieri, translated by Robin Kirkpatrick. *Review Saturday Guardian,* March 25, 2006, 18.

Logan, William. *Reputations of the Tongue: On Poetry and Poets.* Gainesville: University Press of Florida, 1999.

Maier, Carol. "Teaching the Literature of the Spanish Civil War in Translation." In *Approaches to Teaching the Spanish Civil War,* edited by Nöel Valis, 248–57. New York: Modern Language Association of America, 2007.

McGann, Jerome. *The Scholar's Art: Literary Studies in a Managed World.* Chicago: University of Chicago Press, 2006.

Mira, Alberto. "Being Wildean: A Dialogue on the Importance of Style in Translation." In *The Translator as Writer,* edited by Susan Bassnett and Peter Bush, 196–207. London: Continuum, 2006.

Mistral, Gabriela. "The Alien" [La extranjera]. Translated by Kate Flores. In *The Defiant Muse: Hispanic Feminist Poems from the Middle Ages to the Present: A Bilingual Anthology,* edited by Angel Flores and Kate Flores, 51–52. New York: Feminist Press, 1986.

———. "The Foreigner" [La extranjera].Translated by Doris Dana. In *Selected Poems of Gabriela Mistral: A Bilingual Edition,* 101–2. Baltimore: Johns Hopkins University Press, 2001.

———. "The Foreigner" [La extranjera]. Translated by Ursula K. Le Guin. In *Selected Poems of Gabriela Mistral,* 192–93. Albuquerque: University of New Mexico Press, 2003.

———. "The Stranger" [La extranjera]. Translated by Langston Hughes. In *The Other Voice: Twentieth-Century Women's Poetry in Translation,* edited by Joanna Bankier, Carol Cosman, Doris Earnshaw, Joan Keefe, Deirdre Lasgari, and Kathleen Silver, 157. New York: Norton, 1976.

Prins, Yopie. *Victorian Sappho.* Princeton, NJ: Princeton University Press, 1999.

Pym, Anthony. "The Translator as Author: A Review of Two *Quixotes.*" *Translation and Literature* 14, no. 1 (2005): 171–81.

Rabassa, Gregory. *If This Be Treason: Translation and Its Dyscontents.* New York: New Directions, 2006.

Remnick, David. "The Translation Wars." *New Yorker*, November 7, 2005, 98–109.

Stanton, Edward F. "Translation or Trampoline? Translation and Teaching." In *Estudios en honor a Enrique Ruiz Fornells*, edited by Juan Fernández Jiménez, José Labrador Herráiz, and L. Teresa Valdivieso, 620–24. Erie, PA: ALDEUU, 1990.

Tolstoy, Leo. *Anna Karenina*. Translated by Richard Pevear and Larissa Volokhonsky. New York: Viking, 2001.

Tymoczko, Maria. "Wintering Out with Irish Poetry: Affiliation and Autobiography in English Translation." *The Translator* 6, no. 2 (2000): 137–48.

Vanderschelden, Isabelle. "Why Retranslate the French Classics? The Impact of Retranslation on Quality." In *On Translating French Literature and Film*, edited by Myriam Salama-Carr, 1–18. Amsterdam: Rodopi, 2000.

Venuti, Lawrence. "How to Read a Translation." *Words Without Borders* (May 22, 2010). http://wordswithoutborders.org/article/how-to-read-a-translation/.

———. "The Pedagogy of Literature." In *The Scandals of Translation: Towards an Ethics of Difference*, 88–105. New York: Routledge, 1998.

Translation Theory and Its Usefulness

Françoise Massardier-Kenney

Teachers and readers of texts in translation seldom reflect on the fact that translators have been key intermediaries who create literary "value" and greatly contribute to the creation of notions of "literature" (especially "great literature") by introducing new forms and authors who often become part of the canon that defines the readers' culture (Casanova 27). This situation is caused by a number of factors, the major one being the current unquestioned belief that literatures have strict national boundaries—a belief reflected in corresponding institutional divisions into "English" departments and "foreign language" departments, rather than departments of "literature" or "letters." This situation also reflects the increasing monolingualism prevalent in North American culture and the fact that writers, editors, readers, and teachers of literature in the past typically knew several languages, whereas now they often don't. Moreover, most students have not been trained in the languages and literatures that have most affected their own culture, let alone the languages and literatures of more distant cultures. Even when we, North American academics and students, seem to show a great interest in the "other," that other is all too often one who speaks the same language we do.

Under these circumstances, one can legitimately ask why readers of literature in translation should know anything about "translation theory." How can it help them make sense of their reading experience? Which theories should they know? The exponential growth of "translation studies" as an academic discipline (with its corresponding flurry of specialized seminars, conferences, journals, anthologies, etc.) might well seem overwhelming to an instructor, but that instructor does not need to read extensively in translation theory to become a more sophisticated reader of literature in translation. Although many essays, books, and fragments are labeled "theories," they often are anything but that: rather than developing a systematic account of translation productions, roles, or descriptions, they offer prescriptions about translation that are anchored in specific (not to say narrow) historical, cultural, institutional, and political contexts, and they have little bearing on the reading of texts that do not belong to those same contexts. In addition, many "translation theories" do not apply to literature as a specific field. They are either theories of texts in general, and their focus on the communication of objective information brings little understanding to the reading of literary texts; or they focus on research methodologies (e.g., the use of corpus linguistics, text typologies, etc.) that have little relevance to the production or reading of literature in translation.

However, a number of texts reflect directly on the general principles and issues bearing on literary translation. These texts include translator's commentaries, writer's essays, letters, fragments, and critical (sometimes theoretical) works. The most useful of these bring to light some of the major assumptions that have shaped the production of translations throughout the ages in the Western world; attempt to provide general principles that can be used to explain or assess the specific choices that translators make, and their effects on the texts we read; or reflect upon the act of translation as a creative activity.

It is useful to know that different conceptions of what it means to translate, how one should translate, and what kinds of translations are produced at given times are influenced by four intertwined sets of hierarchical relationships: thought/language, culture of the center/culture of the periphery, culture/literature, and literature/translation. For the purpose of our analysis, these strands need to be described separately, but they are interrelated and should be considered together when assessing a specific translation practice, criticism, or theory.

The first set of hierarchical relations has to do with the relation between thought and language. From the Greeks until the early nineteenth century, most thinkers conceived of language as expressing preexisting thoughts. They considered that thoughts were autonomous and could be separated from the linguistic, material expressions they may be "dressed in," and they believed that language was a means to communicate thoughts that were already there. Within this model (represented by the notion of Platonic Forms as well as the "ideas" of the empiricists or the Enlightenment), it made sense to consider translation merely as the transfer of thought contents that could be expressed in another language. Whether discussions of translation advocated translating "sense for sense" (i.e., focused on the transfer of general mean-ing) or "word for word" (i.e., translations rendering the individual concepts represented by individual linguistic units), the underlying assumption was the same: language was a "vehicle for the exchange of thought," to use An-dré Lefevere's expression. Even today a number of critics or theorists work from this older paradigm and speak of "equivalence of message," although such discussions may seem obsolete within a theoretical context (that of the philosophy of language) in which the notion of thoughts free from any linguistic expression has been abandoned.

As André Lefevere explains in his essential essay "Translation: Its Ge-nealogy in the West," during the period when this conception of "thought before language" flourished, both producers and readers of translation were bilingual and often multilingual. Thus, readers of translation did not read translated texts for information but as exercises in pedagogy or cultural ap-propriation. This is important to remember because even if some writers, translators, and readers still espouse the thought-first model, the concomitant process of cultural appropriation described by Lefevere is no longer possible, because readers are now monolingual readers of translation and thus cannot appropriate what they do not perceive.

This thought/language paradigm was quietly overturned in the late eigh-teenth century when German philosopher Johann Gottfried von Herder started arguing that thought was dependent on and bounded by language.[1] According to Herder, one cannot think unless one has a language, and one can only think what one can express linguistically. A word's meaning depends on its usage, not on predetermined ideas or concepts. In other words, all thought is dependent on language, and meanings and concepts are integral to word usage. This view had major implications for translation: now, repro-ducing a work's meanings in a different language required reproducing the original word usages, not disembodied meanings; if these word usages did not exist in the target language, they somehow had to be recreated through a "bending" of the word usages in existence in the target language.

It is not surprising that this idea took root at a time of nascent nationalism. Herder closely linked nation and language, and language thus came to repre-sent the idea of a nation, a people. The idea that a word's meaning depends on its usage led to a type of translation—advocated and practiced in Ger-many by Schleiermacher, von Humbolt, Goethe, Schlegel, and Hölderlin—in which the target language (in their case, German) is transformed in order to accommodate word usages that do not already exist in it. Schleiermacher's famous distinction between bringing the writer to the reader (which he rejects) and bringing the reader to the writer—which has now been popularized and (overly) simplified as a distinction between "domestication" (making the foreign text fit the norms of the target language) and "foreignization" (bending the target language to allow the foreignness of the source text to be visible)—is but the application of Herder's focus on word usage. Similarly, the other major distinction popular in translation studies—Peter Newmark's opposition between semantic translation, which focuses on the source text by providing equivalent semantic contents (i.e., an equivalent meaning), and communicative translation, which focuses on creating a text easily read by the target readers—is another version of Schleiermacher's distinction, although the notion of communicative translation uses word usage to fit the reader's expectations rather than to understand the source text. In a much more subtle and useful way, Antoine Berman's essential comments on translation also reflect the Herderian revolution, especially when he reminds us that although a literary work may contain information, its purpose is not to transmit this information; rather, its purpose is "to open onto the experience of the world" (71), an experience that translation attempts to transfer in its corporeality (i.e., Herder's "usage") into the target language.

The second set of hierarchical relations that is crucial for our understanding of translation theory involves the struggle of various cultures at different times to occupy a position of power. At the heart of this struggle we find the use of vernacular languages and translations from other, more prestigious cultures to create political, linguistic, and literary resources in the receiving cultures. For instance, in order to fight against the authority of the Church of Rome and the hegemony of the Italian humanists, King François I of France advocated the use of French (the "language of the king") as opposed to Latin, Italian, or various local dialects, and French poets of the Renaissance strengthened French through the systematic transposition and adaptation of the resources of Latin rhetoric.[2] Later, when French reached a position of superiority, won the linguistic battle against Latin, and became the universal language of culture in Europe, the systematic use of literary structures from Latin came to a halt, and the focus of translations shifted to making texts conform to the rules of proper French. Rather than assimilating new forms and coining new words in order to enrich French, translations tended to transfer foreign texts into Gallic forms, which explains why the French translations of Shakespeare from the nineteenth century are in alexandrine verse and omit the gory scenes. In the late twentieth century, a similar pattern could be observed with English. Specific translation practices can thus be explained by reference to general relations of power, and the significance of a given general tendency in translation can only be understood within the general context in which it occurs: the French Renaissance's reliance on Latin forms and lexis is less of a sign of respect for the "other" than it is an attempt to carve out a space for its own culture.

Similarly, rather than submitting to the authority of a culture of the center, as Pascale Casanova calls those cultures that occupy a position of prestige and whose language and values are all-powerful (e.g., Rome, Paris, and now New York or perhaps Hollywood), cultures of the periphery (e.g., London in the fifteenth century, Germany in the nineteenth century, and Middle Eastern countries today)—whose peoples and cultures are not yet recognized politically and culturally—can aspire to literary and political equality (111) through the transfer of prestigious cultural forms that can be used to expand the possibilities of their own culture. The German Romantic emphasis on translations of ancient Greek and Latin can be explained as an effort to shrug off the hegemony of French as a universalist culture, and modern writers of Arabic from various countries have adopted Western forms such as the realist novel or free verse (which are not traditional in their own culture) in order to gain access to the literary scene. One only needs to think of such writers as Nobel prize winner Naguib Mahfouz, the great Syrian poet Adonis, or a number of north African writers who have transformed their language and gained prestige for their work through their appropriation of Western forms.

Clearly, translation has been the most important process that has allowed the dissemination of varied literary forms and lexical innovations and has shaped the contours of what we call national literatures, but we should not forget the converse truth: the *lack* of translation flows from the periphery to the center deprives us of a broad understanding of the different ways in which cultures make sense of the world and write about it. For instance, anthropologist Mary Douglas has recently showed that Westerners are unable to recognize, let alone appreciate, what she calls "ring composition" (as opposed to linear composition, which we think is the only way to organize facts, thoughts, essays, or novels), a major form of literary composition and thinking found in a number of epic works from non-Western cultures (including many Chinese novels).[3] Our inability to gain access to different experiences of the world through their depictions in other literatures limits our understanding of human thought and language, resulting in our holding beliefs that are not sufficiently tested. It is thus not surprising that a recent major challenge to Chomsky's theory of a universal grammar is being presented by an American linguist and translator through the study of a little-known Amazonian language called Pirahã.[4]

Thus, the relation we have called culture of the center/culture of the periphery intersects with the thought/language relation. The lack of enlightened translations flowing from the periphery to the center leads to a lack of understanding of major human thought processes, and a major strategy for a literature of the periphery to enter the center is to appropriate linguistic and literary forms through translation. This movement from periphery to center also occurs within a culture when a specific literary work, form, or movement gains value through being translated into a prestigious language and, thus anointed, can reenter the culture of origin. Famous examples include Poe, who could only be taken seriously in America as a writer after he was translated into French by Baudelaire, or Beckett, whose exile to France and self-translations greatly aided his fame and influence in Great Britain. Inversely, recent translations into English (the current language of power, needless to say) of contemporary French Caribbean writers or Latin American writers has contributed to their acceptance by French and Hispanic cultures. A final, less positive example concerns the translation of Russian literature during the Cold War, which focused on politically motivated works written by dissidents and which created a narrow, inaccurate image of Russian literature during that time, a view that has only started to be modified through the translation of other major authors who were neglected because they did not fit into the Cold War paradigm of Russian literature that was acceptable in the United States.

This leads to the third set of hierarchical relations that affects our understanding of translation: culture/literature. Throughout the ages, literature was perceived as a major indicator of the degree of culture of a specific country or nation, and literature functioned as a major embodiment of national identity; but that situation has changed. Although today no one could deny that the United States is a hegemonic culture, within this culture literature has been displaced as the defining embodiment of national identity (as English literature was for England, or German literature for Germany). Literature has even become a marginal activity with increasingly less cultural capital, which has major consequences for the significance of translation. Because the role of literature in the United States is ancillary, the role of translations from other languages is necessarily minor. Translation studies scholars lament the lack of translations from other languages into American English—in 2005, only 3.54% of new fiction titles published in the United States were translations, as opposed to 42.7% for France[5]—but we must remember that these numbers have little significance in and of themselves. Even if more foreign novels were published in English, the increase would say nothing about the status (or rather the lack of status) of American literature within American culture.[6] The culture/literature relation is slightly different in other countries, such as France, where literature is still seen as linked to national identity, and numbers reflect the stronger status of literature. For instance, 2006 saw an enormous number of novels published in French, although French critics still decried the state of French literature. It is significant that out of a total of 727 novels published in France in 2007, 234 were foreign ones, according to Alain Beuve-Mery of Le Monde.[7]

This leads to the last set of hierarchical relations to consider when thinking about literature in translation: that of literature and translation. The relative power of translation in relation to literature has changed throughout the ages and varies from region to region. As we have seen, translation has been acknowledged as playing a crucial role in the development of individual literatures, but its current status in American institutions (universities, the press, publishing houses) is one of inferiority. The modernist obsession with originality, linked with the emergence of the United States as a monolingual world power, has led to a kind of literary amnesia in which the contributions of translations have remained unacknowledged or devalorized. This obscurity explains why American translators are seldom given the opportunity to preface their translating work and why the infrequent translations that appear in the United States can rarely afford to call attention to themselves as translations, whereas in other periods or other countries translation's more prestigious status is likely to lead to translators openly identifying their work as translations.[8]

An awareness of these theoretical considerations will allow the readers of translations to understand why certain choices have to be made at certain times and to appreciate the constraints under which translators operate at different times and in different countries. However, readers should also understand that these general principles are manifested for the most part as unconscious tendencies on the part of translators and translations' professional readers, i.e. critics.

NOTES

1. Michael N. Forster claims that Herder can be considered the founder of both the modern philosophy of language and the modern philosophy of interpretation (hermeneutics) and translation. I agree with Forster's assessment, especially because all the important texts on translation from the nineteenth century onward are heavily influenced by Herder, even if they don't quote him. Nor is it a coincidence that both André Lefevere's and Pascale Casanova's works acknowledge the influence of Herder, even though his name seldom appears in recent anthologies of translation theory or readers in translation studies. See Michael N. Forster, "Herder's Philosophy of Language, Interpretation, and Translation: Three Fundamental Principles," *Review of Metaphysics* 56 (2002): 323–56.

2. For a history of these world struggles of cultural and literary appropriations, see Casanova, *The World Republic of Letters.*

3. See Mary Douglas, *Thinking in Circles: An Essay on Ring Composition* (New Haven: Yale University Press, 2007).

4. See John Colapinto's article about linguist Dan Everett, "The Interpreter: Has a Remote Amazonia Tribe Upended our Understanding of Language?" *New Yorker,* April 16, 2007, 12–37.

5. Jascha Hoffman, "Data," *New York Times Book Review,* April 15, 2007, 27.

6. The sobering figures provided by the Association of American Publishers document the decreasing importance of literature: 48% of all paperbacks are romance fiction, while the rest is taken up by self-help books and other nonfiction. The most popular American novelists seem to be those who do not write literary fiction, such as Tom Clancy, Stephen King, or James Patterson. A recent *New York Times Magazine* article on the subject of Patterson's popularity is particularly striking: http://www.nytimes.com/2010/01/24/magazine/24patterson-t.html.

7. See "Traducteur, un métier précaire," *Le Monde,* September 14, 2007. According to statistics provided by the French booksellers magazine *Livres Hebdo,* the number of novels published during the *rentrée littéraire* (the beginning of the literary season each September) in France was 488 in 1996; this figure rose to 683 in 2006 (including 208 translations).

8. See, for instance, the situation in South Asia as described by Christi Merrill's chapter in this volume.

RECOMMENDED READING

Appiah, Kwame Anthony. "Thick Translation." In *The Translation Studies Reader,* edited by Lawrence Venuti, 389–401. London: Routledge, 2000. Appiah's study of the translation of African proverbs is also an excellent introduction to the theoretical and pedagogical issues surrounding the translation of oral literatures that are perceived as inferior to Western literatures.

Baker, Mona, ed. *Routledge Encyclopedia of Translation Studies.* London: Routledge, 2008. This encyclopedia is very useful for finding definitions used in translation studies.

Berman, Antoine. *Pour une critique des traductions: John Donne.* Paris: Gallimard, 1995 (*Toward a Translation Criticism.* Kent, OH: Kent State University Press, 2009). The theoretical section of this book should be required reading for anyone interested in translation. Many people have read Berman without acknowledging his influence.

Calderbank, Anthony. "Translator's Introduction." In *Blue Aubergine,* by Miral Al-Tahawy, translated by Antbony Calderbank, vii–ix. Cairo: American University Press of Cairo, 2002.

Casanova, Pascale. *The World Republic of Letters.* Translated by M. B. Debevoise. Boston: Harvard University Press, 2005. Casanova's interpretation of literature outside of national boundaries is crucial for reading in translation.

Caws, Mary Ann. *Surprised in Translation.* Chicago: University of Chicago Press, 2006. In this volume, Caws provides essays on translations—her own and those of others—that have surprised her.

Christ, Ronald. "Extravag(r)ant and Un/erring Spirit." In *E. Luminata,* by Diamela Eltit, translated by Ronald Christ, 205–34. New York: Lumen Books, 1997.

Ghanoonparvar, M. R. *Translating the Garden.* Austin: University of Texas Press, 2001. The author analyzes his own work as the translator of Shahrukh Miskub's *Goftogu dar Bagh* from Persian into English.

Lefevere, André, ed. *Translation/History/Culture: A Sourcebook.* London: Routledge, 1992. This anthology provides prefaces and essays by famous author/translators from the Romans to the late nineteenth century.

———. "Translation: Its Genealogy in the West." In *Translation, History, and Culture,* edited by Susan Bassnett and Antoine Lefevere, 14–28. London: Pinter Press, 1990. This is a concise, precise history of translation patterns in the West.

Schleiermacher, Friedrich. "On the Different Methods of Translation," translated by André Lefevere. In *German Romantic Criticism,* edited by Leslie Willson, 1–30. New York: Continuum Publishing Company, 1982. This highly influential essay summarizes the major options for translation.

Weaver, William. "The Process of Translation." In *The Craft of Translation,* edited by Rainer Schulte and John Biguenet, 117–24. Chicago: University of Chicago Press, 1989. This essay by a foremost translator is a window onto the mind of the translator at work.

"Toto, I've a Feeling We're Not in Kansas Anymore": Reading and Presenting Texts in Translation from "Familiar" Cultures

Isabel Garayta

The difficulty in confronting any literary text, translation or not, is relative to our distance from it in any of the myriad ways we might define "distance." Most critical and pedagogical approaches to literature attempt to shed light on particular aspects of a work in the hope that illuminating a text or some aspect of it will shorten the distance between it and the reader, or at least enable the reader to traverse the distance on surer footing. One way to gauge the distance between reader and text may be, on the simplest level, to ask how "foreign" a text seems to a reader and to his or her experience. Under this trope, what critics and teachers attempt to do is move text and reader closer together in order to help the reader bridge some of the text's distance or "foreignness" and better understand its "language," even if not completely. The challenges presented by texts in one's native language, written as they are within a culture and literary tradition in which one has grown up and been educated, almost inevitably multiply in the case of a text from a foreign culture and language, for in addition to the distance that must be traversed between any reader and a text written in her own language, the reader of a translation will almost certainly find herself separated from the source text by further distances—of geography, language, culture, historical viewpoint, and literary genre and its expectations, to name only a few types of "alienation." Thus, readers of translations can be said to be at two removes of foreignness from the original text.

Although reading translated texts from what might be called "familiar" cultures (for example, French, German, Italian, and Spanish, which for historical reasons have a strong presence in North American culture) requires less effort than reading texts from cultures that seem more distant, it is also important to recognize that a sense of familiarity might entail a false sense of comfort. A reader might be lulled into thinking that she "knows things" about the translated text, its characters, and its message that she in fact does *not* know. Moreover, when moving around in cultures that seem "not so foreign," one may find that a sense of familiarity is not reliable. Even though there may be shared history, politics, or even geography, the reader may be less conversant with the *literary* culture and tradition from which the text emerges. To return to a trope I used earlier, one's footing may be less sure on this literary ground than one assumes, and approaching the text as "transparent" (in both language and "content") may lead to misreading or underreading it. If and when the realization comes that there is something odd about the work or one's experience of it, the "we're not in Kansas anymore" syndrome may have set in: the language sounds familiar, and the world looks *sort of* like what one thinks it should, but some things seem slightly off, and one begins to find oneself in unfamiliar territory, whose rules are not quite clear. Fortunately, this discomfort may be the first step toward an awareness that one is reading a translation.

Curiously, if this sense of oddness or unfamiliarity does not arise as one reads a text from a familiar yet foreign culture, then the reader would be well advised to ask, "Why not?" She should also try to become alert to how the mediation of translation has robbed her of that experience of "otherness" that is one of the reasons we prize translations—robbed because the familiar but distant has been reduced, for the reader's "comfort," to the identical or the known.

In the following pages, teachers will find suggestions for ways to help students approach these translated texts with a better understanding of the mediation wrought upon them (specifically as a result of translation, but also of publishing practices). Without an awareness of that mediation and a sensitivity to the difference or "otherness" that the translation may have elided, hidden, or camouflaged, a reader is deprived of the experience of "otherness" that is one of the gifts the reading of a foreign text offers.

No matter the degree of distance students experience with respect to a text in translation, the first step in approaching it must be an overt recognition of the fact that they are reading a translation, or reading *in* translation, and concurrently, that an act of mediation has brought the work into their language and culture. This elementary recognition may seem just that—elementary—but anyone who doubts the invisibility of translation in academia has only to try, I predict fruitlessly, to remember the names of the translators who gave them access to the texts they consider central to their education. Likewise, I would venture to say that few readers can remember many class discussions on the subject of the translations themselves, even for texts that have had a significant and exciting history of translation. Even more troubling than translation's invisibility in the classroom, however, is the fact that translation, when it does become a topic of discussion, is usually treated only in passing, with the conversation often reduced to the instructor's lament that students, as readers, are reduced to an undesirable dependence on this sort of mediation. So, in a class where translated texts will be read, taking the time at the beginning to discuss a couple of essays on the subject of translation is invaluable, as it will open students' eyes to this mediation and begin to validate the discipline for them (see Venuti; Biguenet and Schulte; Schulte and Biguenet).

Once the fact of the translation's existence *qua* translation has been established, it falls to the instructor to begin contextualizing the source text of the translation under discussion: its author; its immediate and more distant literary tradition and culture; the work's allegiance to or subversion of the micro- and macroliterary tradition of the country or culture or language in which it originated; the historical, social, and cultural context within which the work appeared, and the author's attitude(s) toward these contexts. These are, in short, the same issues and conditions that surround the study of a "native" text, but for a foreign text, the ground is more or less unfamiliar, and the relevant material needs to be explicitated and deliberately brought forward and examined. Contextualizing the source text within its originating culture will help bring it to life as a multifaceted work and will make real the backdrop against which it came into existence. In this process, the translated text will also come more clearly into focus *as* a translation, as well as a work of literature, history, and social comment that must, in turn, be contextualized within the translator's own receiving culture. As Venuti has explained (1995), it is essential to maintain this double critical vision, in which both source text and translation must be contextualized. It may also be helpful as part of the contextualization of the source text to examine the "canonicity" of the author and of the text, because this canonicity may well have played into how the translator has approached the text and how ready she has been to move away from it or, on the contrary, to produce, out of respect (or editorial demands), an extremely close version.

Another issue that also necessitates contextualization of both the source and the translated text is the question of the relative prestige of genres in differing literary systems. The importance of the novel of political commitment in Latin America, for instance, is quite different from the literary (un)importance of that genre in U.S. letters. Therefore, not just the literary but also the social impact of, for example, the highly political novels of Carlos Fuentes, Reinaldo Arenas, Augusto Roa Bastos, and others should be examined and contrasted against the backdrop of the Anglo-American literary tradition with which students are probably familiar, but which in any case this exercise provides an opportunity to review.

Students' initial encounter with the translated text itself should include a careful look at the paratextual matter. Translators, especially of texts intended for academic adoption, often append a translator's note to the text, which may offer insights into the text's translational possibilities and the choices this particular translator has made. While a careful reading of a translator's note is undoubtedly key to understanding a particular translation, we should take advantage of the fact that it may also open the door to explorations of philosophical or "ideological" positions vis-à-vis translation in general. Sometimes, too, publishers provide introductions and other front and back matter that helps not only to contextualize the work but also to shed light on decisions about which elements of the text and the work were stressed. Glossaries and footnotes might serve as a clue to how much or how little "foreignness" or difficulty the translator or publisher perceived in the text, or chose to preserve. When choosing texts published with this sort of material, rather than texts that give every physical appearance of being works in the original, teachers can emphasize the translated nature of the text.[1]

Instructors often use texts that have been translated more than once. Sometimes when teachers do not require students to use a specific edition or translation of a work such as the *Odyssey* or *Don Quixote,* students themselves, in the normal course of a class discussion, will begin to note the differences in the translations they have bought or taken from the library. Very fruitful insights into the mediation and the work itself may emerge as students question what the "essence" of a work is (must poetry be translated as poetry?), what the challenges and limits of translation are, and how the fashions of translation have changed over time.[2] To help students recognize the differences brought to the "same" text by different translators at different times, the teacher can specifically compare translations of a single source text to elicit the pattern of translational strategies at work. Such a comparison will almost certainly lead the discussion into many aspects of both translation and the work itself, as different translators inevitably emphasize differing aspects of the work.

One such exercise could be done using three contemporary translations of *Brevísima relación de la destrucción de las Indias* by Fray Bartolomé de las Casas (Briffaut 1974, Griffin 1992, and Hurley 2003). All of these editions include translator's notes that, when examined together with each of the translations, will allow students to see clearly how divergent readings or positions vis-à-vis the source text inevitably render different translations. Ideally, students will not only be comparing readings but also tracing how a critical reading is reflected in the translation and how theory becomes practice.

A good place to begin is with Andrew Hurley's note on his translation of *An Account, Much Abbreviated, of the Destruction of the Indies,* in which he argues that the distance between today's reader and Fray Bartolomé de las Casas is even more temporal and cultural than linguistic. Here the translator discusses his reasons for, and the practical effect of, his decision to "archaize" the language of the translation by adhering to pre-1560 vocabulary as a way to "restore to Las Casas a certain kind of otherness—the otherness of a historical moment when what he said was challenging, shocking, and controversial in the extreme—which, in the course of time and fame, he has lost" (Hurley liv). Ultimately, Hurley tells us that he has employed this translational strategy—which will require a slow, attentive reading—as a way to breathe life back into a text that familiarity has dulled for us, and in the hope that "by seeming 'old' or 'other' it will also seem new and perhaps even challenging, shocking, and controversial, and will be read for what it actually says, not what we think—because we've heard so much about him—it says" (Hurley liv).

The resulting translation becomes an interesting point of departure for comparisons with other versions as students can assess first whether and to what extent the translator has achieved his goal. They can then assess whether the other versions do in effect elide the "otherness" to which Hurley alludes and instead force text and reader together by either anachronistically endowing the sixteenth-century writer with a comforting and contemporary political correctness or by shortening sentences and modernizing the style to make Las Casas's text more fluent and palatable to today's students and readers.

In a class, poetry is often the easiest and quickest way to explore how translators emphasize, or privilege, one aspect of a text over another; again, looking at differing versions of the same text makes this patent. A simple exercise aimed at understanding how the translator's purpose or operative definition of "fidelity" determines the practice of translation, with its con-crete translational choices, is to look at an interlinear or literal translation of a poem (what is commonly called a "crib" or "trot"), in which the main objective is to communicate what (not *how*) the poem says, and where sense takes precedence. (With even minimal knowledge of the source language, a class can usually produce its own interlinear version of a simple poem.) This "poem" can then be compared to a freer, less literal and more "poetic" rendering of the same poem, and the contrast between the versions will make evident how fluid the definition of "fidelity" is. Translations of poems by poets are often exciting to look at, because poets seem more willing to translate freely in the interest of creating their own literary piece.[3] At the end of this exercise, even a quick look at the hilarious translations into French of Mother Goose ("*Un petit d'un petit/S'étonne aux Halles,*" by van Rooten) and Shakespeare ("*Tout pille or, note, tout pille, date hisse de caisse tiens!*" by Hulme) can provide a humorous moment and bring home the point that in translation, any given element of a text (even sound, to the exclusion of sense) may be privileged over all the others—sometimes with absurd results.

Continuing with the use of poetry in the classroom, but moving beyond the elements of sound and sense, a teacher might choose to look at how a particular literary tradition or genre determines the formal aspects of the original so that students can then see more clearly the choices the translator had to make when moving into an alternate tradition. This interrogation can raise questions about differences in genres between one literary system and another and serve as a springboard for class discussion or to stimulate student research into and comparison of these systems. In Spanish, for ex-ample, prosody is syllabic, whereas in English, the tradition is metric; thus, the changes that occur in the poetry and its effects when moving from a hendeca-syllabic line in Spanish to an iambic pentameter in English is an interesting area for discussion, as are decisions about rhyming and other acoustic effects. Likewise, the Spanish sonnet is both similar to and different from the several types of English or Italian sonnet; discussion of the differences can make for a fruitful exploration of literary tradition, innovation, and influence, leading students into a discussion of what happens when texts are moved out of and into different literary traditions.

Another way to broach a discussion of the evolution and cross-fertilization of literary systems and the development and change of genres is by com-paring and contrasting literary movements across national (or language) boundaries. For example, the chronological influences and lags of German and Anglo-American Romanticism, French *symbolisme,* and Latin American and Spanish *modernismo* might be explored when reading authors from the German, English, French, and Spanish-language traditions of the late eighteenth, nineteenth, and early twentieth centuries. Texts in translation make this exploration relevant and interesting on both literary and translational grounds. Also, the role of translation itself as a major force in "consecrating" texts and gaining them entry into the "world of letters" (Casanova) is an important aspect that merits discussion.

Once the work has been contextualized in the many ways it is possible to do so, the translated text can begin to be read by the class as a literary work much like any other, but *also* in translation. Here, the teacher needs to briefly review for her class the notion of "fidelity" and its many manifestations and deviations, and she should touch on two concepts, closely related to one another, that are used to describe broad strategies employed by translators: (1) "foreignization" or "resistant translation," and (2) "domestication." These terms describe how a translator chooses to bridge the distance between reader and text, a distance in which language is obviously the first but certainly not the only hurdle. Reader and text must meet, and inevitably this meeting must take place either in the "land" of the source text or the "land" of the reader. Thus, either the reader (suddenly endowed by translation, as though by Solomon's legendary ring, with the ability to understand the language) is transported to the foreign world of the text, or the text is transported to the world of the reader and rendered as if it were "native" to the reader's language and culture.

The first approach provides a sense of the "otherness" that one would experience traveling in another culture; it is embraced by translators who value the experience of the foreign and who may see translation as a way of enriching their native culture, literature, and even language, as a route toward cross-fertilization and a desirable hybridization. These translators privilege the source language and culture; they may choose not to translate things such as street names, food names, and key concepts (*amour propre, dignidad, dolce far niente*) inextricably embedded in the source culture. Their English may reflect peculiarities derived from the source language; they may write in a way that does not sound "native" but that instead reflects "interference" from the source language, as a way of underscoring difference and of allowing the reader to hear the traces of the foreign language beneath the English. Most importantly, these translators refuse to mask the fact that this is a translated, foreign text.

The second approach leads to a "domesticated"—or, more positively put, "communicative"—version of the text, which makes for more comfortable reading and thereby contributes to the sense of false familiarity mentioned earlier; but it puts readers more completely at the mercy of the translator's mediation and ultimately deprives them of much of the experience of the foreign. This approach has been in vogue for much of the twentieth century in Anglo-American publishing, where the push has been to hide the foreign origin of texts and to sell them as if they had originally been written in English, an English that is smooth and "fluent," as the jargon has it.

Once students have begun to contextualize the source text, once they have been introduced to some of the basic concepts of translation such as "fidelity" and its variant interpretations, once they have thought about what possibilities are open to translators in their quest to bring foreign text and native reader together, and once their preconceptions about translation as a mechanical activity or naturally occurring artifact begin to crumble, they are ready to look at a translated text with new eyes.

Class discussion might begin by eliciting from students details about their familiarity with the source culture to be portrayed in the work they will be reading—what they "know" about elements of the foreign culture that they will encounter, such as the setting; customs; kinship relations; the status of women, men, and children; and concepts of time. Later, after students have read the assigned work, referring back to this inventory of "knowledge" can help them focus on how the text at hand has disconfirmed some of those "certainties" and can lead to a discussion of new insights into the source culture provided by the text. One effective approach for the study of texts rich in cultural referents is to focus first on "surface" aspects of the culture (elements such as eating, dress, and geography) and then move on to more complex aspects, such as history—for example, how a certain historical figure or event in the work is seen by the originating culture in contrast to how that figure is seen in the students' culture. Students will thus be able to begin to gauge how what they know about the source culture, and the differences between it and their own culture, have been either boldfaced or erased as they are carried over in the act of translation. Throughout, the emphasis of the analysis should be to pinpoint clues to the translator's mediation by becoming alert to patterns and deviations, so that the translator's hand is laid on the table.

Concretely, students might explore whether culturally bound elements have been translated or left in the original language and culture, and they can discuss the effects of these practices and what the translator's motivation might have been for each decision. They can ask themselves, for example, whether obvious elements like food, proper names, and specific places have been replaced with things and names familiar to the reader. Have street names been translated or left in the original? They might theorize that while leaving a name like rue de Rivoli or Via Veneto or Unter den Linden untouched in a translation could respond to the common practice of leaving well-known names in the original, leaving intact a lesser-known (less highly valued?) proper name such as Calle Muralla may respond to a number of rationales. For instance, the translator may want to change that common practice of leaving well-known names in the original (based as it is upon assumptions as to what street names an "educated" reader should recognize) or even to undermine the snobbish hierarchy of which streets and languages our culture recognizes as "important." Conversely, a decision to translate a street name or landmark—to render el Malecón, for example, as "the street that runs along the oceanfront"—may be traced back to a translator's (or editor's) view of what may be too difficult for a target reader, whose $18.95 may be more important to the translator or publisher than being an agent of cultural change.

Intertextual allusions or references also provide an important window into a translator's approach. Students will discover, at one extreme, those who simply translate the words of the allusion into English and leave the allusions themselves unexplained or unglossed; at the other extreme, they will encounter those who replace the entire allusion with an "equivalent" one from the readers' culture—what is called "finding the dynamic equivalent." Eugene Nida, one of the foremost exponents of the "dynamic equivalence" or "equivalent effect" strategy of translation, states that a translation "of dynamic equivalence aims at complete naturalness of expression, and tries to relate the receptor to modes of behavior relevant within the context of his own culture; it does not insist that he understand the cultural patterns of the source-language context." An example of translating the Bible for a contemporary American, Nida has written, might be rendering "greet one another with a holy kiss" (the literal translation of an original biblical passage) with "give one another a hearty handshake all around" (Nida 129–30). Again, these translational decisions point to a considered approach on the part of the translator, one which—in the absence of an explicit statement from the translator—a thoughtful reader should be able to infer.

Likewise, texts with historical allusions may provide an opportunity to examine the treatment of historical events and figures, especially the angle they are being presented from. Often the key to the point of view assumed by the translator can be found in the language used to name historical events or places. Think, for example, of the Anglo-American viewpoint that is assumed when shorthand such as "the Cuban Missile Crisis" is employed, or when a translator makes the choice between using the term "Bay of Pigs" versus Playa Girón, or when las Islas Malvinas is translated as "the Falkland Islands."

Observations such as these make students aware of the importance of focusing on the translator's language (and culture-centric) choices. To direct the students' thinking about this topic, the teacher might pose such questions as: Does the language of the translation seem to echo the sort of language that would have been used at the time of the writing of the original? That is, does the translation "modernize" or "archaize"? Does it contain anachronisms (verbal or conceptual), or does it seem to attempt to avoid them? What might the arguments be for modernization versus faux historicization? If the author is known and applauded in his native culture as a stylist, does the style of the translation give any sense of that virtuosity, or is it merely "literary"? Is the vocabulary of the translation inventive or relatively mainstream; broad or limited; recherché or plain? What about sentence length and complexity? Do sentences in the translation reflect the original as described by critics and reviewers who have discussed the original, or have they been made to fit the reading habits of the target audience? Does dialogue reflect contemporary English usage, or has it been "treated" to reflect some notion of foreignness or datedness or other type of distance? Here, reviews and scholarly discussions of the translation's style versus the original's style, together with close reading, can help the class assess the stylistic approach of the translator to the text. In what students might be encouraged to see as "detective work," they can uncover differences between the original and the translation, and they can gain some idea of the strategy (the "modus operandi") that has been employed.

Once students understand that there is no such thing as one correct translation (excepting, of course, mistakes that may be the result of a translator's ignorance or oversight), that different translators may approach a text with a different readership or purpose in mind, and that, consequently, translators shape or emphasize different aspects of the source text, the focus of interest rightly shifts to *how* a translator has approached the language of the text. Here again it is useful to look at multiple translations of the same text and especially at special uses of language, such as in poetry or jokes, where "fidelity" must be redefined with the understanding that however much the language was stretched in the original, so also must the translation be allowed to stretch.

We know that instructors often begin with the a priori assertion to their classes that the experience of reading a translated text, if the students recognize the translation at all, will always be somehow diminished and less than perfect, and that students' inability to read the original will always stand between them and a "native" experience of the text. An attitude such as this, so frustrating for students and so detrimental to learning, is undoubtedly in conflict with the true spirit of education; but with pedagogy refocused in the ways I have suggested here, this attitude can be replaced with a positive, inquiring attitude, under which translation is approached not as a necessary evil, not even as merely a necessary route to a desired end, but as an exciting intellectual endeavor to be more fully explored in its own right.

NOTES

1. An example of an "encounter" such as the one suggested here might occur with *The Answer/La Respuesta* by Sor Juana Inés de la Cruz, critical edition and translation by Electa Arenal and Amanda Powell. Even before reading begins, a careful examination of the text with the students should reveal several key things to them: first, that Arenal and Powell see the roles of critic and translator as inseparable—a position that will bear further discussion as the translation is examined; second, that, as evidenced by the chronology included in the book's front matter, it is the translators'/critics' intention to contextualize the author and the work within the history of women's contributions to the arts, sciences, and religion; third, that, as stated in the preface and revealed by the choice of publisher (Feminist Press), the translators/critics will focus on the author's feminist ideology; fourth, that the extensive use of footnotes, bibliographical material, and annotations all emphasize the scholarly attention accorded this author; and fifth, that the translators'/critics' efforts are aimed at ensuring Sor Juana a place in the international canon of feminist writings.

2. André Lefevere's in-depth discussion of the several translations of Catullus 32 in *Translating Literature: Practice and Theory in a Comparative Literature Context* can also serve as an excellent model for this classroom strategy, as can Peden's discussion of the translations of Sor Juana Inés de la Cruz's "Poem 145."

3. While not from a "familiar" culture, *Nineteen Ways of Looking at Wang Wei* (Weinberger and Paz, eds.) is a charming and revelatory example of such an anthology, consisting of translations of the same poem by a number of translators, some of them poets in their own right, which might be used for discussing translation strategy and "re-creative poetics" in general.

WORKS CITED

Biguenet, John, and Rainer Schulte, eds. *The Craft of Translation*. Chicago: University of Chicago Press, 1989.

Casanova, Pascale. *The World Republic of Letters*. Translated by M. B. DeBevoise. Cambridge, MA, and London: Harvard University Press, 2004.

Casas, Bartolomé de las. *An Account, Much Abbreviated, of the Destruction of the Indies*. Edited and with an introduction by Franklin Knight. Translated by Andrew Hurley. Indianapolis and Cambridge, MA: Hackett, 2003.

———. *The Devastation of the Indies: A Brief Account*. Translated by Herma Briffault. Baltimore: Johns Hopkins University Press, 1992.

———. *A Short Account of the Destruction of the Indies*. Edited and translated by Nigel Griffin. Introduction by Anthony Pagden. London and New York: Penguin Classics, 1992.

Cruz, Sor Juana Inés de la. *The Answer/La Respuesta*. Translated and edited by Electa Arenal and Amanda Powell. New York: Feminist Press, 1994.

Hulme, John. *Guillaume Chequespierre and the Oise Salon*. New York: Harper & Row, 1986.

Lefevere, André. *Translating Literature: Practice and Theory in a Comparative Literature Context*. New York: Modern Language Association of America, 1992.

Nida, Eugene. "Principles of Correspondence." In *The Translation Studies Reader*, edited by Lawrence Venuti, 126–40. London and New York: Routledge, 2000.

Peden, Margaret Sayers. "Building a Translation, the Reconstruction Business: Poem 145 of Sor Juana Inés de la Cruz." In *The Craft of Translation*, edited by John Biguenet and Rainer Schulte, 13–27. Chicago: University of Chicago Press, 1989.

Rooten, Luis d'Antin van. *Mots d'Heures: Gousses, Rames*. New York and London: Penguin Books, 1980.

Schulte, Rainer, and John Biguenet, eds. *Theories of Translation*. Chicago: University of Chicago Press, 1992.

Venuti, Lawrence. "The Pedagogy of Literature." Chap. 5 in *The Scandals of Translation: Towards an Ethics of Difference*. London and New York: Routledge, 1998.

———. *The Translator's Invisibility: A History of Translation*. London and New York: Routledge, 1995.

———, ed. *The Translation Studies Reader*. London and New York: Routledge, 2000.

Weinberger, Eliot, and Octavio Paz, eds. *Nineteen Ways of Looking at Wang Wei*. Mount Kisko, NY: Moyer Bell Ltd., 1987.

"Take it with a Grain of MSG": Reading Translated Literatures from Other Shores

Yunte Huang

In this age of globalization, transcoding is prevalent, ranging from adopting Unicode as the universal standard for digitizing all the scripts in the world to thematizing a foreign literary text as if it were a local story but scripted in a different language. In both cases, the other's mode of inscription or structure of meaning is regarded as dispensable or secondary to the content, or data, to be processed and distributed by the megamachine that levels out all the differences of codes, temporalities, and localities. Against such a technocultural background, I propose in this essay that literatures translated and read in contexts radically different from the ones in which they were composed may teach us important lessons about the perils of transcoding and may prepare us, in the words of Gayatri Chakravorty Spivak, "for a patient and provisional and forever deferred arrival into the performance of the other" (13). Between impatient transcoding and patient response, Spivak reminds us, "there is a world of difference" (13).

Because my expertise in foreign literature is limited to Chinese, I will confine my discussion in this essay to two kinds of Chinese literary work: classical poetry and transnational literature. In both cases, I suggest that it is not enough for North American instructors and students simply to look for and rely on a good translation that reads elegantly and smoothly in English. The more important tasks lie in teaching and learning the ideographic quality of Chinese characters, the history of literary genres, and the cultural functions of these genres in given historical contexts. Better still, in the case of classical Chinese poetry, there is in North America a very long history of translation and reception that has literally made Chinese poetry part of the English-language literature. Similarly, some of the Chinese literary works produced by immigrants to North America have made their way into the literary canon here after being translated. Even though this canon still maintains an imperial English-only policy, the multilingual view of North American literature has gained increasing currency in recent years and will create a double imperative for us not just to read those immigrant texts in translation and to know their literary and cultural specifics, but also to regard those specifics as part of North American literature.[1] Aware of the importance of shifting contexts, I will now discuss how to read translated classical Chinese poetry in light of the entangled history of reception and appropriation by Anglo-American modernism, and I will address what to look out for when we read a text such as one of the Angel Island poems discussed below, which were originally written in Chinese but are now known almost exclusively in English translation.

In the history of cross-cultural literary appropriation, nothing may sound as outrageous as T. S. Eliot's assertion that Ezra Pound was "the inventor of Chinese poetry for our time" (xvi). Seen in a different light, however, Eliot may be right: he does qualify his claim by calling Pound the inventor of Chinese poetry "for our time." That is, Pound did not invent Chinese poetry as such, but rather Chinese poetry in English translation. This is not the place for a full account of the invention to which Eliot refers, but it would be impossible, or at least delusional, for us to believe that we could come face to face with a Chinese poem directly or through translation without knowing the basic premises of that invention, because our understanding of poetry in general has been shaped by Anglo-American modernism, which in turn was shaped partly by its translations and appropriations of other poetic traditions, such as the Chinese.

Take, for example, the following poem by Wang Wei (701–761), titled "Wei City Tune":

渭城朝雨浥輕塵
客舍青青柳色新
勸君更盡一杯酒
西出陽關無故人

Translated literally, the poem reads:

Wei City's morning rain wets the light dust
The guest-inn blues with new willow hue

Asking you to drink one more round
West of Yang Gate, not friend to be found

Ezra Pound, in *Cathay* (1915), renders it as:

Light rain is on the light dust.
The willow of the inn-yard
Will be going greener and greener,
But you, Sir, had better take wine ere your departure,
For you will have no friends about you
When you come to the gates of Go.

The liberty Pound took with the original has made his version quite controversial, and scholars are divided as to how to evaluate the reliability of his translation. But I think his so-called mistranslations or errors are more interesting and may teach us more about Chinese poetry than a "faithful" translation.

As I have argued elsewhere, a seemingly simple instant of translation of a poem contains a long history of dislocation and transformation of cultural meanings across linguistic boundaries. In the case of Pound's translation of Chinese poetry, I have called that history a process of transpacific displacement, starting from the Chinese originals, through Japanese interpretation, to Ernest Fenollosa's reconceptualization, and finally to Pound's reinvention.[2] One mistake Pound made in his version of "Wei City Tune," for instance, is the word *Go*. Despite its alliteration with "gates," *Go* is actually Pound's misreading of *Yo*, written in Fenollosa's cursive hand in the notebook Pound was working with, and *yo* is the Japanese pronunciation of the Chinese character *yang*.

These so-called mistakes or misconceptions do not just constitute an important record of cross-cultural poetics; they also bring forth the poetic quality of the originals, which are often suppressed by the attempt to create syntactical and semantic equivalence in other translations. For example, Pound's assertion that Chinese uses an "ideogramic method" of writing is often dismissed by scholars as a misrepresentation of the nature of the language. But if we adopt a Poundian (mis)reading, the above poem may yield unexpected poetic rewards unobtainable in translations that allow English to transcode Chinese. 輕 (light) originally refers to "light carriage." The radical on the left, 車, is a picture of a carriage seen from the side, 輈 (the two strokes on the sides are wheels). Pound's line "light rain on the light dust," which would have been unjustifiable semantically, does capture the sense of "carriage," as if the rain is riding on the dust. In the same vein, Pound's addition of "yard" to "inn," which alone would have been an sufficient equivalence to 客舍, foregrounds the spatial dimension of the second character, which is a picture of a house with a roof on top. Other Chinese words that are noticeable to a Poundian eye but would not have made a difference to a transcoding process include 青 (*qing*, meaning blue or green; 靑, a picture of wood on fire, causing "blue" flame); 盡 (*jin*, meaning empty; the lower radical 皿, or 𤮄, is a vessel, i.e., an "empty" vessel); and 西 (*xi*, meaning west; 㢴, a picture of a bird sitting on its nest—time for rest or sun setting in the "west").

While the same ideogramic quality of Chinese writing should continue to draw our attention when we turn to Angel Island poetry, other factors, such as genre and literary tradition, may appear more important with the new body of work because they may easily get lost in the liminal crossroad of culture contact, where Chinese meets Chinese American and where an active recontextualization, as I will argue, is especially needed. Writing about the African American tradition, Henry Louis Gates Jr. reminds us that "the black Africans who survived the dreaded 'Middle Passage' from the west coast of Africa to the New World did not sail alone. Violently and radically abstracted from their civilizations, these Africans nevertheless carried with them to the Western Hemisphere aspects of their cultures that were meaningful, that could not be obliterated, and that they chose, by acts of will, not to forget: their music, their myths, their expressive institutional structures, their metaphysical systems of order, and their forms of performance."[3] Gates's reminder is equally applicable to Chinese immigrants who crossed the Pacific and managed to maintain aspects of their culture, including language, poetry, and literary traditions.

The poems written by Chinese immigrants on the wooden barracks walls of the detaining station on Angel Island, off the coast of San Francisco, can be read as important records of a shameful, racist chapter of U.S. immigration history. Between 1910 and 1940, many Chinese were detained there as a result of the 1882 Chinese Exclusion Act, which virtually banned legal immigration of Chinese laborers, allowing only family-based immigration and a few other categories. While waiting for their cases to be processed, many of these immigrants, out of frustration, anger, or boredom, scribbled poems on the walls of the barracks. In the first anthology that published these poems in bilingual versions, the editors/translators divided them into thematic categories: "Voyage," "Detainment," "About Westerners," and so on. The editors/translators stated their clear preference for the semantic over the formal in their treatment of the poems: "The form [in our translation] is oftentimes compromised in order to retain the content, which we for historical reasons feel is our first priority" (Lai 31). As a result, the poems in translation pose little challenge to English readers, and scholars have characterized them as "artlessly direct" works whose significance would have to derive from their contents alone (Wong 253).

But I want to suggest that the illusion of these poems' transparency is created by the translators' disregard for their modes of inscription. Granted that these are important historical records and that there is a political urgency nowadays to publish a body of underrepresented ethnic minority writing; but by choosing content over form, data over code, the translators gain short-term effect by "getting the stories out" at the expense of the long-term efficacy of carrying over other aspects of literary culture.[4] In other words, in order to have a better view of where these Angel Island poems stand at the intersection of cultures, we need to know not only the historical facts of Chinese immigration to the United States, but also the Chinese literary tradition out of which these poems originated and against which they must be interpreted.

My insistence on the importance of knowing the contingent origins of cultural practices in our study of translated literature derives from my belief that, as Masao Miyoshi has put it, "genres, like most other things, are specific to history and geography" (28). Therefore, it is necessary for us to recognize what Miyoshi has called "the form's native visage and lineage" (36). Angel Island poems should be read as examples of 題壁詩 (*tibishi*). Literally meaning "poetry inscribed on the wall, *tibishi* has been an important form of composing and disseminating poems in Chinese literary history. The space for inscription is actually not limited to "walls"; poems written on cliffs, rocks, doors, windows, rafters, and even snow fields also belong to this genre. At inns and roadside pavilions where travelers usually stopped for a rest, there were even special kinds of "poetry boards" set up for the convenience of the poetically inspired.[5] On the walls of the wooden barracks where the Chinese immigrants were detained, there were no "poetry boards," although the sense of transition one felt at a modern-day detaining station was surely as strong as that felt at the roadside pavilions of ancient times;

and the poetic desire thus inspired was equally deep. The detainees carved poems with knives and used brushes to paint them over so the words would be legible. Many of these poems self-consciously address themselves and the other poems as *tibishi*:

> Over a hundred poems are on the walls.
> Looking at them, they are all pining at the delayed progress. (62–63)

Or,

> There are tens of thousands of poems composed on these walls.
> They are all cries of complaint and sadness. (66–67)

And they are all meant to be read by the other detainees who will stand on exactly the same spots where the poems were composed and who share the same experiences of incarceration, frustration, and humiliation:

> Let this be an expression of the torment which fills my belly.
> Leave this as a memento to encourage fellow souls. (121–22)

Or,

> My fellow villagers seeing this should take heed and remember,
> I write my wild words to let those after me know. (162–63)

This feature of *tibishi*, in calling attention to writing as set on something (the wall) and absorbed in its material relations to its intended readers, raise questions about the politics of transcription, translation, and reading.

These poems have now made their way into the American literary canon, appearing in collections such as the *Heath Anthology of American Literature*. They are printed only in English translations and made to look clean, conforming to the horizontal linearity of English poetry (the Chinese originals on the walls are mostly written vertically, from right to left), and they are made easy to understand with the help of editorial annotations. As such finished products ready for private consumption by a modern-day reader, they are a far cry from their obscure, marginalized provenance on the walls of an immigration detaining station. I am not trying to fetishize the materiality of these poems, but as *tibishi,* they do challenge us to confront the material properties of the graphic space. If the existence of masterpieces in literary history relies explicitly or implicitly on the notion of an abstracted and infinitely transmissible text independent of modes of inscription, *tibishi* calls this notion into question. It seems that these poems achieve their efficacy more as a result of their physical traces, rather than in spite of them; they draw attention to the act of their saying, and not merely to what they say. A translation that does not take into consideration this feature of *tibishi* and merely transcodes the content will thus fail to elicit what is truly significant about these poems in their full historical materiality.

But ultimately, even materiality is not as important as the shifting contexts for these poems, which would in turn require an active recontextulization on the reader's part. While emphasizing the importance of knowing the origins of cultural practices in our study of translated literature, I also understand the practical needs of a reader to whom such origins remain foreign and remote. Hence, if direct access to cultural knowledge is unobtainable, a route of indirect knowing or recontextualization may be attempted, with caution. With Angel Island poems, for instance, one may think of their similarity to a form of writing more familiar to most of us: graffiti. When labeled as vandalism, graffiti constitute a crime of writing. By means of defacement, graffiti intentionally violate property rights. "They draw attention to themselves," writes Dick Hebdige. "They are an expression both of impotence and a kind of power—the power to disfigure."[6] As such, graffiti exhibit, in the words of Susan Stewart, "a stylization inseparable from the body, a stylization that, in its impenetrable 'wildness,' could surpass even linguistic reference and serve purely as the concrete evidence of an individual existence and the reclamation of the environment through the label of the personal."[7] When conceptualized as artwork, however, graffiti join the ranks of commodity and lose their signature of cultural resistance. The so-called tags, which used to provide clues for the police to track down and arrest inveterate vandals, have now become signatures of commodifiable authenticity. The history of collecting, editing, and anthologizing *tibishi* shows a similar process of personalization and depersonalization, legitimization and delegitimization. Poems by canonical authors are often copied and preserved, whereas poems by anonymous authors get ignored and erased. Hence, canonization of *tibishi* is also a process of commodification that changes the nature of the scriptural economy associated with "writing on the wall," relocating traces of inscription from the site of destructive "doodling" to the domain of productive labor.

Angel Island poems were on the brink of destruction because the park ranger's superiors considered them meaningless graffiti (let us remember that maintaining a public park requires erasing unauthorized inscriptions from public space and erecting in the same space such utterly oxymoronic signs as "DO NOT WRITE ON WALLS"). The process of transcribing and publishing these poems is inevitably in danger of replicating the process of legitimization and delegitimization that the original inscriptions have questioned with their defiant opacity, with their status as vandalistic graffiti and not just reproducible poems with recuperable themes and thoughts. The potency and efficacy of these poems thus come from their form rather than their content, from their occupying an ambivalent space between a form of vandalism to be condemned and a form of historical record to be preserved. That ambivalence is what the efforts of transcribing, translating, and publishing these poems have hitherto missed.

For readers who lack a direct knowledge of the history of *tibishi,* a comparison with graffiti, a form more familiar to them, would have elucidated some of the features of Angel Island poems that have unfortunately been rendered invisible by current translations. Such an indirect way of knowing through recontextualization is not just another case of transcoding; it is an active response that mobilizes one's own imagination. A few decades ago, Jerome Rothenberg proposed "total translation" as a way to deal with poetic traditions unfamiliar to North American English readers: "Everything in these song-poems is finally translatable: words, sounds, voice, melody, gesture, event, etc., in the reconstitution of a unity that would be shattered by approaching each element in isolation. A full and total experience begins it, which only a total translation can fully bring across" (91). If the traditional idea of translation, as evidenced in the treatment of Angel Island poems, involves merely a shift in code to present a common meaning to a linguistically different audience, Rothenberg's total translation is meant to understand the past form through a present parallel, "making something present, or making something as a present—for his own time and place" (92).

It may seem that the notion of indirect knowing and the ideal of total translation are at odds with each other, but both acknowledge the original as a full present, not to be transcoded and conquered by assigning it a language familiar to us. "Each poem, being made present and translated," says Rothenberg, "flies in the face of divisive ideology" (75).

NOTES

1. For the best examples of multilingual perspectives on American literature, see Werner Sollors and Marc Shell, eds., *Multilingual Anthology of American Literature* (New York: New York University Press, 2000), and Werner Sollors, ed., *Multilingual America: Transnationalism, Ethnicity, and the Languages of American Literature* (New York: New York University Press, 1998).

2. See my book *Transpacific Displacement: Ethnography, Translation, and Intertextual Travel in Twentieth-Century American Literature* (Berkeley: University of California Press, 2002).

3. Henry Louis Gates Jr., *The Signifying Monkey: A Theory of African-American Literary Criticism* (New York: Oxford University Press, 1988), 3–4.

4. Once again a comparison with African American literature may be applicable. During the Harlem Renaissance, leading African American writers were divided over the use of black vernacular in their work. One side argued for the adoption of standard English, mastering the form in order to achieve short-term results, and the other side promoted the use of vernacular as deformation of the mastery in order to achieve long-term efficacy.

5. In English, Judith T. Zeitline's recent essay "Disappearing Verses: Writing on Walls and Anxieties of Loss" contains wonderful case studies of *tibishi*.

6. Dick Hebdige, *Subculture: The Meaning of Style* (London: Routledge, 1979), 3.

7. Susan Stewart, *Crimes of Writing: Problems in the Containment of Representation* (New York: Oxford University Press, 1991), 212.

WORKS CONSULTED

Eliot, T. S. "Introduction." In Ezra Pound, *Selected Poems,* xvi. London: Faber and Faber, 1928.

Gates, Henry Louis, Jr. *The Signifying Monkey: A Theory of African-American Literary Criticism.* New York: Oxford University Press, 1988.

Hebdige, Dick. *Subculture: The Meaning of Style.* London: Routledge, 1979.

Huang, Yunte. *Shi: A Radical Reading of Chinese Poetry.* New York: Roof Books, 1997.

———. *Transpacific Displacement: Ethnography, Translation, and Intertextual Travel in Twentieth-Century American Literature.* Berkeley: University of California Press, 2002.

———. *Transpacific Imaginations: History, Literature, Counterpoetics.* Cambridge, MA: Harvard University Press, 2008.

Lai, Him Mark, Genny Lim, and Judy Yung, eds. and trans. *Island: Poetry and History of Chinese Immigrants on Angel Island 1910–1940.* Seattle: University of Washington Press, 1991. First published 1980 by the HOCDOI Project.

Miyoshi, Masao. *Off Center: Power and Culture Relations between Japan and the United States.* Cambridge, MA: Harvard University Press, 1991.

Pound, Ezra. *Cathay.* London: Elkin Mathews, 1915.

———. *Selected Poems.* London: Faber and Faber, 1928.

Rothenberg, Jerome. *Pre-Faces and Other Writings.* New York: New Directions, 1981.

Sollors, Werner, ed. *Multilingual America: Transnationalism, Ethnicity, and the Languages of American Literature.* New York: New York University Press, 1998.

———, and Marc Shell, eds. *Multilingual Anthology of American Literature.* New York: New York University Press, 2000.

Spivak, Gayatri Chakravorty. *Death of a Discipline.* New York: Columbia University Press, 2003.

Stewart, Susan. *Crimes of Writing: Problems in the Containment of Representation.* New York: Oxford University Press, 1991.

Wong, Sau-ling C. "The Politics and Poetics of Folksong Reading: Literary Portrayals of Life under Exclusion." In *Entry Denied: Exclusion and the Chinese Community in America, 1882–1943,* edited by Sucheng Chan, 253. Philadelphia: Temple University Press, 1991.

Zeitline, Judith T. "Disappearing Verses: Writing on Walls and Anxieties of Loss." In *Writing and Materiality in China: Essays in Honor of Patrick Hanan,* edited by Judith T. Zeitline and Lydia Liu, 73–132. Cambridge, MA: Harvard University Press, 2003.

Fictional Texts as Pedagogical Tools

Rosemary Arrojo

I have assumed the mysterious obligation to reconstruct, word for word, the novel that for him was spontaneous. This game of solitaire I play is governed by two polar rules: the first allows me to try out formal or psychological variants; the second forces me to sacrifice them to the "original" text and to come, by irrefutable arguments, to those eradications. . . . In addition to these first two artificial constraints there is another, inherent to the project. Composing the *Quixote* in the early seventeenth century was a reasonable, necessary, perhaps even inevitable undertaking; in the early twentieth, it is virtually impossible. Not for nothing have three hundred years elapsed, freighted with the most complex events. Among those events, to mention but one, is the *Quixote* itself.

Jorge Luis Borges, "Pierre Menard, Author of the *Quixote*"

Readers of translations who have no access to their source texts generally ignore the gaps and differences that separate the two, tending to view translated texts as if they were indeed originals. However, if readers are invited to seriously consider the fact that a translation is necessarily another text that has been produced in another language, time, and context, they are bound to encounter an array of complex issues that are associated with the relationships usually established between the original and its derivations, and between authorship and translation, or even between what is domestic and what is foreign. At the same time, when readers of translations happen to be well-acquainted with the languages of their originals and are able to compare them, they often realize that the versions available may not reflect the same reading of the original that they have in mind.

Translation, which has the potential to reveal that the original is plural and ever-changing—and which, therefore, may undermine our general belief in the alleged stability of meaning and the possibility of identical repetitions—is essentially subversive. Moreover, as we realize that any translation is first and foremost an interpretation of the original that is written in another linguistic and cultural context by someone who is (usually) not its author, and that it is nonetheless offered to us as the original's legitimate replacement in our own language, we might begin to wonder why translated texts are often viewed with some degree of suspicion, and, therefore, why the general discourse on translation has been dominated by prescriptive statements that emphasize issues associated with respect and fidelity in an attempt to make sure that translators do not transgress the often unclear limits between translation and authorship.

In contrast to the conventionally sober discourse of theory and scholarly texts, works of fiction tend to make more explicit the darker side of translation and the responses that it seems to trigger, which, precisely because they involve desires and feelings, usually complicate the relationships that are normally acceptable between originals and their interpretations, and between authors and interpreters. Fictional texts that explore representations of translation introduce readers to characters who have to deal with the ethical dilemmas associated with the relationships usually established between originals and their reproductions; as such they constitute excellent material for the discussion of fundamental issues directly related to translation and interpretation. Because their plots bring practical illustrations of the main theoretical issues that have dominated the academic discourse about translation, they can be quite efficient, for example, in stimulating students to compare and evaluate some of the theoretical concerns that have occupied specialists. Their use for pedagogical purposes is especially suitable for students who are not familiar with the discourse of translation theory or with the kinds of research currently conducted in translation studies. To the extent that they bring us characters who are involved with translation and interpretation issues and who belong to communities that tend to criticize and often condemn their work, these fictional texts can inspire even nonspecialists to reflect on the processes involved in writing, reading, and translating, and hopefully also to problematize their own notions about the production, reproduction, and reception of texts.

Jorge Luis Borges's well-known short story "Pierre Menard, Author of the *Quixote*" is the quintessential fictional text about translation, and it can be extremely effective at raising questions and stimulating productive discussions on the most recurrent notions associated with originals and their reproductions. First published in Argentina in 1944, it is a perplexing story in the format of a short review essay that is also an alleged tribute to Pierre Menard, who, we learn from the narrator, is an obscure French symbolist author who has recently died. The narrator is a critic who claims to have catalogued all the "visible" works left by Menard: nineteen pieces (monographs, translations, scholarly essays, drafts, sonnets) that are described in a sarcastic and, at times, almost cruel manner suggesting that a mediocre but ambitious intellectual and writer is being profiled (89–90). However, it is the characterization of Pierre Menard's "invisible" work—"the writing of a few fragments from Cervantes's *Don Quixote*" (91)—that has attracted so much attention to Borges's story. Menard's "invisible" project, to which he "dedicated his scruples and his nights 'lit by midnight oil'" (95), turns out to be the translation of excerpts from Cervantes's masterpiece, even though the word "translation" is never used to describe it. We are told, though, that Menard's work, which involved "infinite complexity" and which was "perhaps the most significant writing of our time" (90), was in fact the repetition "in a foreign tongue of a book that already existed" (95).

The peculiar relationship that Menard establishes with Cervantes's text, and all the intriguing relationships that the story allows us to examine—between the original and its repetition, the author and the translator, the translator and his reader, the reader and the translation, or even between Menard and don Quixote as characters—constitute valuable material for reflection on the issues pertaining to the nature of language, meaning, texts, and the subject, which have been central to Western thought for the last two millennia. And yet, some of the fundamental issues concerning translation and interpretation that are raised by Menard's "interminably heroic production" (90), such as the status and (in)stability of the original, the translator's (in)visibility, and the ambiguity of faithfulness, can be productively discussed on many levels by both translation scholars and nonspecialists alike. For example, students of literature and readers of translations who are not familiar with translation studies but have been introduced to the main tenets of poststructuralist and postmodern thought will find in the story a good-humored illustration of the fundamentals of contemporary, post-Nietzschean linguistic and textual theories, such as the conventional nature of meaning and hierarchical oppositions, the instability of texts, and the inevitably productive character of interpretation, which they can then associate with their reflection on translation.[1]

The story can also be quite useful for introducing students who are not familiar with formal theories in general to the basic theoretical issues related to translation. One could start, for instance, with a discussion of traditional, common-sense notions of fidelity and then invite students to reexamine them in the light of the translation strategies devised by Menard to reproduce Cervantes's original. At first, as we are informed, "his method was to be relatively simple: Learn Spanish, return to Catholicism, fight against the Moor or Turk, forget the history of Europe from 1602 to 1918—*be* Miguel de Cervantes" (91). We might argue, among other things, that in his initial plan to become Cervantes and to fully repeat the text of *Don Quixote,* Menard was actually taking quite seriously (and, in a way, literally) the usual recommendation that translators should be invisible in their work and thus attempt to produce translations that fully reproduce the same meanings of their originals.

Borges's amusing illustration (and implicit sarcastic critique) of our traditional conception of how translations should relate to their originals becomes even more precise in Menard's further elaboration of his method. As the narrator tells us, our French symbolist "discarded" his initial idea of turning into Cervantes on the grounds that it was "too easy" (91). Understandably enough, "being, somehow, Cervantes, and arriving thereby at the Quixote . . . looked to Menard less challenging (and therefore less interesting) than continuing to be Pierre Menard and coming to the Quixote *through the experiences of Pierre Menard*" (91).[2] Students can be invited to associate the laughable, seemingly absurd terms in which translation is described in Borges's story with our usual conceptions of translation ethics, which, we may conclude, are just as absurd or impossible as Menard's. Menard's choice to continue being himself while composing exactly the same text written by Cervantes in another time and in another language makes him seem to be a model translator who is literally following the ethical guidelines typically prescribed by tradition. In this way, Menard is also an illustration of the quixotic mission translators are expected to accomplish in our culture.

Any discussion of Pierre Menard's strategies to repeat Cervantes's text and their relationship with translation ethics will have to take into account the story's climactic point, which probably is one of the most inspiring moments in twentieth-century fiction: the narrator's comparison of the two verbally identical fragments from part 1, chapter 9 of *Don Quixote,* one by Cervantes, and the other by Menard: "truth, whose mother is history, rival of time, depository of deeds, witness of the past, exemplar and adviser to the present, and the future's counselor" (94).[3] As the narrator presents his different readings of the two fragments that are "apparently" the same, we can reflect on what a text actually is, what kind of relationships it establishes with reading and interpretation, and, finally, how the (in)stability and the status of the original, and of texts in general, can be related to an ethics of interpretation. After all, even though Menard has produced a translation that seems to be a perfect reproduction of the original—that is, a translation that has managed to keep the exact same words, and, paradoxically, even the exact same language of the original—it is still read by the narrator as a different text. Therefore, although Menard dies with the conviction that he has indeed been totally faithful to Cervantes's words, his alleged repetition of the original cannot truly recover it. Could we say, then, that Menard has been truly faithful to Cervantes? Has Borges's narrator been faithful to Menard's version, or even to his declared intentions? How can reading, interpreting, and translating be controlled? Can they ever be controlled?

Besides stimulating instructors and students to inquire into mainstream notions of translation ethics and the kind of expectations they place upon the translator's task, Menard's peculiar relationship with Cervantes and his masterpiece will also give interested readers the opportunity to reflect on closely related issues such as the status of translations and originals in our culture, and the ways in which we tend to respond to both. In order to approach such issues, one could further explore Borges's plot with questions such as the following: Why is the word "translation" never used to describe Menard's work? Why is his translation project "invisible"? Considering Pierre Menard's obsessive desire to repeat Cervantes's text, how is Borges's story addressing the recurrent cliché of the translator as frustrated author? How are authorship and translation being treated in the story? How does Borges's narrator treat the deceased Pierre Menard and his quixotic project? What kind of conclusions would the plot of Borges's story allow us to reach about translation in general?[4]

Even though I have not been actively searching for texts that focus on representations of translators and translations, over the years I have come across pieces from different cultures and traditions that have helped me refine and deepen my own thinking about translation and particularly about the ways in which our culture tends to respond to translators and their craft.[5] Some of these texts are not available in English and unfortunately cannot be used with students who do not have access to other languages. In spite of that, though, at least two of them deserve to be mentioned here. One is a delightful short story written in the 1930s by Hungarian author Dezsö Kosztolányi, originally published in his 1933 collection *Kornél esti,* which I read in Ladislao Szabo's 1996 Portuguese version, "O tradutor cleptomaníaco" ("The Kleptomaniac Translator").[6] The other is Claude Bleton's recent novel *Les Nègres du traducteur,*[7] which I read in the Spanish version, titled *Los negros del traductor,* by María Teresa Gallego, Andrés Ehrenhaus, Miguel Sáenz, and Jesús Zulaika. *Los negros del traductor* was published in 2004, the same year as the original.[8]

Like Borges's "Pierre Menard, Author of the *Quixote,*" Kosztolányi's and Bleton's texts offer readers an amusing exploration of recurrent commonplaces associated with translators and their relationships with originals and their authors. Also, like "Pierre Menard," these pieces feature a complex relationship between translator and author, in which the first is attracted to translation as the opportunity to occupy someone else's authorial position. However, unlike Borges's character, whose desire to become Cervantes results in an "invisible" writing project that is apparently harmless, Kosztolányi's and Bleton's fictional translators are shown to threaten the integrity of the originals or authors they translate. Gallus, the kleptomaniac in Kosztolányi's story, is a frustrated writer who accepts the job of translating a second-rate English novella nobody else wants to touch because he desperately needs the money. Even though (or precisely because) his skillful writing turns the trashy English text into elegant Hungarian prose, he is accused of stealing objects and characters from the original and is forever ostracized from the circle of writers to which he aspired to belong. While Gallus is severely punished for having dared to take an authorial position in his work as a translator, Aaron Janvier, Bleton's narrator/translator in *Les Nègres du traducteur,* manages to turn upside down the traditional hierarchical opposition between originals and translations, and between authors and translators, transforming his authors into subservient ghostwriters who are in charge of faithfully writing the Spanish "originals" to the French "translations" he sends them. Moreover, as some of his authors start rebelling against his outrageous demands, he does not hesitate to kill them off, and he even gets away with it for a while until he is finally caught by an attentive reader.

The motif of the translator or interpreter as a disruptive agent can also be examined in two texts originally published in Portuguese, for which there are available English versions. I am referring to "Notas ao pé da página" ("Footnotes," in Clifford E. Landers's English version), a hilarious short story published by the Brazilian Moacyr Scliar in the mid-1990s, and *História do Cerco de Lisboa*, a 1989 novel by Portuguese author José Saramago, whose English version, *The History of the Siege of Lisbon*, was written by Giovanni Pontiero. While Scliar's story introduces us to a powerful, self-confident translator who literally takes the place of the author he is translating, Saramago's novel brings us a lonely, bitter proofreader who resents the authors whose manuscripts he is (under)paid to read. At the same time, though, and in spite of their differences, Scliar's and Saramago's plots explicitly associate authorial power to male sexual prowess, adding yet another twist to the motif of the translator as an unwelcome intruder or incorrigible betrayer. The successful translator in Scliar's story expresses his authorial voice in five footnotes to his "invisible" translation of a poet's diaries. With the excuse of clarifying some points of the original, to which we do not have access, the footnotes provide us with details of the asymmetrical relationship between the translator and the author, in which the latter needs to beg the former to translate his text. The footnotes also inform us about the love triangle in which the translator gets involved with the poet's mistress, a story that ends happily for the translator, who marries the poet's former lover. The poet, however, could not bear the heartache and ends up dying.[9]

As Scliar's character takes on an explicitly authorial position, which is also equated with his ability to seduce his author's lover, he finds a parallel in Saramago's Raimundo Silva, the proofreader who changes his life as soon as he finds the courage to subvert a historical text about medieval Portugal, titled *History of the Siege of Lisbon*, which he has accepted for proofreading. When Raimundo adds a "no" to a crucial sentence that clearly states that the crusaders will help the Portuguese to recover Lisbon from the Moors, he not only changes the history of his country but also begins to change his own. As he dares to make himself visible as an author, Saramago's proofreader attracts the attention of his editor, a beautiful and intelligent woman who falls in love with him and encourages him to write his own manuscript, a novel appropriately titled *History of the Siege of Lisbon*.[10]

The motif of the translator or interpreter as a frustrated author who turns into a power-seeking, disruptive agent is also central in Italo Calvino's well-known novel *Se una notte d'inverno un viaggiatore,* first published in 1979, and whose English version, *If on a winter's night a traveler,* by William Weaver, appeared in 1981. Calvino's plot is especially efficient as an illustration of the power relations that often underlie the relationships usually established between authors, translators, editors, and readers. It introduces us to three main male characters: the Reader, who is the protagonist; Silas Flannery, an author figure who can no longer write; and Ermes Marana, the translator who manipulates and misplaces originals and their translations. All of them are sexually attracted to Ludmilla, the female reader, and as their pursuit of the original coincides with their pursuit of her affection, issues of fidelity and betrayal in sexual relationships become entangled with textual relations and the ethics of reading and translating.[11]

Calvino's association between woman and text is a revealing illustration of the gendering of textual relations that is a recurrent motif in our patriarchal culture, serving as a mirror for the feelings and prejudices that tend to be involved in the production and reproduction of meaning.[12] Possessing and controlling textual meaning, or the text as a woman, is thus presented as a male prerogative and as the main objective of the male characters involved in the plot. In addition, since texts, like women, tend to be fickle and unstable (as the rationale behind these associations seems to imply) and thus often at risk of surrendering to the seductive/interpretive advances of ambitious intruders, they need to be protected from the temptations of infidelity by a legitimate and strong male authorial figure. The unscrupulous Ermes Marana, Calvino's exemplary *traduttore/traditore,* is described as a swindler who flaunts his authorial/sexual desire and whose blatantly unethical behavior finds an obvious reflection in his very name. Appropriately, Ermes is also Hermes, the Greek god known to be a a mercenary and a master of deceit, who is usually associated with interpretation (hermeneutics) and mediation. He is also known for his brand of Aphroditic eroticism, which is inclined towards brief sexual encounters and multiple partners rather than marriage and family life (c.f., for example, Friedrich 205). Likewise, we can relate Calvino's character to Don Juan de Marana, Alexandre Dumas's early version of the widely known amoral seducer of women.[13] From this perspective, the sly translator is not simply unethical and uncommitted to the original when he inappropriately, and temporarily, takes the author's place; he also devotes his time and efforts to a kind of textual activity that is basically illegitimate and ultimately sterile.

Besides helping us elaborate on the widespread resistance to textual reproduction that is part and parcel of a culture that would like to count on the possibility of forever-stable meanings, these fictional translators function as key elements in plots that also feature the idealization of originals and authorship. In fact, the valorization of originals as a privileged form of text production—and, most importantly, the valorization of those who are in charge of creating them—go hand in hand with the kind of suspicious attitude toward interpretation and translation, or any form of text reproduction, that emerges in fictional texts that portray translators as thieves, assassins, or sexual predators.

Such issues can be examined more closely, for example, in Edgar Allan Poe's intriguing tale "The Oval Portrait" (originally titled "Life in Death"), first published in 1842, in which we will find another opportunity to further reflect on the hierarchical opposition between originals and their reproductions that seems ingrained in the fabric of our Platonic culture. Its plot introduces us to a painter and his passionate dedication to a portrait he is painting of his beloved young wife; it can also be read as a story about an original and its repetition, in which it is possible to view the lovely model as yet another representation of the text, or the original, as a woman.[14] The story allows us to examine the recurrent metaphor of the translator as a painter, which is often invoked to suggest that translation fails to reproduce the life of the original, particularly for those who do not have direct access to its language and therefore who cannot come into direct contact with whatever makes it worth reading.[15] Contrary to this notion that any form of reproduction, such as translation or portraiture, is typically unsatisfactory because it fails to bring us the spirit or the soul of the original, the painting in Poe's story seems to be miraculously (and tragically) superior to the model as it somehow literally captures, or even steals, the life and beauty of the painter's bride.

As the plot suggests, this astounding result is directly associated with the painter's passionate devotion to his art. He is so "wild" about his craft and becomes so absorbed in the painting of his bride that he completely disregards her well-being, failing to notice that while he devotes his time and energy to his work, her life and beauty are actually being transferred to the portrait. Only when his project is finally finished and he is able to come back to his senses does he realize that his lovely model—his "original," so to speak—is dead: "And then the brush was given, and then the tint was placed; and, for one moment the painter stood entranced before the work which he had wrought: but in the next while yet he gazed, he grew tremulous and very pallid, and aghast, and crying with a loud voice, 'This is indeed Life itself!' Turned himself suddenly round to his beloved who was dead. The painter then added: 'But is this indeed Death?'" (737–38).

Instructors and students might find it enriching to compare the miraculous achievement of Poe's painter to Pierre Menard's *Quixote* in Borges's story, as both characters seem to have produced translations that appear to be totally faithful to their originals. However, even though in both plots the extraordinary translations are shown to be not only quite different from their originals but also independent texts that can be read or admired for their own sake, Poe's story adds a perplexing twist to our reflection on the allegedly subversive vocation of translations and their ambivalent relationship with originals. While Menard's "more subtle" *Quixote* does not invalidate or erase Cervantes's, in "The Oval Portrait" the rearticulation of the usual opposition between the original and its repetition brings out the supposedly destructive thrust of reproductions. Because the model in Poe's story turns into a corpse at the very moment when the portrait is finished, it is not in the dead, decaying original but in its superb translation that the beauty of the painter's bride lives on and can be cherished.

In addition, as the painter/translator is implicitly blamed and sternly punished for the tragic outcome of his excessive dedication to the portrait— and, therefore, for having failed to protect his bride and model from his own authorial passion—Poe's tale also seems to suggest that the traditional oppositions between original and reproduction, and between author and translator, should have been kept within their proper hierarchy. Therefore, in order for translation as portraiture to be "safe" as a form of textual reproduction, and in order for the original to be adequately protected from the dangers brought about by repetition, the translator should be fully devoted to the original and refrain from recreating it in another cultural environment and in another time. In other words, the translator's task should be clearly distinguishable from the author's, just as the reproduction should maintain its submissive bond to the original, aspiring to resemble it but never to replace it.[16] Because in this story creative power is equated with the divine ability to manipulate life and death, we might also conclude that what is improper about the painter's behavior is precisely his attempt to go beyond the limits of his humble task

and to emulate God, the ultimate Authorial figure. Finally, as it associates
the tragic outcome of the painter's project to his improper attempt at playing God, an attribution that is implicitly viewed as the author's prerogative,
Poe's tale takes us back to the myth of Babel, which depicts the exemplary
punishment bestowed upon the descendants of Noah.

"The Oval Portrait" is instrumental in illustrating the underlying association between translation and transgression that is at the basis of Western
culture and its longing for absolute originality and stable meaning, an association that appears to be even stronger when we consider that the "danger"
represented by translation is paradoxically greater when the translator actually does a good job of replacing the original in another context and another
language or medium. As the story suggests, because a perfect reproduction
could surpass or literally kill the original, and because a painter/translator
can actually create life instead of simply reproducing it, the process of translation tends to challenge and destabilize our comfortable distinctions between
what is true and what is false, what is real and legitimate and what is not, or
even between life and death. Thus, it seems that what is truly "dangerous"
or worrisome about translation is precisely the impossibility of keeping it
in its "proper" place.

The common thread that unites all the plots briefly discussed above is the
way in which translations and translators cannot help but get mixed up with
originals and authors. In the pieces by Borges, Kosztolányi, Scliar, Saramago,
Calvino, Poe, and Bleton commented upon here, students will be able to
examine exemplary illustrations of the undeniably authorial role translators
must play as they negotiate some kind of compromise between the foreign
and the domestic, or the source and the target texts, in order to make translation possible. At the same time, though, because these fictional texts also
bring us strong reader figures, and, therefore, because they also expose and
explore complex relationships between readers and texts, readers and authors,
or readers and translators, these stories will allow students to reflect on their
own authorial role in the reception of both originals and translations. They
might start by examining how the readers and narrators featured in these
plots actually determine the ways in which texts and translations are read
and judged.

Hopefully, when students consider, for example, that in Borges's story it is
actually the reader/narrator who determines that Menard's apparently perfect
translation of Cervantes's *Quixote* is in fact quite different from the original,

they can begin to evaluate how the reader's role involves the production of textual meaning in a way that is certainly comparable to both the author and the translator. As students give up the illusion of the original as a stable entity that can be fully recovered and repeated, and as they become aware of their own role as interpreters, they will be also more willing to accept translation as a form of writing and to examine the visibility of translators without the usual prejudices that our culture has cultivated around their task. Finally, one should hope that as students develop a greater awareness of their own interpretive role, they will have not only a greater openness to the interpretive role of others, but also a more sensitive approach and a more generous attitude toward difference in general.

NOTES

1. Similarly, those who have been exposed to basic notions of psychoanalysis or contemporary theories of influence will be able to learn from Pierre Menard's desire to be Cervantes and to write (not simply to rewrite) the Quixote, and they could be encouraged to consider the implications of such desire for translation, or even to think of translation as a response to influence. For an elaboration of these issues, see Arrojo, "Translation, Transference, and the Attraction to Otherness: Borges, Menard, Whitman." For other readings of Borges's story, see Kristal (29–31) and Waisman (93–109).

2. It might be useful to compare Menard's approach to formal, prescriptive statements on translation ethics from different times and traditions. In Alexander Fraser Tytler's "The Proper Task of a Translator," first published in 1791, for example, we can find several statements such as his "laws of translation," which are uncannily similar to Menard's method: "I. That the translation should give a complete transcript of the ideas of the original work. II. That the style and manner of writing should be of the same character with that of the original. III. That the translation should have all the ease of original composition." Tytler's reflection on the difficulties of the translator's task is also reminiscent of Borges's text. The following excerpt is particularly compatible with what we know about Menard's conceptions: "The translator . . . uses not the same colours with the original, but is required to give his picture the same force and effect. He is not allowed to copy the touches of his own, to produce a perfect resemblance. The more he studies a scrupulous imitation, the less his copy will reflect the ease and spirit of the original. How then shall a translator accomplish this difficult union of ease with fidelity? To use a bold expression, he must adopt the very soul of his author, which must speak through his own organs" (209–11).

3. In my discussions of this story with groups of students on different levels and in different contexts, I have also found it quite productive to call their attention to the content of Cervantes's (and Menard's) fragment. For example, an exploration of

the implications of the notion that history is the mother of truth may prove useful for further reflection on the (in)stability of texts and its relationship to Menard's accomplishment and failure.

4. Instructors may find it helpful to use other texts by Borges that focus on translation. His essays "The Homeric Versions" and "The Translators of the Thousand and One Nights," for example, both published in the 1930s, can stimulate students to further elaborate on some of the issues raised in "Pierre Menard" and can familiarize those who are new to translation studies with more formal texts on translation theory and commentary. For general discussions on the texts by Borges (fiction and nonfiction) that deal with issues of translation and interpretation, see Kristal and Waisman.

5. In "Fictionalising Translation and Multilingualism," published as a special issue of *Linguistica Antverpiensia*, a Netherlands-based journal devoted to the study of language, translation, and culture, the reader will find several articles that focus on representations of translation and translators in fiction written in different languages and from different traditions. See, for example, Baer, Wakabayashi, Feltrin-Morris, and Curran.

6. A French version, "Le traducteur cleptomane," was published in 2002. In "Writing, Interpreting, and the Power Struggle for the Control of Meaning," I have proposed a dialogue between Kosztolányi's piece and two other stories—Borges's "Death and the Compass" and Kafka's "The Burrow"—which has allowed me to discuss some consequences of the representation of the original as the author's private property or special refuge, and of the translator or interpreter as a thief or unwelcome intruder.

7. In "Translation and Impropriety—A Reading of Claude Bleton's *Les Nègres du traducteur*," I have discussed Bleton's exploration of a few clichés associated with postmodern textual theories, such as the "death" of the author, and how they can be related to translation ethics and to representations of the translator as a frustrated author.

8. The role of the translator in both Kosztolányi's and Bleton's texts has also been discussed by Anderson.

9. For a detailed discussion of Scliar's story, see my "The Gendering of Translation in Fiction: Translators, Authors, and Women/Texts in Scliar and Calvino."

10. For a detailed discussion (in Portuguese) of Saramago's novel, see my "A relação exemplar entre autor e revisor (e outros trabalhadores textuais semelhantes) e o Mito de Babel."

11. For a detailed discussion of representations of texts as women, and their relationship with traditional notions of fidelity in Calvino's book and well as in Scliar's story mentioned above, see my "The Gendering of Translation in Fiction."

12. For a general discussion of the gendering of translation, see Lori Chamberlain's groundbreaking "Gender and the Metaphorics of Translation."

13. For a detailed examination of Ermes Marana's name and its relationship to Calvino's plot, see my "The Gendering of Translation in Fiction," 88.

14. For readings of Poe's piece as a story about translation, see my "The Power of Originals and the Scandal of Translation—A Reading of Edgar Allan Poe's 'The Oval Portrait,'" as well as Caws and Kennedy.

15. An exemplary illustration can be found in a well-known statement by Joachim du Bellay, which first appeared in 1549. According to him, all "the splendors of poetry . . . can hardly be expressed in translation, any more than a painter can represent the soul with the body of the person whom he attempts to represent from nature" (104).

16. As I have argued elsewhere, this conclusion also seems to be supported by Poe's epigraph to the story, "*Egli 'e vivo e parlerebbe se non osservasse la rigola del silentio*" (He is alive and would speak if he did not observe the rule of silence), which is "an inscription beneath an Italian Picture of St. Bruno" (734). In other words, like the picture of St. Bruno, the painter's work should have "observed the rule of silence" and therefore should not have been able to "speak" in the place of the original (Arrojo, "The Power of Originals," 174).

WORKS CITED

Anderson, Jean. "The Double Agent: Aspects of Literary Translator Affect as Revealed in Fictional Work by Translators." *Linguistica Antverpiensia*, n.s., 4 (2005): 171–82.

Arrojo, Rosemary. "The Gendering of Translation in Fiction: Translators, Authors, and Women/Texts in Scliar and Calvino." In *Gender, Sex and Translation—The Manipulation of Identities,* edited by Jose Santaemilia, 81–95. Manchester, UK: St. Jerome, 2005.

———. "The Power of Originals and the Scandal of Translation—A Reading of Edgar Allan Poe's 'The Oval Portrait.'" In *Apropos of Ideology—Translation Studies on Ideology—Ideology in Translation Studies,* edited by Maria Calzada Perez, 165–80. Manchester, UK: St. Jerome, 2003.

———. "A relação exemplar entre autor e revisor (e outros trabalhadores textuais semelhantes) e o mito de Babel: alguns comentários sobre *História do Cerco de Lisboa,* de José Saramago." Especial *D.E.L.T.A.* 19 (2003): 163–74.

———. "Translation and Impropriety—A Reading of Claude Bleton's *Les Nègres du traducteur.*" *TIS—Translation and Interpretation Studies,* 1, no. 2 (2006): 91–109.

———. "Translation, Transference, and the Attraction to Otherness—Borges, Menard, Whitman." *Diacritics, 34, no. 3/4 (2004): 31–53.*

———. "Writing, Interpreting and the Power Struggle for the Control of Meaning." In *Translation and Power,* edited by Maria Tymoczko and Edwin Gentzler, 63–79. Amherst and Boston: University of Massachusetts Press, 2002.

Baer, Brian James. "Translating the Transition: The Translator-Detective in Post-Soviet Fiction." *Linguistica Antverpiensia,* n.s., 4 (2005): 243–54.

Bleton, Claude. *Los negros del traductor.* Translated by María Teresa Gallego, Andrés Ehrenhaus, Miguel Sáenz, and Jesús Zulaika. Madrid: Editorial Funambulista, 2004.

Borges, Jorge Luis. "Death and the Compass." Translated by Andrew Hurley. *Collected Fictions,* 147–56. New York: Penguin Books, 1998.

————. "The Homeric Versions." Translated by Esther Allen, Suzanne J. Levine, and Eliot Weinberger. *The Total Library—Non-Fiction 1922–1986*, edited by E. Weinberger, 69–74. New York: Penguin Books, 2001.

————. "Pierre Menard, Author of the *Quixote*." Translated by Andrew Hurley. *Collected Fictions*, 88–95. New York: Penguin Books, 1998.

————. "The Translator of *The Thousand and One Nights*." Translated by Esther Allen, Suzanne J. Levine, and Eliot Weinberger. *The Total Library—Non-Fiction 1922–1986*, edited by E. Weinberger, 92–109. New York: Penguin Books, 2001.

Calvino, Italo. *If on a winter's night a traveler*. Translated by William Weaver. New York: Harcourt Brace and Company, 1981.

Caws, Mary Ann. "Insertion in an Oval Frame: Poe Circumscribed by Baudelaire." Pts. 1 and 2. *French Review* 56 (1983): 679–83; 56 (1983): 885–95.

Chamberlain, Lori. "Gender and the Metaphorics of Translation." *The Translation Studies Reader*, edited by Lawrence Venuti, 314–29. New York: Routledge, 2000.

Curran, Beverley. "The Fictional Translator in Anglophone Literatures." *Linguistica Antverpiensia*, n.s., 4 (2005): 183–99.

du Bellay, Joachim. "The Defense and Illustration of the French Language." Translated by James H. Smith and Edd W. Parks. In *Western Translation Theory from Herodotus to Nietzsche*, edited by Douglas Robinson, 102–5. Manchester, UK: St. Jerome, 2002.

Feltrin-Morris, Marella. "No Book to Call One's Own: Perspectives on Translation and Literary Creation in Francesca Duranti's *The House on Moon Lake*." *Linguistica Antverpiensi*, n.s., 4 (2005): 255–64.

Friedrich, Paul. *The Meaning of Aphrodite*. Chicago: University of Chicago Press, 1978.

Kafka, Franz. "The Burrow." Translated by Willa and Edwin Muir. In *Franz Kafka—The Complete Stories*, edited by Nahum N. Glatzer, 325–59. New York: Schocken Books, 1971.

Kennedy, J. Gerald. *Poe, Death, and the Life of Writing*. New Haven and London: Yale University Press, 1987.

Kosztolányi, Dezső. "Le traducteur cleptomane." In *Le traducteur cleptomane et autres histoires*, translated by Adám Peter and Maurice Regnaut. Paris: Viviane Hamy, 2002.

————. "O tradutor cleptomaníaco." In *O tradutor cleptomaníaco e outras histórias de kornél esti*, translated by Ladislao Szabo, 7–10. Rio de Janeiro: Editora 34, 1996.

Kristal, Efraín. *Invisible Work—Borges and Translation*. Nashville: Vanderbilt University Press, 2002.

Poe, Edgar Allan. "Life in Death [The Oval Portrait]." In *The Unabridged Edgar Allan Poe*, 734–38. Philadelphia: Running Press, 1983.

Saramago, José. *The History of the Siege of Lisbon*. Translated by Giovanni Pontiero. London: Harvill, 1996.

Scliar, Moacyr. "Footnotes." Translated by Clifford E. Landers. *ATA—Source* 23 (1997): 9–13.

Tytler, Alexander Fraser. "The Proper Task of a Translator." In *Western Translation Theory from Herodotus to Nietzsche,* edited by Douglas Robinson, 208–12. Manchester, UK: St. Jerome, 2002.

Wakabayashi, Judy. "Representations of Translators and Translation in Japanese Fiction." *Linguistica Antverpiensia,* n.s. 4 (2005): 155–69.

Waisman, Sergio. *Borges and Translation—The Irreverence of the Periphery.* Lewisburg, PA: Bucknell University Press, 2005.

Between Reading and Writing

Sergio Waisman

What are the many [versions] of the *Iliad* . . . if not diverse perspectives of a moveable event, if not a long experimental assortment of omissions and emphases?

> Jorge Luis Borges, "Las versiones homéricas"
> ("The Homeric Versions")

When we assign a translation in class, how do we convey to our students that there is something different about the literary text they have before them? One thing we can do is take advantage of that first sign of difference and exploit it for all of its worth, for all its richness and potential. For what is translation, after all? Translation is the text we see, the text we have before us (the target), but it is also the text alluded to (the source). Translation is that strangest of literary artifacts, as it is always defined as being more than one. This may very well be the nature of literature itself, given the ultimately ambiguous nature of literary language, but this may not always be as easy to witness as it is in translation. Translation is *différance* personified, if you will.

What exactly does one read when one reads a translation? What does it mean to say that we are reading Homer or Dante or the *Bhagavad Gita,* when what we have in front of us is a text in English? There has been much debate in recent decades about the role of the author and of the reader, but very few of these discussions include translation. And yet, one relatively quick way to illustrate for undergraduates the infamous concept of the "death of the author" may just be to call forth the image of the translator, that mischievous Janus-faced character who has perhaps been blamed more often for single-handedly

killing off the author—by betraying the original or the author's intentions—
than any other force known in literature.

Furthermore, even once readers (including students at all levels) are made
aware of the presence of a translator in a text, even once readers are made
aware of the presence of a translator as one of the mediators in the text—and
in literature in translation as perhaps *the* determining mediator in the text—
then we are still left with a tremendous and perhaps unanswerable question: is
there a way for a reader to detect the presence of the translator?[1] And if there
is a way for a reader to detect the presence of the translator, then how does
detecting such a presence—how does evoking or bringing forth translators,
so that they do not remain mysteriously invisible mediators—contribute to
our range of possible readings of the text being read? Readers of literature
in translation must seek ways to address these crucial questions, else the text
before them will remain impossibly unapproachable. Among other things,
this essay provides a number of strategies for approaching these issues.

Whether one believes that translation is possible (with thinkers from Jakobson to Steiner to Paz) or that translation is an inherently flawed endeavor (as did
Nabokov or Ortega y Gasset), one thing seems clear: translation is undoubtedly
a strange literary task, especially from the point of view of modern conceptions of authorship and originality. Indeed, translating a text is a thoroughly
odd experience: you produce an entire text that is yours, *you* write it, you put
it down on paper, you undertake your stylistic and syntactic decisions—but
when you are done, you sign *someone else's name* to it instead of your own.
Or, equally startling, you sign your name *in addition to* someone else's. Thus,
the text—assuming that the translator is recognized at all—gains a double or
phantom authorship. More than strange, this erasing or doubling of authorship is thoroughly destabilizing. By signing your words over to someone else,
by putting another's name to your language, you willingly sacrifice yourself.
Handing over your identity card, you make yourself invisible; and not only
do you assure that the author is not dead, you actually reinstate Him in all
His pre-Barthesian grandeur. Such self-effacement might seem like too high a
price to pay, but many would say that it is the necessary duty of the translator,
whose task, after all, is to serve the original at all costs.

In fact, one of translation's most common truisms is that translation is by
definition an altruistic task, one undertaken out of love, in which translators
give themselves over to the original (in the best of cases) or to the demands
of the market (in the worst of cases). Because translators dedicate them-

selves entirely to a text that is not theirs, in principle translators abandon their own voice and style, and sometimes even their ideas and ideologies, in an attempt to recreate those of the author of the original. Regardless of the methodology used by translators, almost all histories of translation state that translators remain at the disposal of the source: whether translators consciously or unconsciously set out to domesticate or foreignize the text,[2] their role is assumed to be secondary to the concerns of the original, or of the reader, or somehow of both. Translators themselves most commonly define their tasks in modest and humble terms, as selfless and secondary to the author they are serving.[3]

But is it really so clear that literary translation is an altruistic task, that the literary translator is a figure who sacrifices everything for the original? I do not believe so. Translation is always at least partially selfish, because translation is a mode of reading that is, by definition, a mode of appropriation. Translation may be an attempt at careful reproduction; translation may involve a hermeneutic motion intended to "compensate" or "restitute" or "recompense" meaning, such that the target successfully transfers the meaning of the source into an analogous text (as George Steiner details in *After Babel*), but as a number of thinkers have discussed, translation always necessarily distorts and transforms the text. In the words of Octavio Paz: "Translation always implies a transformation of the original. This transformation cannot but be literary because all translations are operations that utilize the two modes of expression to which, according to Roman Jakobson, all literary procedures can be reduced: metonymy and metaphor" (*Traducción* 13–14).[4] In fact, it may be precisely in those transformations—in those "creative infidelities," as Borges calls them, in those "transcreations," as Haroldo de Campos calls them (Balderston and Schwartz 4)—that the irreverent potential of translation resides.

The problem is that as long as we compare originals and translations, we will come almost at once to talk about fidelity, and then we will have a very difficult time getting away from the demands of fidelity, which turns out to be an extremely constraining parameter. The problem is that as long as we compare originals and translations, the translation will always lose to the original, and fidelity will never be achieved. Whether one strives for letter or for spirit, for form or for meaning, for a domesticating version or for a foreignizing version, the target will never measure up to the source text. Fidelity is a measuring stick by which the original is guaranteed to maintain its superiority over any and all attempts at the inferior reproductions of the translations—its upstart, mongrel children. Fidelity is Prospero's seemingly perfect, deterministic power over Caliban's rebellious imperfections.[5] Demands that the translator be faithful to the original—as old as the practice of translation itself[6]—also run the risk of masking serious issues of authorship and originality raised by translation, questions relevant not only in literature but also in many other cultural political arenas.

Commenting on the appropriation that always comes to the forefront when one considers translation, Ricardo Piglia has said: "I have always been interested in the relationship between translation and property, since the translator rewrites an entire text that is his/hers, and yet is not. The translator finds him/herself in a strange place, somewhere between plagiarism and citation. Translation is a strange exercise of appropriation. . . . In language there is no such thing as private property. Language is a circulation with a common flow. Literature disrupts that flow, and perhaps that is precisely what literature is" ("Lost in Translation," n.p.).

By postulating that translation lies somewhere between the (supposedly legitimate) practice of citation and the (supposedly illegitimate) practice of plagiarism, Piglia questions what are commonly thought to be distinct borders. Translation lays bare the appropriation of literature, and in so doing challenges the hypocrisy of modern beliefs of authorship and even such notions as the inherited classic.[7] Translation puts us in an in-between space, a very productive area from which one can ask some of the crucial questions of literature— questions about who owns texts and language. The answers, Piglia suggests, are that no one owns language and that literature may just be there to reclaim language—and that perhaps one of the reasons that so many thinkers have been interested in translation through the ages may be this characteristic of translation, its ability to "disrupt the flow" of language, as Piglia says.[8]

So there is a contradiction: translation is selfless, translation is selfish. Translation is altruistic, translation is an act of appropriation. But which is it? I believe we can say that it is neither or that it is both. And we can add that the real issue is what happens when we gain awareness of such contradictions about translation in the United States. Or, rather, we can ask what the implications are of such a contradiction—of the fact that translation is always simultaneously *both* an act of giving and of taking—for practicing and reading translation in and into English in the United States.

One way to get at this question is to analyse why translators translate. Here I can only speak in the first person. Why do I translate? Is it to serve others, so that others may have access to certain Spanish-language texts in English? Yes, in part, but as I have already intimated, I do not believe that translation is only an altruistic task. So why does one translate? What does it mean for someone in the United States to say that this or that text or writer needs to be translated into English? What are translators looking for, what do they want, what are translators missing in their own tongue that makes them go toward the tongue of the other, consume it, give it voice and life anew in their own? Rather than asking for whom translators translate or what kind of service translators are rendering by translating, let us ask: what are they after for themselves?

I believe that translation reveals a lacuna, a lack, in the target language and culture—and in the translators themselves. One might say that translators translate not only to say what has not yet been said in their own culture, in their own language, but also to say what they have not yet been able to say at all. Translators have a need for that other text in that other language, and they desire to fill a void, an unfillable gap. Translating is an attempt to say the unsayable. Translation thus emerges as a form of contraband, rebellion or resistance in and against social, linguistic, and cultural norms. And that just may be the task of the translator.

On a similar note, Argentine poet Diana Bellessi has said: "If the poem appears first as rhythm, and only later unfolds meaning in its own way, then translation is above all an attempt at alterity. Alterity of the body, breathing the music of another language and of the utter uniqueness of a speaking voice. A double effort founded, no doubt, on love, that permits the translator to identify with the text on a variety of levels. . . . Translation always provokes a meditation on one's own language—on its powers and limits—and on language itself" (26).

Our need—or desire—for alterity, then, would factor in as a significant player in our need for translation. Similarly, it follows that our fear or anxiety over alterity (over all forms of otherness) is part of what prevents translation, what makes the more xenophobic aspects of U.S. culture exclude translation into English in any significant way. Conversely, because translation reveals a lacuna, a lack, it creates desire. If I say that writers like Ricardo Piglia and Diamela Eltit (the contemporary writers from Argentina and Chile, respectively, whose texts I have worked on) need to be translated, what I have in mind is that their texts contain a certain value—in Spanish—which I am proposing to bring into English. The question becomes: can such value—a value that combines the literary, cultural, and political—be translated into English? Can it be imported to the United States, at the center of power? How does such cultural capital travel from the margins to the center? And if such value and quality are reproduced, will our need, our lack, in the center be resolved?

One could establish critical criteria to determine why this or that writer or text merits being translated into English. Such criteria would raise issues about the role of translation in questions of canon formation and reception. But for my purposes here, as I explore the more intangible, mysterious mechanism behind the act of translation, I wish to look at the subjective side of the issue: just because someone says that Piglia and Eltit have value in Spanish and need to be translated, that does not mean that *I* need to translate them. And yet, in the cases of Piglia and Eltit, I have decided that I need to translate them, to try to translate what I see as the important, challenging, innovative, disruptive—in a word, the valuable, poetic, and political qualities—in their texts.[9] Thus, when I speak in the first person, as I seek to describe my personal need to translate Piglia and Eltit, I draw a connection between this concept of need that I have presented here—as a desire for alterity driven by lacunae in language and culture—and the role that the translator always plays as a key mediator in the text. But the question remains: where might the reader see the subjective need of the translator in action? The answer lies in the marks that each individual translator leaves behind in the translated text. In other words, the translator's personal need is played out in the translator's individual decisions and practices, which in turn become how he or she is manifested as the mediator of the text.[10]

Let me turn to examples of my own marks as a mediator in the texts of translations I have done, first of Ricardo Piglia and then of Diamela Eltit. Of the many challenges in translating *The Absent City,* Piglia's extremely complex multilayered novel, one of the hardest may have been the word *nudos* in the section titled "Los nudos blancos." There are two ways to translate *nudos* in English: as "nodes" (as in the nodes of a system or a computer program), or as "knots" (as in the knots one weaves or ties). In Piglia's novel, the *nudos* are the textual places where the multiple narratives of the text—as well as the individual and collective memories they encapsulate—are condensed and in turn intersect with other *nudos*. However, when one tries to localize any given *nudo,* the specific location of any of the many microstories of the novel, then the text explodes, so to speak, and it becomes impossible to fix the *nudo* or the center of any of the stories of the novel, or of history itself. In terms of the novel's plot and development, this is seen in the way that Elena—who used to be a woman but is now a machine—in the museum is never silenced, even though the state apparatuses are constantly seeking to disconnect her (the female machine). Therefore, given the two lexical possibilities for the word *nudos,* I opted to forgo the "knots" (which here would have been Penelope's knots) and to insist instead on "the white nodes," hoping—at least in that section of the novel, with that particular *nudo*—to underscore *The Absent City*'s connection with William Burroughs and a certain North American counterculture that may have otherwise not come through as clearly in the English translation.[11]

In the case of Diamela Eltit, the question becomes how to bring into English a text that itself challenges Spanish from the very limits of Chilean culture and society; in other words, how to import a text that utilizes fragments and remainders of Chilean culture and society, to give voice (in English, as Eltit does in Spanish) to the "minor figures" of that society, the "minor characters" faced with the overwhelming presence of the political, economic, historical, and cultural legacy of the Chilean dictatorship and its continuing neoliberal wake.[12] In addition, from the perspective of a translator in the North, there are actually two issues of marginality at play here. The first is in what sense Latin America (and Spanish from a South American country) functions as peripheral in the global context. The second issue of marginality is how Eltit is marginal—or, better yet, minor—within that periphery and that peripheral language. The question, for me, is how to translate a marginality that is specifically related to its relationship to language (in Spanish) into a language (English) that is itself the language of the center of empire (in the United States).[13]

In my work with *Los trabajadores de la muerte* (Laborers of death),[14] by far the most challenging voice to translate is that of the mother, a strange, late-twentieth-century Chilean woman whose thoughts and actions at times remind us of the classical Medea. Throughout the novel, Eltit delves into issues such as rape, incest, mutilation, insanity, and death to completely deconstruct any possibility of a romanticized figure of the mother. These moves, framed by references to an aggressive and destructive marketplace, suggest an unsettling darkness that contrasts starkly with the neoliberal success story usually spouted with regard to Chile. An additional question that I have not yet confronted is how my attempt to translate this mother's stream of consciousness might be affected by my own gender.

In discussing my experiences with translating Piglia and Eltit, I have at times fallen into a habit that is all too common in translation studies: comparing the source with the target texts. This is meant to be useful, as, among other things, it allows us to better read the original through the translation. As critics have often pointed out, a translation is always a reading—an interpretation—of the original.[15] A discussion of source and target texts can serve as a way to better understand the original; it can form part of a productive hermeneutic process. This, combined with instructors' efforts to raise their own and their students' "translation awareness," will help enrich the experience of reading literature in translation.[16] But still this is not enough. Regardless of one's best intentions, the usefulness of the original-translation comparison quickly runs its course. I therefore return now to one of the most basic concepts in the study of translation—fidelity—but in doing so I will suggest a way in which readers at all levels can go beyond the limitations implied by this oldest of translation terms.[17]

There are two major modern thinkers who can help us go beyond the two-text model of comparison (original vs. translation): Walter Benjamin and Jorge Luis Borges. In Europe and the United States much more has been said about Benjamin's theoretical contributions in this regard, so I will only mention him briefly here and will then devote the next few pages and my conclusion to Borges. As several critics have pointed out,[18] one of the most radical contributions of Walter Benjamin's seminal "The Task of the Translator" (1923) is Benjamin's rejection of the traditional comparative dichotomy of original vs. translation. He instead views translation as a mode that serves as a pointer toward that "pure language" of which Benjamin messianically dreams.[19]

The other crucial thinker in this respect is Borges. Translation was a key theme and practice throughout his oeuvre, and he dedicates two major essays to translation (the first of which I strongly recommend for any course on translation): "Las versiones homéricas" ("The Homeric Versions," 1932) and "Los traductores de Las 1001 noches" ("The Translators of The Thousand and One Nights," 1935).[20] In these, Borges challenges many of the basic tenets of traditional translation theory, finding potential where others find loss.[21] It is worth repeating the best-known quotation from "The Homeric Versions," as much for Borges's humor as for its subversive questioning of notions of originality and of its first cousin, authorship: "To presuppose that every recombination of elements is necessarily inferior to its original, is to presuppose that draft 9 is necessarily inferior to draft H—as there can be only drafts. The concept of the *definitive text* corresponds only to religion or fatigue" (*Obras completas* 1:239; italics in the original).

If all texts are "drafts," the traditional model of comparing (what are almost always considered the inferior) translations with their (what are invariably determined to be the superior) originals simply ceases to make sense. It is not necessarily that translations are automatically considered as good as the originals, either. Rather, in Borges's ironic formulation, the concept of originality is thoroughly destabilized, opening the way for translations to gain as much potential legitimacy as originals. Or perhaps more directly put: Borges sees literature as consisting of a series of drafts, of versions, one after the other, their order determined as much by the randomness of time and place as anything else.

The implications of Borges's questioning of the "definitive text" in "The Homeric Versions" become even clearer when he discusses translation of the classics. Borges insists that a text's value is not determined by chronology, as he leans toward a configuration in which all versions are hypothetically legitimate and full of potential. Thus, the different existing translations of Homer, Borges states, are all "sincere, genuine and divergent" (*Obras completas* 1:240). This idea is suggested in the very title of his essay: "The Homeric *Versions*." Borges observes that not knowing the source language of the original is precisely the condition that allows him as a reader to enjoy a vast number of versions of it. Such an observation may strike monolingual readers as reassuring, and it is. But it is actually reassuring to all of us who have ever read literature in translation, as we are always dependent on the translator at such a moment. The surprising aspect of Borges's stance, of course, is that he does not bemoan this condition of not knowing the source, but rather celebrates its potential.

In fact, it is notable that Borges compares translations of the *Odyssey* without attempting to refer back to the original. By deviating from the approach of comparing the source with the target, Borges avoids the traditional, usually unproductive practice of simply listing what is lost in translation. In addition, he declares that, in his own case, "the *Odyssey*, thanks to my opportune ignorance of Greek, is an international library of works in prose and verse" (*Obras completas* 1:239–40). Borges works with paradox here to turn an apparent lack—not knowing the source language—into an unexpected gain: the potential to create multiple versions in the target language and his ability to read them. This statement also points to the importance of the reader and the context in creating this "international library" of Homeric versions.

To illustrate these ideas, Borges compares a brief section from six differ-ent translations into English of the *Odyssey*. He proceeds in order from the most to the least literal of the translations, commenting on individual styles of the translators and identifying, in each, the kind of aesthetic "pleasures" that accompany the corresponding manner of translating (*Obras completas* 1:241–43).[22] After comparing these Homeric versions, Borges asks which is the most faithful. Until this point in the essay, Borges has mostly sidestepped the question of fidelity as it is traditionally treated by stating that translations are not necessarily inferior to the original, and by suggesting, as I mentioned before, that the concept of the "definitive text" is a fallacy. But now he faces the question of fidelity head-on. The answer he gives—once again in paradoxical terms—is "all or none." If fidelity must be what belongs to "the imaginations of Homer, to the irretrievable men and times that he represented," then none of these versions are faithful from our point of view, for we cannot possibly aim to reproduce Homer's cultural and historical context. Such an effort would be equal to a kind of "original repetition" or perfect mimesis, which would be impossible even without a change in languages. Whereas if fidelity is construed as faithfulness to Homer's intentions ("to his objectives"), then all of these can be said to be faithful, except for the literal ones, for according to Borges these derive their aesthetic value entirely from their "contrast with current uses" of language. By saying that all the Homeric versions but the most literal ones are basically faithful to the poet's intentions, Borges reiterates his belief that translation is not accompanied by loss. Instead, Borges identifies an unexpected gain in the multiplicity of versions of the now-unreachable original.

In addition to the many theoretical implications of Borges's essay, this text can also be put to practical use in the classroom. Borges's critical reading of the "international library" of Homeric versions that he is able to draw upon thanks to his "opportune ignorance of Greek"—much as he later does with respect to Arabic in "The Translators of *The Thousand and One Nights*"—suggests several wonderful exercises that can be done in class, whether it be a class in literary translation, comparative literature, or a number of other modern or "foreign" literature courses. Students could read and analyze different transla-tions of the same source text, much as Borges does in "The Homeric Versions" and in "The Translators of *The Thousand and One Nights*." This can be done with classical texts (e.g., passages from the Bible, Homer, Dante, etc.) or with more "modern" texts of which there are multiple translations (in one course, for example, I found twelve versions of Neruda's poem "Walking Around.")

Much can be done with this kind of exercise, individually or in groups. For example, students can be asked to compare the different versions, to analyze the texts as autonomous productions, and to find criteria to evaluate the value of a translation *when they have no access the original.*

The class can then be asked to consider some of the following questions: What does it mean to have more than one translation of the same original? (And to know that it has been published?) How do the various translations compare among each other? How are they different at different points in time? How do the different versions affect our concepts of such issues as originality and authorship? Does reading multiple versions of the same text affect our concept of the "essence" of that text? If so, how, or why? How does this exercise affect our conception of reading, or of tradition, or of the transmittal of texts through time and across languages and cultures? And finally—and perhaps most importantly—in what ways might the translators be said to have acted as mediators in the various texts, even if as readers we are only able to read the literature in translation? Doing this activity and assigning Borges's essay "The Homeric Versions" together is a good idea. At the very least, the professor should have read "The Homeric Versions" and "The Translators of *The Thousand and One Nights*" before making this lesson plan. In a bilingual class the students could also compare and analyze the translations and then go to the original *after* they have come to some conclusions about the translations.

Clearly, Borges's take on the issue of fidelity reveals a complicated playfulness and the insightful sensibilities of an active translator and an extremely innovative writer. It is not enough to speak of fidelity in general. We must ask to what elements of the source text the translator is expected to be faithful, and not only how the translator should achieve such faithfulness, but perhaps more importantly, why? How is the translator's ability to achieve fidelity related not only to the value of the source text but also to its very originality? Does the translator not, in a way, actually "create" what is "original" about the source text—in a move analogous to how writers "create" their precursors, as Borges explains in "Kafka and His Precursors"—by deciding which elements of the source merit an attempt at "faithful reproduction," however such a thing is defined?

Borges goes on to explore the potential gain that accompanies translation in his 1935 essay "The Translators of *The Thousand and One Nights.*" Here, Borges disregards traditional demands for fidelity by suggesting that the merit of a translation may just lie in how well the translator makes use of the *infidelities* that inevitably occur when one transposes a text from one language and context into another. In his discussion of Richard F. Burton's version of the *Arabian Nights,* for example, Borges identifies the countless substitutions, rewritings, alterations, omissions, and interpolations that Burton undertakes, and Borges praises these falsifications, which improve on the original, he argues (*Obras completas* 1:405). Of another translation of the *Nights* (the 1889 version into French by J. C. Mardrus), Borges states: "To celebrate Mardrus's fidelity is to omit Mardrus's soul, it is to not even speak of Mardrus. It is his infidelity, his *creative and joyful infidelity,* with which we should be concerned" (*Obras completas* 1:410; emphasis added).

At some level, all translations "betray" the source text. As Borges saw early on, however, this betrayal need not lead to despair or anxiety; it need not cause a "misery of translation" (as Ortega y Gasset frightfully put it). Each moment of translation is a site of potentiality. Even if most such moments are wasted, even if most "infidelities" are neither "creative" nor "joyful," translation is still rife with potential, and some of translation's infidelities luckily turn out to be both "creative and joyful." So what is translation? Something between reading and writing, an exercise in alterity and communication, an exploration of self and other, a giving and taking, at play in the endless rooms and reflections of the library. At the beginning of "The Homeric Versions," Borges states: "There is no problem as consubstantial to literature and its modest mysteries as that posed by a translation." And there may in fact be no better point of entry into literature and its "modest mysteries" than the study of translation—whether we are able to answer these questions or not.

NOTES

1. Rachel May studies precisely this question for Russian literature in English translation in *The Translator in the Text.*

2. The domesticating vs. foreignizing debate is excellently traced by Venuti in *The Translator's Invisibility.* As part of his study, Venuti makes no secret that he strongly favors foreignizing translations into English in the United States so as to preserve or carry over the "foreign" elements of the original in the translation.

3. See, for example, Rabassa's *If This Be Treason.*

4. Likewise, as Derrida has said: "Une bonne traduction doit toujours abuser" (Lewis 261).

5. See Pires Vieira's "Liberating Calibans," a crucial study about the history and uses of mistranslation in Brazil. I borrow the image and use it in a much lighter tone here.

6. If the Italian proverb *traduttore, traditore* dismisses the translator as a traitor outright, there is a misogynistic French proverb that more subtly suggests that it is only the disloyal (and female-gendered!) translator who will achieve any beauty: *La traduction est comme une femme: si elle est belle, elle n'est pas fidèle.* I thank Masha Belenky for sharing this French proverb with me.

7. There is already a broad range of criticism on Piglia's work. For an excellent collection, including texts that discuss these issues, see the essays in *Ricardo Piglia.*

8. It should also be noted that such appropriation is necessarily different depending on where the translator is situated. As Lawrence Venuti argues in *The Scandals of Translation,* the "possible motives and effects [of translation] are local and contingent, differing according to major or minor positions in the global economy" (158). Discussing what he terms the "ethics of location," Venuti goes on to observe that "the cultural authority and impact of translation vary according to the position of a particular country in the geopolitical economy. In the hegemonic countries, metaphysical concepts of authorial originality and cultural authenticity denigrate translation as second-order writing, derivative and adulterated. . . . In developing countries, translation accrues cultural as well as economic capital" (*The Scandals of Translation* 187). Also, as I have mentioned elsewhere, the translator's responsibility in the United States—the ethics of translation from the center, if you will—seems to be to know what one can betray and what one must not betray. See my "Ethics and Aesthetics North and South."

9. To date, I have translated *Assumed Name* (Latin American Literary Review Press, 1995) and *The Absent City* (Duke University Press, 2000), plus a handful of short stories, by the Argentine Ricardo Piglia. I am in the process of completing a translation of *Los trabajadores de la muerte* (Laborers of death), the 1998 novel by the Chilean Diamela Eltit.

10. In *The Scandals of Translation,* Venuti refers to this as the "remainder" in the text.

11. I also hoped that the use of "node" would resonate with the theoretical concept of the "rhizome," in Deleuze and Guattari's sense of the term, but this was a smaller consideration. See Piglia's comments about Burroughs and other U.S. writers with whom he considers he is dialoguing in his "Afterword" to my translation of *The Absent City.* Another relevant point to mention about *The Absent City* in this context is that this novel has everything to do with translation, reproduction, and mediation, even before it is translated from the source into the target language. Although a full discussion of *The Absent City* falls outside the scope of this essay, Piglia's novel is actually a wonderful book to read and study when thinking about the issues at hand. I mention this because my translation now makes this crucial novel (one of the most important Latin American novels of the last twenty years) available to English-speaking readers. For a discussion of the role of translation in *The Absent City,* see Masiello (164–68) and my own "Ethics and Aesthetics North and South."

12. I am using the term "minor" here in the specific sense that Deleuze and Guattari have given it in recent years. See, for example, their *Kafka.*

13. In his brilliant translation of Eltit's *Lumpérica,* Ronald Christ talks about partaking in an *"engagé* translation of an *engagé* novel," by which he means *engagé* at all levels—politically, formally, structurally, and linguistically—in addition to literally and culturally. His translation invites us, as readers, to partake in this very kind of reading. In his "Translator's Afterword," he carefully details how he proceeded to create such a translation for us. In other words, he seeks to tell us how he functions as the mediator in the text of *E. Luminata* (the title of Christ's translation of Eltit's novel).

14. This is a working translation of the title.

15. Steiner refers to translation as a "hermeneutic motion" and details the various step-by-step processes that must occur in an "equitable" transmittal of meaning (296–413).

16. White makes a nice argument in this regard in "Translation and Teaching." The standard on this topic is Venuti's *The Translator's Invisibility.* See also May's excellent study, *The Translator in the Text,* which analyzes the role of the translator as mediator in Russian literature in English.

17. As a number of critics have observed, fidelity is the basic underlying question in just about every theory of translation, and it remains one of the major issues in the field to date. George Steiner articulates this point clearly and convincingly when he states: "It can be argued that all theories of translation—formal, pragmatic, chronological—are only variants of a single, inescapable question. In what ways can or ought fidelity to be achieved? What is the optimal correlation between the A text in the source-language and the B text in the receptor-language? The issue has been debated for over two thousand years" (*After Babel* 275).

18. See, in particular, Corngold's "Comparative Literature."

19. We can also note that for Derrida, Benjamin's vision in "The Task of the Translator" assists him in seeing translation as the complement of the original, as the complement of an original that is now (thanks to the translation) seen as a (previously) incomplete and unstable text. Thus, for Derrida, translation has the potential to temporarily reveal the destabilized original even while it complements it, leading Derrida to speak of the paradoxical nature of translation as both necessary and impossible, a necessity that is impossible ("Des tours de Babel" 170–72).

20. "The Translators of *The Thousand and One Nights*" is included in Venuti's *The Translation Studies Reader.* Borges's entire oeuvre is available in English, but other than Venuti's praiseworthy efforts, Borges's texts on translation are hardly ever included in anthologies on or about translation in the United States. The issue of the history of the translation of Borges's work into English is complicated and falls outside the scope of this essay. English-speaking readers interested in these and other prose texts by Borges are encouraged to seek out the recently published volumes by Viking, which are now considered the best available—in particular the *Selected Non-Fictions* and *Selected Fictions.*

21. Borges wrote about translation in several essays, and translation was often present in a significant fashion in his fictions (on this, see my *Borges and Translation*). Borges was also a prolific translator throughout his life. Borges translated entire works or

individual pieces by William Faulkner, Virginia Woolf, André Gide, Henri Michaux, Walt Whitman, Herman Melville, Franz Kafka, Edgar Allan Poe, Jack London, Robert Louis Stevenson, James Joyce, Oscar Wilde, Nathaniel Hawthorne, and others.

22. In his comparison of these versions, Borges translates the samples from English into Spanish himself. Borges's skills as a translator truly shine here, as he demonstrates his ability to reproduce and recreate linguistic constructions from one language to another. As Suzanne Jill Levine observes, the piece give Borges "an excuse . . . to give a virtuoso performance of different styles and eras of Homer" ("Some Versions of Homer," 1135). By seeking archaic effects at times or using Gongoresque inversions and hyperboles for Pope, for example ("Some Versions of Homer," 1138), Borges beautifully recreates the vocabulary and syntax of the various translators, and of the languages of their specific time periods, in Spanish.

WORKS CITED

Balderston, Daniel, and Marcy E. Schwartz. "Introduction." In *Voice-Overs: Translation and Latin American Literature,* edited by Daniel Balderston and Marcy E. Schwartz, 1–12. Albany: State University of New York Press, 2002.

Bellessi, Diana. "Gender and Translation." In *Voice-Overs: Translation and Latin American Literature,* edited by Daniel Balderston and Marcy E. Schwartz, 26–29. Albany: State University of New York Press, 2002.

Benjamin, Walter. "The Task of the Translator." In *Theories of Translation: An Anthology of Essays from Dryden to Derrida,* edited by Rainer Schulte and John Biguenet, 71–82. Chicago: University of Chicago Press, 1992.

Borges, Jorge Luis. *Obras completas.* 4 vols. Barcelona: Emecé Editores España, 1996.

Christ, Ronald. "Translator's Afterword." In *E. Luminata,* by Diamela Eltit, 205–34. Translated by Ronald Christ. Santa Fe: Lumen, 1997.

Corngold, Stanley. "Comparative Literature: The Delay in Translation." In *Nation, Language, and the Ethics of Translation,* edited by Sandra Bermann and Michael Wood, 139–45. Princeton, NJ: Princeton University Press, 2005.

Deleuze, Gilles, and Félix Guattari. *Kafka: Toward a Minor Literature.* Minneapolis: University of Minnesota Press, 1986.

Derrida, Jacques. "Des tours de Babel." In *Difference in Translation,* edited by Joseph Graham, 165–207. Ithaca, NY: Cornell University Press, 1985.

Jakobson, Roman. "On Linguistic Aspects of Translation." In *Theories of Translation: An Anthology of Essays from Dryden to Derrida,* edited by Rainer Schulte and John Biguenet, 144–51. Chicago: University of Chicago Press, 1992.

Levine, Suzanne Jill. "Some Versions of Homer." *PMLA* 107 (1992): 1134–38.

Lewis, Phillip E. "The Measure of Translation Effects." In *The Translation Studies Reader,* edited by Lawrence Venuti, 256–75. 2nd ed. London: Routledge, 2000.

Masiello, Francine. *The Art of Transition: Latin American Culture and Neoliberal Crisis.* Durham, NC: Duke University Press, 2001.

May, Rachel. *The Translator in the Text: On Reading Russian Literature in English.* Evanston, IL: Northwestern University Press, 1994.

Nabokov, Vladimir. "Problems of Translation: *Onegin* in English." In *Theories of Translation: An Anthology of Essays from Dryden to Derrida,* edited by Rainer Schulte and John Biguenet, 127–43. Chicago: University of Chicago Press, 1992.

Ortega y Gasset, José. "Miseria y esplendor de la traducción." *Obras completas,* 5:431–52. Madrid: Revista de Occidente, 1961.

Paz, Octavio. *Traducción: literatura y literalidad.* Barcelona: Tusquets Editores, 1981.

Piglia, Ricardo. *The Absent City.* Translated by Sergio Waisman. Durham, NC: Duke University Press, 2000.

———. "Lost in Translation: Ricardo Piglia, Daniel Balderston, and Sergio Waisman in Dialogue." Reading and lecture. Berkeley: University of California, Berkeley, March 4, 1998.

Pires Vieira, Else Ribeiro. "Liberating Calibans: Readings of *Antropofagia* and Haroldo de Campos' Poetics of Transcreation." *Post-Colonial Translation: Theory and Practice,* edited by Susan Bassnett and Harish Trivedi, 95–113. London and New York: Routledge, 1999.

Rabassa, Gregory. *If This Be Treason: Translation and Its Dyscontents: A Memoir.* New York: New Directions, 2005.

Rodríguez Pérsico, Adriana, and Jorge Fornet, eds. *Ricardo Piglia: Una poética sin límites.* Pittsburgh: IILI, 2004.

Steiner, George. *After Babel: Aspects of Language and Translation.* Oxford: Oxford University Press, 1992.

Venuti, Lawrence. *The Scandals of Translation: Towards an Ethics of Difference.* London: Routledge, 1998.

———. *The Translation Studies Reader.* 2nd ed. London: Routledge, 2000.

———. *The Translator's Invisibility.* London: Routledge, 1995.

Waisman, Sergio. *Borges and Translation: The Irreverence of the Periphery.* Lewisburg, PA: Bucknell University Press, 2005.

———. "Ethics and Aesthetics North and South: Translation in the Work of Ricardo Piglia." *MLQ (Modern Language Quarterly)* 62 (2001): 259–83.

White, Steven. "Translation and Teaching: The Dangers of Representing Latin America for Students in the United States." In *Voice-Overs: Translation and Latin American Literature,* edited by Daniel Balderston and Marcy E. Schwartz, 235–44. Albany: State University of New York Press, 2002.

Translation Transvalued

Ronald Christ

The existence of subventions for publication proves that our culture values literature in translation; the need for subventions proves that our culture does not value literature in translation.

William Vesterman

I do not pretend to understand the ultimate causes of the decisive paradox formulated above by Vesterman, but I can draw upon my own experiences as student, teacher, translator, and publisher to illustrate some of the ways it affects the state of the art.

Mark Van Doren once deflected a question of mine with a casual remark, and in so doing inflected my life—as he undoubtedly did for many others. An undergraduate in his graduate course Comedy and Tragedy, I caught up with him on the stairs after class: "Professor, for the Nietzsche, which translation should I read?" He stood, appropriately, a tall two treads above me and turned with some little exasperation and a smile: "It doesn't matter; we're concerned with ideas, not translations." I stood stunned, facing the wrong way in a lane of eagerly descending students.

It was as though Van Doren had declared to a Christian believer that we should be concerned with the spirit, not its incarnation. Yet I already knew his fond preference for Motteux's Cervantes over whatever newer versions reigned in 1955, and more than half the readings in that course were translations.

That same year in a beginner's Spanish class with Gregory Rabassa, I overheard that this kind and amusing teacher had been turning to translation work in order to make alimony payments. (Years later I would hear him say: "The only thing that gets lost in translation is the money.") Decidedly, then, the topos of translation was a-building in my mind as a fleshly necessity of at least two sorts—an impression confirmed and extended by Raskolnikov's hack work in *Crime and Punishment,* my first knowing encounter with the established topos of the larger mind confined to the implicitly negligible task of translation in order to eat: a seedy task it seemed, in a dead end alley just off . . . Grub Street.

Translation, the topos declares, is a necessity: "we" need it in order to know what we need to know about certain writers, to mitigate our provincialism, to feed our curiosity as well as our responsibility to their fame, individual and national, in the world;[1] "they" need it just to be fed. Not right, surely, but Brecht, as translated by Marc Blitzstein, enjoined: *First feed the face, then talk right and wrong*[2]—whether that face be intellectual or merely carnal. Such controlling literary images do not stimulate the *emulation* of translation's rank and wealth.[3] If you doubt the vitality of this topos, tell me how many instances are there of a translator in books or movies whose work is admirable, rewarding. I think of Jerome in Greenaway's *The Pillow Book,* yet while he promises translation in some six or seven languages (!), he is not shown actively engaged as a translator.[4]

Economics, I came to see back then, was at the cold heart of the matter, but I had still to discover the major element: the ever-present missing middle; for no more does the farmer ordinarily raise his crops directly for my table than does the translator usually render his labor straight ahead for the public or student maw. No, translation was, is, an art-trade in whose nexus the publisher serves as gatherer and distributor. With few exceptions, the "product" is ultimately the publisher's. (There are exceptions, farmer's markets, odd presses.) Translators may earn a living, even earn it well, translating—a few do; readers may store up untold wealth from the translations they read; but it is the publishers who might grow rich.

And they sometimes have done so, and sometimes not. I know: I'm one of the latter. Most publishers, of both categories, insistently claim the cost of translation as the determining consideration for not publishing foreign works in English; then, as a back-up, we will say: the market's so small, we'll never regain our costs, let alone make a profit. So we require grants, subventions.

Years after my stairwell illumination, I came to know intimately a program devoted to promoting a limited sector of translation in this country, to blunting both horns of that economic dilemma; and while there are wondrous and scandalous things to be cited from that experience, finally none compares to my discovering how very little money, directly spent, was required in order to ensure the successful translation of a work into English.[5] I believe that $3000 (in the mid-1970s) was the highest subvention ever offered by the program. No matter: what the program labored and excelled at was finding or creating a readership, i.e., a market, for the translated works: reporters and reviewers were cultivated; readings, lectures, roundtables, radio, TV programs, and university courses supported; a journal established; books of criticism and bibliographies published; and information combined with service offered whenever possible. At every point we found that production was less difficult than developing a market, a readership. Things have not changed.

Today, publishers are still hung up on those same horns of producing translations of belles lettres and (not) finding readers for them. Books and newspaper stories about the dearth of translations published, the piddling readership encountered, almost proliferate into the commonplace. The genus of solutions remains constant, as do the species of facts, figures, comparisons—almost all coming down to a dubious economic proposition: increased production of translations will increase demand from readers; almost all resulting in an identical fix-it: larger grants and subventions for the publication of more translations. This noble-seeming solution has not worked very well. It is not likely to work very well, ever.

"The law of natural selection, as applied to human institutions, gives the axiom: 'What is, is wrong.'" By "human institutions" Thorsten Veblen refers to our habitual attitudes and ways of thinking, which "inevitably lag behind the changes in the material universe to which they reluctantly adjust."[6] Instead, then, of considering, once again, how to increase those numbers, I will set three small scenes of translation and make several passing suggestions, encouragements really, for improving its conditions of conception and realization—long range, long haul, tough row, and all that. I will place the chief burden of this idealistic goal on academia, on the readers of this book. Specifically, I will aim at departments of literary study and, most especially, departments of English, the so-called target language for translation in the United States.

Before I do, however, let me note that there is no national prize for translation for which the author (if indeed a contemporary or living author) is jointly honored—a structural split in our perceived value of translation as literature. To this end, Lumen Books recently initiated a Writer in Translation Award, which may develop, but there is no such Pulitzer Prize (how could there be? though Hungarian-born, Pulitzer emphasized the American), no National Arts Award, nothing. At most, the Banff Center's program of opening joint residencies for translators and authors points the way.

When I began teaching in 1960 as a member of the Department of English and World Literature, English literature was persistently embedded in Goethe's "world" context, one that in my part of the world no more included Eastern literatures than had my Great Books–derived undergraduate studies. Yet at both schools literature was ventilated—perhaps artificially respirated is more accurate, the method no less life-giving—inspired by the crosswinds of international writing.[7] At that time, liberal arts students were required to take four years of World Literature (as well as four years of history, art and music, philosophy, and moral theology), so books accumulated an international past and present. Translations mixed so naturally and necessarily with works in English within this complexly allusive, multiply durational sequence that after my especially vigorous do on *Paradise Lost,* a student treated me to the finest compliment of my teaching life, a brilliant inversion of the reviewer's most damaging praise of a translation: *so well translated it might have been written in English.* The student said, "That was really great, Professor, but next time you teach Milton, please, use a better translation." Precisely. An *aperçu* of the most acute order. Faulty, as *aperçus* are apt to be, but inexpensive for us both and generously indicating the value, scope, and possibility of translation.

Eight years later, in the Department of English at Rutgers University, I found my higher-ups curtailing the teaching of translated works: *you can't close-read a translation.* Doubling my salary and halving my hours, my economic advancement had also, and characteristically, closed the linguistic border to immigrant works. Yet, as time went by, a minimal passage was opened, and eventually I was invited to offer a graduate seminar on reading in translation. The question I proposed—What is the *experience* of reading a book in translation?—largely remained as unanswered at the end of that seminar (and still is) as at the beginning, although we had accumulated a memorable quantity of data and case histories, as well as one empirical test: deviant diction and style most predictably provoked the experience into awareness ("sounds like a translation"), just as it had with my Milton student; and we found that nothing in our training had prepared us for this experience. Yet the rhythm of norm and deviancy is surely the systole and diastole of style, but in a strunked and whited world. The circumstances, the scene of translation in our literature departments, seldom direct readers to a deeply attentive appreciation of translation, process, or product, as a literary art and source of understanding and inspiration for our native writings. Not only is the translator invisible, as Lawrence Venuti made us see, but translation is kept invisible as well.[8]

But my colleagues in that seminar taught me that training and expertise in their disciplines had nowhere led them to applying their skills and scholarship to the editing of translations, which, despite any indignation, is most often these days practiced (when practiced at all) by editors who do not "know" the foreign language in which the original work was written. Fulfilling, positively instrumental work, and a job opportunity to boot.

Classical education was based on translation, inter- and intralingual. One effect we may cause when we now teach from translation, going in either or both directions, is the inducement, increase, enhancement of an attitude toward translated works. We cultivate—better said etymologically, we *recruit*— an audience for translations; we even cause translated books to be sold, albeit on a sort of command-performance basis, and this in a nation known for its manifest destiny of indifference to such works and their fostering cultures. We do these things provided that we do not restrict our service to flogging translations for miserable faults and flaunting our corrections and revisions. (Quiz: recall as many instances as you can when a teacher of literature studied a passage as good translation as opposed to faulting it or virtuosically revising it. Heed the noble error of Perrault's translator, who gave Cinderella a slipper made of glass instead of the author's original squirrel skin. What would the world be without a glass slipper?)

No less than the causes of global warming, the economic problems of translation in this country have long been known, often shelved for and by further study, and scarcely ever addressed. When a National Endowment for the Arts survey discovered in July 2004 that fewer than half of America's adults read literature (defined as novels, short stories, plays, and poetry), were you surprised?[9] I was. Among people I know, that percentage is way too high, nonfiction having captured everyone's attention. One translator, a prize-winning and internationally recognized intellect, told me: "These days, I read only nonfiction, for pleasure or any other purpose—except in our reading group, where they want to read a novel every month." The monthly uplift, then, may account for literature with a section of the reading public as much as it does among graduate students, who often report that they have no time for novels and poems, so consecrated are they to criticism, theory, and biography. Among the latter types of book, a fair number are translations or are translation-derived; but these titles of course do not number with literary works in translation. In departments of English, novels and poems, let alone novels in translation, are displaced; in departments of foreign language and comparative literature, where a novel might be studied in linguistic as well as literary detail, translations are looked down upon as a make-do, because the original is mystically not present. We have institutionalized an incubator where many teachers of our teachers-to-be discredit literature and doubly discredit literature in translation.

So when the major publishers of literature in translation—which means minority, independent presses, small as my own (1.5 persons, part time), or large ones, such as Dalkey Archive (around 50 people)—clamor for subventions because the return on sales is so low, who is to wonder? And when the big, appropriately labeled commercial presses equally complain and for the same reason, what is to be remarked?

The statistics now and for past decades are drear, as well-known as they are grave. Study after study, wail after wallow has proclaimed the same: in the United States, about 3 percent of the books published each year are translations, which comes recently to about 300 titles, of which as few as 0.4 percent are adult literature.[10] (Take heart, confirm your prejudice: the figures are about the same in Great Britain.) For those translated books, with occasional exception, the reviews are scarce, the bookstore space limited, if available. Of the literary works published in translation, very few come close to earning back half the cost of producing them. In short, without financial subvention and noble intention, publishers do not publish translations because in the United States there is virtually no market for translation (translate: virtually no readers). That is a very plain fact. Its causes and history are many-storied and much worried about.

To date, most studies and pleas recommend more subventions, whether from foundations or national governments. (The most notable of those recommending the latter is John O'Brien's four-part series in *Context*, because O'Brien is straightforward, concrete, incisive, and prescriptive, as well as admissive of others' arguments.[11]) The thinking is, the books don't sell, so let's print a larger variety and number of them with the financial risk of production reduced or removed. This thinking comes from business, for profit or not for profit; still, I ask, what other business would think this way? (Were there space, I would compare our production of more and more Ph.D. students in English, sponsored by fellowships and grants, with fewer and fewer job opportunities for them—a lamentable situation repeatedly argued against by William Vesterman.) It does not take a Veblen to perceive that this solution chiefly addresses the marketplace, not the market; it does nothing for habits of thinking about translation.

Nasty facts first. Translation itself is not the recognized major cost in presenting a book from a foreign language. Look at this breakdown of typical costs, generously and publicly supplied by O'Brien:

Author advance	$3,000
Translation	$4,000
Editing	$4,000
Production, design, printing	$10,300
Marketing	$6,900
Operating	$2,700

Editing here costs the same as translation, and the item does not include proofreading: for that Dalkey calls upon a squad of unpaid interns from the University of Illinois at Urbana-Champaign. My experience over the last forty years teaches that the editing, may I say the ultimate englishing? of the translation, when it is undertaken, almost always costs more than the translation itself; but because that cost is usually figured as an in-house expense, whereas translation is an out-of-house cost, it is seldom figured to count against publishing translations. Again, this is where skilled graduates in English might see possibilities for employment.

In the case of Lumen, Inc., which I suspect is closer to the average for small presses, the typical paperback in an edition of 1,500 will cost approximately:

Author advance	$1,000
Translation	$5,000
Editing*	$7,000
Production, design,* printing	$6,000
Marketing	$3,000
Operating	$1,000
*unpaid cost of contributed labor	

Our production costs are lower because we print only paperbacks. Also, our editions are small (1000–1500), and our advances are lower, usually 10 percent of the net price of one copy multiplied by 1000. For example, a recently negotiated contract stipulates an advance of $1700 based on an estimated net price of $17. (Low as that price may seem, it is well above what major chains declare to be the limit at which an unknown author will sell: $14.) Long-range costs, such as warehousing, representation at book fairs, and subject catalogues, are difficult to figure, and they arise chiefly because we are dedicated to keeping translations in print—first, because we believe in our books, and second, because a literary work must remain in print in order to build an academic audience. Whereas most publishers figure their return on an initial printing over a sixteen- or eighteen-month period, we extend that period over many years. But should we sell out of that $17 book in eighteen months, our gross return on the initial $23,000 cost would be $25,500 minus the following deductions, rounded off:

Bookstore discount (40%)	$11,575
Distributor (27% of 55%)	$3,000

This yields about $10,000 net income—a 50% loss—from which then must be deducted hidden costs, the most egregious being what are known in the trade as "hurts": copies returned by bookstores for credit and rendered unsaleable, most frequently because the store has applied a bar-code sticker that damages the book when removed. Such books may go to the distributor's recycling program, or, because we have paid the shipping, they come back to us for giving away to libraries, prisons, and the like.

How is the deficit made up, if it is? First, grants come to mind, such as those from the NEA, to both translators and publishers. I have had one such NEA translation grant, which went entirely into publication costs, but Lumen's two recent applications have been rejected, reportedly because our project was considered too ambitious and because the judges were confused by our publishing both architecture books and works in translation. We have had grants from the Trubar Foundation in Slovenia and the Spanish Ministry of Culture, both of which paid 50% of translation costs; and, when we were located in New York, we received generous developmental support from the literature program of the New York State Council on the Arts. In truth, we have been funded by what at Manhattan College I learned to call a *living endowment:* one of us part-timers takes no salary, the other receives a token fee that barely covers the purchase of hardware, software, and materials. Recently, Helen Lane's bequest to the press, resulting in Helen Lane Editions, enables us to undertake a limited number of additional projects.

Grants are, at present, the most efficient and effective means of subsidizing the losses from publishing translations in this country. On the other hand, asking foreign nations to increase their subsidies for our translations, as John O'Brien does, seems a curious inversion of our nation's problem with drugs. We unsuccessfully expend millions to eradicate, say, Colombia's drug production, because Colombia is viewed as the source of our supply; while we do little or nothing, really, to limit the market here. Therefore: Colombia should stop exporting drugs because we cannot stop using them; Spain, for example, should increase its already generous subsidies for translation, because we won't buy them.

But let's backtrack for a moment. The example I used above in which my house, Lumen Books, paid a $1700 advance on a novel of 561 pages, masks a fundamental economic fact. Computed at the base translation rate set by the British Arts Council—£80 per 1,000 words—the novel's 192,000 words come to a translation fee not of $5,000 but of $26,000. "I doubt that any American translator gets that," remarked one noted critic and translator; "it will take the translator one year's work to do this translation," commented the novel's author. Put that annual wage alongside the actual substandard salary or fee in this country and you have the translator's economic problem in a nutshell.

Reported figures and budgets, then, are usually faulty, minimally incorrect, as is so often the case in the book business. Having worked through some estimates of the costs of nonprofit publishing as a basis for this piece, Chad Post of Rochester University concluded: "It seems that the more one looks into the financial workings of publishing [translations], the more one realizes that with rare exception, the only financial 'winners' are the shipping companies."

Such, then, is the institutionalized and foundationalized publication of translations at present in the United States: underpaid translators, unsaleable translations. The institution is wrong. The reports, notices, warnings, predictions about its wrongness are plentiful and need no summarizing.(An irregular, cheering, although cautionary counterexample: supertitles for opera. Both the Metropolitan Opera and the New York City Center Opera pay adequate fees to translators, whose work is properly acknowledged in the body of program credits, and not as a small-type afterthought; the Metropolitan even engages a consultant editor of English for rehearsals. As with movies, the provision of these translations by franchise and their concealment by the labels Met Titles and Supertitles compromises their worth to the recognition of translation as creative art; yet the audiences' enthusiasm for the work itself powerfully endorses the product.)

Veblen would note that translation is not a valued commodity in our culture. While there may be, on occasion, a rarified snob appeal, especially one that is *alienating* from the culture—a generalized form of the Anglophilia that tainted English literature studies fifty years ago and earlier—our universities mostly teach by demonstration that translation is an inferior activity when not a literally worthless one. In effect, they concur with the IRS agent who audited my return the year after I received an NEA grant, on which of course I had paid the imposed tax; that was not the agent's point of concern, but she did want to know: "*Why* would the federal government ever subsidize translating a foreign book for publication into the United States?"

Graduate students in English must still pass proficiency exams in one or more foreign languages, usually modern. (The true, unasked test question is *proficiency for what?*) Special cram courses are sometimes offered; once passed, the language will be worse than forgotten, it will be ignored, and its hurdle considered mere hazing for a new scholar, likely to conduct research in English and using critical works translated into English by translators whom the researcher is scarcely able to name, much less evaluate. ("Multicultural" studies have not changed this situation.)

The language exam does not teach proficiency; it teaches a dash of fear, an extra dose of contempt, and, often enough, the rewards of slipping by. The student knows full well that professors themselves can seldom claim translating as legitimate cultural (let alone scholarly) activity; the exam confirms the grinding unprofitability of translation, and if a certain utility is indeed granted, say, for bringing a Derrida into English, well, let George do it.

What if—and this has been suggested before—the exam asked the student to translate a portion of critical writing, an article or chapter, perhaps, for publication and discussion at least within the department? What if, provided the student is imaginative and courageous enough, the condition of proficiency were based on rendering a portion of an untranslated story, novel, drama, or poem? The study of English would be confidently intensified, and its richness increased. The work would be real, the contribution substantial and measurable.

Asked once, and only once, to devise a language test for a teaching assistant, I provided a very short, linguistically straightforward poem by Alfonsia Storni along with approximately two hundred words of biographical commentary from a college-level Latin American anthology. The test did not ask this young teacher to translate anything; it instead *assumed* an ability to read, to use a bilingual dictionary, and to translate, and so asked this teacher to employ his relative language proficiency by preparing an outline of an hour's class based on the poet and her poem, relying on the provided texts for illustrative points of exposition and analysis. A pedagogical exercise vital to students of poetry and feminism, and, yes, pedagogy. The departmental secretary came to my office: "We have a problem. I told him that you mean for him to pass, but he's crying." Genuine work, especially when it is in the day-to-day line of what one has chosen to do in life, is rewarding, neither humiliating nor insurmountable; self-gratifying, not self-denigrating; but nothing in his academic training had prepared the engaged teacher for such an experience. A fundamental, not too imaginative revision of this programmed crisis called a language exam could trigger a revolution in attitude and thinking about translation among our disseminators of thought and attitude—our teachers.

Similarly, translation penetration of our creative writing programs—translation *is* a creative act, at whatever remove—will fecundate both categories of literature. The translator's scholarly, word-by-word, sometimes letter-by-letter scrutiny and the fiction and verse writer's expressive, stylistic impetus by their natures overlap correctively as well as beneficially; a sort of editing, distinguishable from the customary critiquing, may result as a force for bettering the practice as well as the stature of both endeavors. From such crosses might also come much-needed editors of translation, people with literary sensitivity and translation skills, the likes of which most publishing houses have not seen for years.

Cordons sanitaires around the study of English and the study of foreign languages, around practices of creative writing and translation, constrain the development of more enlightened attitudes toward translation, eliminate thinking about the active though diminished role of translation in our present culture, and enforce the outmoded, unproductive arguments about the economics of translation. As the venerable thirteenth edition of the *Encyclopedia Britannica* declares: "At the root of all economic investigation lies the conception of the standard of life of the community." In regard to translation, our standard of living is devalued, disguised.

NOTES

1. "And what about provinicalism in the large nations? The definition is the same: the inability or refusal to imagine one's own culture in *the large context.*" Milan Kundera, translated by Linda Asher, "*Die weltliteratur,*" *New Yorker,* January 8, 2007, 31.

2. Bertold Brecht, *The Threepenny Opera,* trans. Marc Blitzstein, MGM 3121 (LP), 1954.

3. Consider the concept of pecuniary emulation as outlined in Thorstein Veblen, "Pecuniary Emulation," in *The Theory of the Leisure Class* (New York: Penguin, 1967), 22–34.

4. *The Pillow Book,* movie, written and directed by Peter Greenaway (1966); Peter Greenaway, *The Pillow Book* (Paris: Dis Voir, 1996).

5. The literature program of what was then the Center for Inter-American Relations, now the Americas Society, was founded by José Guillermo Castillo. While dedicated to the recognition and promotion of Latin American culture and arts in this country, the center sustained a public affairs program as well, and there were occasional Canadian elements among its interests.

6. Robert Lekachman, "Introduction," in Veblen, *The Theory of the Leisure Class,* viii. The explanation of Veblen's phrase comes directly from Lekachman.

7. Milan Kundera's is perhaps the most forceful recent citation of Goethe's dictum: "National literature no longer means much these days, we are entering the era of *Weltliteratur,* and it is up to each of us to hasten this development." Kundera, "*Die weltliteratur,*" 29.

8. Lawrence Venuti, *The Translator's Invisibility: A History of Translation* (London and New York: Routledge, 1995).

9. Habibul Haque Khondker, "Is Reading Going Out of Fashion?" *Daily Star,* April 2, 2005, http://www.thedailystar.net/2005/04/02/d504021503111.htm.

10. This tiny percentage is persistently noted. I cite Chad Post, quoted by Gary Shapiro, "Around the World in Translation," *New York Sun,* May 27, 2005.

11. See John O'Brien, "A Simple Question," *Context* 14; John O'Brien and Tim Wilkinson, " . . . And More on Translations," *Context* 15; John O'Brien, "Translations, Part 3: The Finnish Know How to Do It," *Context* 16; and John O'Brien and M. A. Orthofer, "Translations, Part 4," *Context* 17. All articles are available at http://www. dalkeyarchive.com/revues/context/. In addition to grants provided through European embassies and ministries of culture, the European Union also offers translation subsidies. Pete Ayrton of Serpent's Tail "claims to be 'the only UK publisher who can understand the EU forms. Some of the dullest weekends of my life have been spent filling them in.'" "New Wave in Translation," *The Bookseller,* March 25, 2005, http://www.marionboyars.co.uk/Amy%20Pages/Bookseller%20Article.html.

PART TWO

Issues and Contexts

IDENTITY AND

RELATIONSHIPS

Identity and Relationships in Translated Japanese Literature

Tomoko Aoyama and Judy Wakabayashi

This chapter explores Japanese concepts of the self and interactions with others as manifested in translated Japanese literature. After outlining how Japanese understandings of self and identity differ from these concepts in the West, we note some of the challenges these differences present to literary translators working in Western languages. The challenges are accentuated by the intimate conceptual relations among ideas of the self, identity, and language, as illustrated in the texts examined here.

Identity encompasses many aspects, such as group identity (traditionally more emphasized in Japan than in the West); the historically more recent focus on individual psychological identity; and geographical, cultural, family, gender, age, political, economic, and religious identity. Race, ethnicity, and nationality do not necessarily coincide with each other or with the native language of the writer or translator. Class is not a major theme in contemporary Japanese literature, given that 97 percent of the population regard themselves as "middle class" (Strecher 298). Class and occupational identities are, however, intimately implicated in the question of the *burakumin,* a social (not ethnic) minority who have long been discriminated against in Japan. Sumii[1] Sué's seven-volume work *The River with No Bridge* (1961–1992; only volume 1 is available in English) is an important work on this topic, as is Shimazaki Tōson's *The Broken Commandment* (1906).

In ancient Japan, it was women writers who dominated genres such as fiction and diaries, so that a generalized woman's "manner of writing, her perceptual stance, and her aesthetic orientation, where they can fairly be gen-eralized at all, have become naturalized in the tradition as its source" (Vernon 6). Although women writers were subsequently eclipsed until the twentieth century, men inherited this tradition, which was "characterized by sentimental lyricism and impressionistic, non-intellectual, detailed observations of daily life" (Ericson 3). Classical literature also lacked clear demarcations between first- and third-person narration, resulting in multivoiced complexity; a blurring among author, narrator, and characters; and an absence of autonomous selfhood. Thus, in translations of premodern works, the use of the English *I*, a term that refers exclusively to one person independent of context, constitutes a fundamental shift in perception from the "contextually and relationally defined" (Miyake 43) nature of Japanese personal pronouns. Even with contemporary works, "There are many first- and second-pronoun forms to choose from in Japanese, each with particular connotative or indexical association with the age/sex/class of the speaker, the relationship to the addressee, and the formality of the context of use" (Shibamoto Smith, 103). In translation into English, however, these associations usually disappear; conversely, the use of overt self-reference and frequent second-person address in translations might make characters seem more assertive than they are in the original Japanese.

In premodern Japan the Confucian moral system took precedence over individualism, which would have undermined the hierarchical social order; but Japan's opening to the West in the 1850s led to a perceived need for self-redefinition as a modernizing nation and for a reconceptualization of the individual "self" in a rapidly changing environment. Stimulated by Western literary models, in the 1880s the translator-writer Futabatei Shimei initiated narrative reforms that detached narrators from characters' and readers' speech situations, and newly available Christian ideas fostered conceptions of the individual as having value and being individuated from others. The new focus on writers' inner lives coexisted with a desire to maintain continuity of the Japanese cultural self, resulting in a "complex negotiation between the formal insistence on the 'I' and the ideological suppression of the self" (Miyoshi, "Against the Native Grain," 155).

Starting with Tayama Katai's *Futon* (*The Quilt and Other Stories*, 1907), the "I-novel" (*shishōsetsu*)[2] subsequently became the dominant novel form in Japanese literature. This introspective, male-created tradition valorizes personal experiences over thought or the presentation of protagonists in confrontation with the social environment in an autonomous fictional world. Japan's subsequent defeat in World War II challenged national identity, questioning the individual-state relationship and destroying many writers' beliefs in themselves and their narrators. The *shishōsetsu* became less influential, but the conflict between this confessional genre and those who reject the possibility or desirability of representing the sincere "self" (Snyder and Gabriel 4) is ongoing, and the genre retains a tenacious hold (e.g., in the writing of Nobel Prize winner Ōe Kenzaburō).

In postwar Japan the failure of family relations and national affluence to act as bases for identity triggered an existential crisis, and the culture's consequent plunge into consumerism and the prioritizing of personal fulfillment proved inadequate compensation for a sense of lack. The writing of internationally renowned author Murakami Haruki is underpinned by a belief that self-definition outside one's role in the system is difficult in Japan today, even as he insists on the individual's right to separateness and continues to seek the self. Works by Korean writers resident in Japan and by bilingual or bicultural writers (e.g., Tawada Yōko and Ian Hideo Levy) challenge essentialist notions of national identity, while Ōba Minako's work imagines a transnational subjectivity based on "alternative communities and relationships" (Hurley 90), such as women's connections with each other.[3]

Today many women writers of all ages are presenting self-images that challenge male writers' representations of women over the centuries. In recent years women (notably Kirino Natsuo) have shown increasing interest in writing detective fiction, with empowered female protagonists as well as an emphasis on issues such as identity and community that reflect "the particular nature of women's lives in Japan" (Seaman 113). The diversity of Japanese women's writing has not, however, been reflected in translation, where they are under- and misrepresented, and few full-length works by women (particularly prewar writers) are available. Coutts (114) notes how the selection and advertising of translated women's works marginalize and objectify women, emphasizing "the eroticism, exoticism and mystery of the 'Oriental' woman," whereas with translations of Japanese male writers the emphasis is on "the quality of the writing, the scholarly reputation of the editors and the importance of the nation's literature, rather than on the gender of the author."

Linguistic and cultural differences play an important role in Japanese-English translation. For instance, Japanese writing today makes use of four scripts: characters borrowed from Chinese, the indigenous *hiragana* phonetic syllabary, the *katakana* phonetic syllabary used mainly for foreign loan words, and the roman alphabet. However, and the effects that writers can achieve via the interplay among the different scripts disappear in translation. Social distinctions conveyed by Japanese honorifics are also often lost or attenuated. Morton (726) observes that "the form of expression in Japanese is affected far more than many other languages by contextual factors: the formality of the setting, the sex and social status of the speech-act participants and so on. Japanese has a highly elaborate honorific system which extends to the use of pronouns (and their avoidance) as well as verbs, vocabulary, etc. This factor . . . reinforces the importance of context, itself a reflection of the nature of Japanese society, which puts great stress on social interdependence." In passages of dialogue, sentence-ending particles help signal the register and the relationship between characters, but this richness often disappears in translations. On the other hand, Japanese sentences often do not have an explicit subject, but English grammar requires that translators supply a subject inferred from the context, making the translation more specific (but less open to interpretation) than the source text. Again, Japanese tense[4] forms are used in ways that often do not match English conventions. Although adherence to the original forms can be effective (as with the historic present in English), often it might simply strike readers as strange, so translators usually "normalize" Japanese tense shifts to match English conventions (harmonizing the tense form with the time frame), thereby countering the impact of Japanese tense shifts. Another feature of much Japanese writing is mimetic expressions, whose frequency and independent lexical status give them greater prominence and impact than English onomatopoeia. Some translators, however, occasionally introduce Japanese onomatopoeia in transliterated form, thereby giving them even more prominence than in the original text and forcing readers to infer the meaning from the Japanese sounds.

In translation the portrayal of identities and relationships can undergo a shift through even "minor" adjustments, such as the use of endearments that lack a close counterpart in Japanese, where indications of love are more subtle. Reflecting Japanese social relations, terms of address and the practice of referring to characters by occupation or descriptive phrases, rather than by name, create a sense of distance that can be magnified when transplanted into an English setting. Intertextual relationships in Japanese literature, with its tradition of allusion, intertextual motifs, quotations, imitation, adaptation, and parody, also present a challenge because of their likely unfamiliarity to Western readers. This problem confronts translators with a decision of whether to add explanations in footnotes or a foreword—visible signs of the translator's own presence in the text.

Translators are embedded within a "cultural structure" that they can perpetuate (West-Pavlov 108) or challenge, and the translator's own identity, values, and individual style are factors in text selection and the translational approach. In turn, reading Japanese literature from "outside" calls not for self-affirmation but for an awareness of positionality (e.g., as a member of "the West" reading a work by a writer from "the East")—as well as a questioning of such dichotomies.

One oft-taught Japanese classic that revolves around relationships is *Genji monogatari* (*The Tale of Genji*), which was written in the eleventh century by a court lady, Murasaki Shikibu (973?–1014?), for a small circle of readers in the imperial court in Kyoto. The tale is narrated in the voice of a gentlewoman or lady-in-waiting to her mistress/empress and other court ladies. Personal names are avoided, as their use was considered rude in the court, and instead characters are usually referred to by rank and position (which change as the story progresses, causing further confusion). In Japan this work has been translated into modern Japanese several times and adapted and transformed into a wide range of genres and forms. The first partial English translation (by Suematsu Kenchō) was published in London in 1882, but it was Arthur Waley's translation (1925–33) that introduced the tale and its "shining" hero, Prince Genji, to the Western world and established its position as a masterpiece of world literature and arguably the world's first "novel" or "psychological novel." The completeness of Waley's translation is debatable, as is the question of whether the Japanese text should be regarded as a novel, but the *Genji* has continued to attract scholarly and popular attention in Japan and, to a lesser extent, in the West.

Waley's translation remains much admired, particularly for its elegance and readability, if not for its accuracy or fidelity. Morris observes that it is "the freest possible type of translation. . . . Indeed the word 're-creation' would be more appropriate; for he has brought Murasaki's novel to life as a great work of English literature in its own right" (283). When Edward Seidensticker's translation appeared in 1976, most reviewers, though fully acknowledging the merits and values of Waley's *Genji*, enthusiastically welcomed the more "complete" translation, which did not omit Murasaki's poems, let alone an entire chapter, as Waley had. Seidensticker's translation also benefited from superior editions of the Japanese text and from scholarly publications not available in Waley's time. The significance and characteristics of the third complete English translation, by Royall Tyler (2001), have not yet been fully discussed, although Kamens comments that "for our time, this is a good *Genji*, the admirable product of ambitious and sensitive work" (339). It too reflects sociocultural and academic changes since the previous translation. For instance, Tyler treats the work's sexual content more overtly than the earlier translations, probably in line with changing attitudes toward gender and sexuality issues.

There are also some partial translations, including Helen Craig McCullough's translation (1994) of ten of the fifty-four chapters, and numerous reference books and critical works in English—e.g., the useful introductory books by Morris, Puette, and Bowring, which provide information about the Heian Period (794–1192) and its sociopolitical, cultural, linguistic, and religious background, as well as more specific reference works such as Shirane (*The Bridge of Dreams*) and Field. Tyler's translation is accompanied by an introduction and useful appendices, including a chronology, glossary, maps, and diagrams. A series of articles by Tyler reveals many aspects of translating this demanding text.

One factor that may interest but confuse *Genji* beginners is its hero's sexual relationships with a number of women (and some men). As Tyler writes, the tale presents "a world neither of languidly elegant wraiths nor of a lecher-hero and his mechanically conquered victims" ("Erotic Entertainment" 68). Hence a simple catalog like Leporello's in *Don Giovanni* would not do. Besides, the text does not clearly name names. This is partly because the ellipsis of sentence subjects and objects is grammatical in Japanese. Even with such linguistic and stylistic ambiguities, Heian readers could identify the topic or person from the honorific language and other signs—many of which, however, require explicitation in translation. Appellation is a major issue in any translation of the *Genji*. Waley and Seidensticker opted to replace the ranks and titles with elegant sobriquets for the characters, usually derived from chapter titles, from poetry by or concerning those characters, or from their residential quarters in the palace or outside. Such clarification helps readers, but Tyler deliberately avoids overclarification and retains the appellations by rank, respecting the Heian gentlewoman's narrative voice.

The intrigue (and interest) in this work derives from the fact that at the core of Genji's sexual activity is his longing for his deceased mother, Kiritsubo. This aspect of the narrative introduces not only a kind of oedipal theme but also a pseudoincestuous relationship with Fujitsubo, the new favorite of Genji's father, the emperor, after Kiritsubo's death. Fujitsubo, just five years older than Genji, physically resembles both Genji's mother and Genji's wife, Lady Murasaki, the tale's heroine, who happens to be Fujitsubo's niece.[5] The strong emphasis placed on the physical resemblances and blood relations among the women Genji loves is outside the norm of modern fiction dealing with relationships. The relationship between Genji and Fujitsubo is far more subversive than romantic, because their son, raised as Genji's half-brother, is to succeed to the throne. The motif of an illicit relationship resulting in childbirth is repeated in later chapters, only this time Genji is the cuckold. The guilty pair are Genji's "child wife," the Third Princess, and Kashiwagi, the best friend of Genji's son. Murasaki Shikibu uses thematic repetition dramatically and effectively to convey the ephemeral nature of life and the dimming of the Shining Prince's radiance.

Knowledge of Heian court life and marriage practices is essential to grasping the complexity of the novel's sexual, marital, and family relationships, as well as their political implications. Buddhism, Shintoism, and folk beliefs, particularly spirit possession, are also important to understanding these personal relationships. There are several times when a character—usually a woman sexually involved with Genji—falls ill or dies suddenly and suspiciously. These events are regarded as a consequence of possession by an evil spirit (often attributed to the Rokujō Lady), and priests are called in to exorcise the spirit. Difficult as it might be for modern readers to accept these turns of events at face value, the theme of spirit possession has invited a range of interesting feminist and psychological readings (e.g., Bargen). Feminist readings have shown that spirit possession is by no means irrational superstition but can be interpreted as "women's weapon" against patriarchal oppression and sexual suppression.

The work's canonicity and the abundance of critical resources surrounding it might intimidate some readers, and its length and complexity might make teachers hesitate to use it in a short nonspecialist course. Although *The Tale of Genji* is a demanding text to read it in its entirety, selected chapters can be used in class, and *Genji* in translation has diverse possibilities as a text for a nonspecialist course. Some chapters, such as "*Yūgao*" ("Evening Face," chapter 4), can be read as interesting short stories. Others, such as the superb "*Wakana*" chapters ("New Herbs" and "Spring Shoots," chapters 34 and 35), might be too complex, yet when understood in relation to other chapters they provide an endless source of reading pleasure.

Just as the *Genji*'s importance is indisputable, no one would deny the significance in modern Japanese literature of Natsume Kinnosuke (1867–1916, conventionally referred to by his pen name, Sōseki), whose works are still widely read both by critics and the general reading public.[6] The text discussed here, *Kokoro*,[7] was published in 1914, a time when Japan was still coming to terms with its changing cultural identity. Kondō Ineko's translation appeared in 1941,[8] followed by Edwin McClellan's 1957 translation, which has been used in many courses around the world for half a century. No other Sōseki novel seems to have attracted as much attention as *Kokoro*,[9] although its "spare, almost stark" (Anderer 498) dramatic power and "language veering toward silence" (499) are partially overshadowed by the slightly stilted and dated language of both translations.

Kokoro is much less intimidating than the *Genji* in size and complexity. There are only four main characters: the first-person narrator (usually referred to as "the student" in secondary sources); his older friend, whom he addresses and refers to as Sensei;[10] Sensei's wife; and Sensei's best friend, "K," who committed suicide when K and Sensei were young. Unlike the Heian tale, Sōseki's text is a modern novel written in modern Japanese and with a clear three-part structure: "Sensei and I," "My Parents and I," and "Sensei and His Testament" (titles from McClellan). As in *Genji*, however, the characters are not normally referred to by name. Instead, in the Japanese text, and to a lesser extent in the translations, we see a constant reminder of the fluidity and relativity of roles and viewpoints within a seemingly straightforward first-person narrative (actually two separate first-person narratives). For instance, Shizu is referred to by name only when her husband (Sensei) addresses her directly.[11] When referring to her in conversation with the student, he uses *sai* (the humble form for "wife"), and the student addresses and refers to her by using the polite version *okusan*. Both Kondo and McClellan translate these terms as "[my, his, your, etc.] wife." However, in part 3, when Sensei recounts his earlier years, Shizu is referred to as *ojōsan* in the Japanese text (Ojosan in the McClellan translation),[12] while her mother is addressed and referred to as *okusan*/Okusan. In *Kokoro* nothing is absolute—not the first-, second-, and third-person viewpoint demarcations, nor personal trust and relationships. The closest and most trustworthy friends and relatives—even one's self—may betray a trust for love or money, and in turn the betrayed may become the betrayer, reflecting Sōseki's view of human nature as essentially evil (Pollack 59).[13]

In the midst of such instability, it is important to note that the narrator of parts 1 and 2 insists that Sensei cannot be called anything else, even though there is no formal teacher-student relationship between them. McClellan slightly simplifies the narrator's remark: "And with pen in hand, I cannot bring myself to write of him in any other way" (1), whereas Kondo, though not without omission, does retain the specific mention of the use of initials: "As for his initial I could never bring myself to resort to such an unfeeling manner of designating him" (1). This aversion to initials is in stark contrast to how Sensei calls his dead friend "K" (the initial of Kokoro) in his final confessional letter to the student.[14] Rather than merely conveying formality, the student's use of the "Sensei" appellation signifies a combination of social codes and personal feelings of warmth, affection, respect, and even sexual attraction.[15] Sensei, on the other hand, maintains a certain aloofness from both the student and his beloved wife.

A comparison of these two translations does not provide as much interest as a comparison among the three *Genji* translations, although a 1990 essay in Japanese by Saitō maintains that Kondo's rendition reflects a deeper understanding of the emotional and spiritual aspects of the novel, while McClellan's translation is more readable but faithful only to the surface structure. In an indirect response to this critique, McClellan ("On Translating *Kokoro*" 18) acknowledges his youth and inexperience as a translator at that time but argues that the dialogue required "little subtlety or experience on the part of the translator to give it an acceptable rendering" and that the main difficulty was "to prevent the surface simplicity of the narrative from becoming banal." There are also some clear differences in the degree to which the two translators cater to English readers. In part, the differing extent to which Japanese words are used and explained in translation reflects changed assumptions over time with regard to English readers' familiarity with Japan. McClellan also felt a need to footnote Sōseki's use of *English* words, presumably because their impact in the Japanese text would otherwise be lost in an English translation. Although the sociocultural differences between Sōseki's time and today are not as large as the differences between the time of *Genji* and today, *Kokoro* continues to invite new interpretations and readings, which—as was the case with *Genji*—might well lead to another translation that takes into account recent scholarship and that also renders the language anew for a contemporary readership.

Very different again is Kanehara Hitomi's contemporary cult classic *Hebi ni piasu* (2003; *Snakes and Earrings,* translated by David Karashima, 2005). By the age of 20 Kanehara had won two literary awards for this disturbing debut novella, which fits within serious literature's tradition of interest in "shocking" youth subculture[16] while resisting stereotypical notions of

Japanese femininity and propriety and underscoring the anxiety generated by women's changing roles—both of the protagonist and of transgressive women authors.[17] Arguably, however, the sensation generated by this "deviant," provocative text conforms to the eroticization/exoticization of Japanese women critiqued earlier.

This unsettling work emerges from a sense of emptiness and disconnection in a consumer-driven society where family relationships are foundering and the body is perhaps one of the few constants under one's control. The self-absorbed, self-loathing Lui evinces a particular lack of purpose. While rejecting family life and seeking out darkness (familiar themes in *shisōsetsu*), the rather nihilistic Lui is curiously unassertive. Her appearance becomes unconventional, but she never develops into a proactive model of female independence, emotionally or sexually, and her masochism positions her as apparently submissive, not unlike women's traditional role. She does, however, take some initiatives, no matter how passive, futile, or bizarre they might seem: modifying her body (albeit in an imitative act), protecting her men, making the risky and shocking choice to remain with a probable murderer, and deciding to go on living. So Lui, although not fundamentally progressive, does challenge stereotypical characterizations of Japanese women. Her relationships with her two lovers take to an extreme the lack of self-disclosure that Shibamoto Smith has identified as a feature of romantic relations in Japanese writing when compared with those in English writing.

Unlike Bad Girls who "revel" in deviance (Miller and Bardsley 1), Lui's sole pleasure derives from physical pain. Experiencing a "rush" (Kanehara 20) as her values are overturned by Ama's forked tongue, Lui gains "cruel pleasure" (39) from being treated sadistically and from the pain of tongue-splitting and a tattoo. (In Japan tattoos have long been associated with *yakuza*,[18] and even ear piercing was frowned upon until recently.) Lui's emotional numbness leads to a desire to be killed, and after Ama's horrific death even the pleasures of physical pain, anorexia, and alcohol abuse offer no escape. Eventually, however, Lui shows signs of returning life, giving the tattooed figures—and herself— "freedom" and commenting that "everything would be all right" (118).[19]

The narrative presents an alternative construction of relationships, and the characters exhibit a complex mixture of values. Such heterogeneity challenges binary notions of good/bad identity, and the text has an inherent ambiguity that could be interpreted as an effective questioning and critique of dichotomies such as passive/active, male/female, adult/child, and mother/ baby, especially in the case of Ama.

Kanehara's novella, which could gainfully be read in conjunction with Tanizaki Jun'ichirō's *"Shisei"* (1910; "The Tattooer,"[20] translated by Ivan Morris), is written in lean, concise, minimalist prose that reflects Japanese pop culture. Karashima adopts a translation approach fundamentally oriented toward domesticating the text linguistically for English readers, using colloquial expressions and occasional four-letter swear words (which have no direct counterpart in Japanese), while also successfully conveying formality when appropriate (47). Culturally, the domestication is less uniform: the accommodation for English readers in the form of an explanatory footnote on page 31 is offset by unexplained references elsewhere, e.g., the allusion to tattoos "for a certain unwelcome section of society" (29; this refers to *yakuza,* but gives no hint about how tattoos are regarded in Japan); an allusion to Akutagawa's story *"Jigoku hen"* ("Hell Screen," translated by Ivan Morris), in which an artist sacrifices his daughter out of a desire to paint a woman burning in hell (33); and literal representations of Japanese body language (55, 57). The translator also introduces the Japanese saying, "Why feed a fish if it's already in your net?" (80). Rather than indicating a deliberate attempt at foreignizing, such features suggest the challenges of conveying to readers of the translation all the background information familiar to Japanese readers—one of the many demanding but satisfying aspects of translating Japanese literature for English audiences.

NOTES

1. Here Japanese names are written according to Japanese convention, with the family name first.

2. For discussion of the I-novel, see Fowler, Hijiya-Kirschnereit, and Suzuki.

3. For fuller discussions of how identity is conceptualized and negotiated in Japanese literature, see Shirane and Suzuki, and Washburn.

4. Strictly speaking, the focus in Japanese is on aspect (the completedness of an action) rather than on tense (occurrence in the past, present, or future).

5. Symbolically, each woman is associated with a purple flower or plant: *kiri* (paulownia), *fuji* (wisteria), and *murasaki* (a plant whose roots yield a purple dye). Purple is associated with nobility in Japan, and Heian aristocrats had a highly developed aesthetic sensitivity to colors.

6. Sōseki was the most popular writer in a poll organized by the literary magazine *Taiyō* in 1909. In a 2000 poll by the *Asahi shimbun* newspaper, he was voted the most popular writer of the millennium, followed by Murasaki Shikibu.

7. The word *kokoro* is usually translated as "heart," but it also encompasses the meaning of "mind." In his foreword, McClellan (vi) notes that "the best rendering of the Japanese word '*kokoro*' that [he has] seen is Lafcadio Hearn's, which is: 'the heart of things.'"

8. This was published by Hokuseido Press, but World War II meant it could not be sent outside of Japan. The edition used here is the Kenkyūsha edition of 1948, in which the translator's name is shown as Ineko Kondo; hereafter we refer to her as Kondo.

9. *Kokoro* has been "one of the most frequently quoted works of modern Japanese fiction in high school *kokugo* (national language education) textbooks" (Sakaki 33, citing Komori Yōichi).

10. This is how it is shown in McClellan's translation—capitalized, no italics, no article. McClellan adds a footnote to the first line of the text: "The English word 'teacher' which comes closest in meaning to the Japanese word *sensei* is not satisfactory here. The French word *maître* would express better what is meant by *sensei*." (1). In Kondo's translation the character is called "the *sensei*," and a footnote ("A Japanese word for teacher. But even the professors of a university are called *sensei* by the students.") is added for the title of the first part "The *Sensei* and I" (1).

11. Grafflin views the "male namelessness" as an attempt to deprive the men other than Sensei of an autonomous identity, whereas Shizu, "as the systematically ignored member of a secondary gender, can be allowed the onomastic trappings of verisimilitude without threatening the grand design" (149). Grafflin also argues that K is Sensei's psychological double (150–56), as does Miyoshi (*Accomplices* 75).

12. Long vowel signs are omitted in both translations. Kondo uses "the *okusan*" but translates *ojōsan* as "(the/her) daughter."

13. Pollack (60) points out that "*Kokoro* presents social situations embodying each of the five cardinal social relationships, only to strip them away in turn until at the end of the novel nothing remains but the isolated 'self.'" These five cardinal relationships, as advocated by the Confucian philosopher Mencius, were:

1. between father and child, "affection" or "love";
2. between ruler and minister, "righteousness" or "duty";
3. between husband and wife, "distinction" or "attention to separate functions";
4. between elder and younger brother, "proper order" or "precedence";
5. between friends, "fidelity" or "faith" or "trust."

14. This is one of the major points of debate between Komori and Miyoshi Yukio, as discussed in Sakaki (42–48).

15. For an insightful study of this aspect, see Dodd.

16. For instance, Ishihara Shintarō's *Taiyō no kisetsu* (1955; *Season of Violence*, 1966) and Murakami Ryū's *Kagiri naku tōmei ni chikai burū* (1976; *Almost Transparent Blue*, 1977).

17. Other women writers who have graphically depicted sexual or physical deviance include Kōno Taeko, Kurahashi Yumiko, Yamada Eimi, and Uchida Shungiku.

18. *Yakuza* are associated with many layers of sociocultural meanings, ranging from real criminals to romanticized cultural icons as both heroes and villains (see Buruma), and tattoos appear in all of these representations.

19. The final paragraph in the English version is based on the Japanese version published in January 2004, but the version subsequently published in the March 2004 *Bungei shunjū* literary magazine as the winner of the 130th Akutagawa Prize is completely different.

20. This is about a tattooer who finds his ideal material in a young woman and transforms her into a sadistic femme fatale by tattooing a spider on her back.

WORKS CONSULTED

Akutagawa, Ryūnosuke. "Hell Screen." Translated by Ivan Morris. In *Hell Screen. Cogwheels. A Fool's Life,* 1–41. Hygiene, CO: Eridanos Press, 1987.

Anderer, Paul. "Sōseki's *Kokoro.*" In *Masterworks of Asian Literature in Comparative Perspective: A Guide for Teaching,* edited by Barbara Stoler Miller, 493–500. Armonk, NY: M. E. Sharpe, 1994.

Bargen, Doris G. *A Woman's Weapon: Spirit Possession in The Tale of Genji.* Honolulu: University of Hawaii Press, 1997.

Bowring, Richard. *Murasaki Shikibu: The Tale of Genji.* Cambridge, UK: Cambridge University Press, 1988.

Buruma, Ian. *Behind the Mask: On Sexual Demons, Sacred Mothers, Transvestites, Gangsters, and Other Japanese Cultural Heroes.* New York: Meridian, 1985.

Coutts, Angela. "The Gendering of Japanese Literature: The Influence of English-Language Translation on Concepts of Canon in the West." *Japan Forum* 14, no. 1 (2002): 103–25.

Dodd, Stephen. "The Significance of Bodies in Sōseki's *Kokoro.*" *Monumenta Nipponica* 53, no. 4 (Winter 1998): 473–98.

Ericson, Joan E. *Be a Woman: Hayashi Fumiko and Modern Japanese Women's Literature.* Honolulu: University of Hawaii Press, 1997.

Field, Norma. *The Splendor of Longing in the Tale of Genji.* Princeton, NJ: Princeton University Press, 1987.

Fowler, Edward. *The Rhetoric of Confession: Shishōsetsu in Early Twentieth-Century Japanese Fiction.* Berkeley: University of California Press, 1988.

Goossen, Theodore, ed. *Oxford Book of Japanese Stories.* Oxford: Oxford University Press, 1997.

Grafflin, Dennis. "Second Thoughts on *Kokoro.*" *Journal of the Association of Teachers of Japan* 18, no. 2 (1983): 145–66.

Hijiya-Kirschnereit, Irmela. *Rituals of Self-Revelation:* Shishōsetsu *as Literary Genre and Socio-cultural Phenomenon.* Cambridge, MA: Council on East Asian Studies, Harvard University, 1996.

Hisamatsu, Sen'ichi. *Biographical Dictionary of Japanese Literature.* Tokyo: Kodansha International, International Society for Educational Information, 1976.

Hurley, Adrienne. "Demons, Transnational Subjects, and the Fiction of Ohba Minako." In *Ōe and Beyond: Fiction in Contemporary Japan,* edited by Stephen Snyder and Philip Gabriel, 89–103. Honolulu: University of Hawaii Press, 1999.

Kamens, Edward. "'A Beautiful, Quiet World'? *The Tale of Genji* and Its English Translations." *Journal of Japanese Studies* 29, no. 2 (Summer 2003): 325–39.

Kanehara, Hitomi. *Hebi ni piasu.* Tokyo: Shūeisha, 2003.

———. *Snakes and Earrings.* Translated by David Karashima. New York: Dutton, 2005.

Karatani, Kojin. *Origins of Modern Japanese Literature.* Translation edited by Brett de Bary. Durham, NC: Duke University Press, 1993.

Katō, Shūichi. *A History of Japanese Literature.* 3 vols. London: Macmillan, 1979.

Keene, Donald. *Anthology of Japanese Literature: From the Earliest Era to the Mid-nineteenth Century.* New York: Grove Press, 1955.

———. *Japanese Literature: An Introduction for Western Readers.* New York: Grove Press, 1955.

McClellan, Edwin. "On Translating *Kokoro.*" In *A Symposium on Natsume Sōseki's* Kokoro: *A Selection from the Proceedings,* edited by Lien-Hsiang Lin, 15–25. Singapore: Department of Japanese Studies, National University of Singapore, 1994.

McCullough, Helen Craig. *Genji and Heike: Selections from The Tale of Genji and The Tale of the Heike.* Stanford, CA: Stanford University Press, 1994.

Miller, Laura, and Jan Bardsley, eds. *Bad Girls of Japan.* Houndmills, UK: Palgrave Macmillan, 2005.

Mitsios, Helen, ed. *New Japanese Voices: The Best Contemporary Fiction from Japan.* New York: Atlantic Monthly Press, 1991.

Miyake, Lynne K. "The Tosa Diary: In the Interstices of Gender and Criticism." In *The Woman's Hand: Gender and Theory in Japanese Women's Writing,* edited by Paul Gordon Schalow and Janet A. Walker, 41–73. Stanford, CA: Stanford University Press, 1996.

Miyoshi, Masao. *Accomplices of Silence: The Modern Japanese Novel.* Berkeley: University of California Press, 1974.

———. "Against the Native Grain: The Japanese Novel and the 'Postmodern' West." In *Postmodernism and Japan,* edited by Masao Miyoshi and H. D. Harootunian, 143–68. Durham, NC: Duke University Press, 1989.

Morris, Ivan I. *The World of the Shining Prince: Court Life in Ancient Japan.* London: Oxford University Press, 1964.

Morton, Leith. "Japanese: Literary Translation into English." In *Encyclopedia of Literary Translation into English,* edited by Olive Classe, 725–29. London: Fitzroy Dearborn Publishers, 2000.

Murasaki, Shikibu. *Genji monogatari*. Translated by Suematsu Kenchō. New edition with introduction by Terence Barrow. Rutland, VT: Tuttle, 1974.

———. *The Tale of Genji*. 6 vols. Translated by Arthur Waley. London: Allen & Unwin, 1925–33.

———. *The Tale of Genji*. 2 vols. Translated by Royall Tyler. New York: Viking, 2001.

Natsume, Sōseki. *Kokoro*. Translated by Kondo Ineko. Tokyo: Kodansha, 1948.

———. *Kokoro*. Translated by Edwin McClellan. Tokyo: Charles E. Tuttle Company, 1957.

Pollack, David. *Reading Against Culture: Ideology and Narrative in the Japanese Novel*. Ithaca, NY: Cornell University Press, 1992.

Puette, William J. *Guide to The Tale of Genji*. Rutland, VT: Tuttle, 1983.

Rimer, J. Thomas. *A Reader's Guide to Japanese Literature*. Tokyo: Kodansha, 1988.

———, and Robert E. Morrell. *Guide to Japanese Poetry*. Boston: G. K. Hall, 1975.

Rubin, Jay, ed. *Modern Japanese Writers*. New York: Scribner's, 2001.

Saitō, Keiko. "*Futatsu no KOKORO: Makureran-yaku to Kondō Ineko-yaku*." *Hikaku bungaku kenkyū* 57, 1990.

Sakaki, Atsuko. *Narrative Performance in Modern Japanese Fiction*. Cambridge, MA: Harvard University Press, 1999.

Seaman, Amanda C. *Bodies of Evidence: Women, Society, and Detective Fiction in 1990s Japan*. Honolulu: University of Hawaii Press, 2004.

Shibamoto Smith, Janet S. "Translating True Love: Japanese Romance Fiction, Harlequin-Style." In *Gender, Sex and Translation: The Manipulation of Identities*, edited by José Santaemilia, 97–116. Manchester, UK, and Northampton, MA: St. Jerome, 2005.

Shimazaki, Tōson. *The Broken Commandment*. Translated by Kenneth Strong. Tokyo: Japan Foundation, 1974.

Shirane, Haruo. *The Bridge of Dreams: A Poetics of 'The Tale of Genji.'* Stanford, CA: Stanford University Press, 1987.

———, and Tomi Suzuki, eds. *Inventing the Classics: Modernity, National Identity, and Japanese Literature*. Stanford, CA: Stanford University Press, 2000.

Snyder, Stephen, and Philip Gabriel. *Ōe and Beyond: Fiction in Contemporary Japan*. Honolulu: University of Hawaii Press, 1999.

Strecher, M. C. "Magical Realism and the Search for Identity in the Fiction of Murakami Haruki." *Journal of Japanese Studies* 25, no. 2 (Summer 1999): 263–98.

Sumii, Sué. *The River with No Bridge*. Translated by Susan Wilkinson. Rutland, VT: Tuttle, 1990.

Suzuki, Tomi. *Narrating the Self: Fictions of Japanese Modernity*. Stanford, CA: Stanford University Press, 1996.

Tanizaki, Jun'ichirō. "The Tattooer." Translated by Howard Hibbett. In *Seven Japanese Tales*, 160–69. London: Secker & Warburg, 1973.

Tayama, Katai. *The Quilt and Other Stories*. Translated and with an introduction by Kenneth G. Henshall. Tokyo: University of Tokyo Press, 1981.

Tyler, Royall. "Lady Murasaki's Erotic Entertainment: The Early Chapters of *The Tale of Genji*." *East Asian History* 12 (1996): 65–78.

Vernon, Victoria V. *Daughters of the Moon: Wish, Will, and Social Constraint in Fiction by Modern Japanese Women.* Berkeley, CA: Institute of East Asian Studies, University of California, 1988.

Washburn, Dennis. *Translating Mount Fuji: Modern Japanese Fiction and the Ethics of Identity.* New York: Columbia University Press, 2007.

West-Pavlov, Russell. *Transcultural Graffiti: Diasporic Writing and the Teaching of Literary Studies.* Amsterdam: Rodopi, 2005.

USEFUL RESOURCES

Three scholarly journals regularly carry reviews of Japanese literature: *Japan Quarterly, Journal of Japanese Studies,* and *Monumenta Nipponica.*

Japanese Literature in Translation Search: http://www.jpf.go.jp/e/culture/media/exchange/translationsearch.html. This is a still-incomplete database of Japanese literature in translation, mainly covering works written or translated since the end of World War II.

Literature as Identity Formation: Reading Chinese Literature in Translation

Michelle Yeh

Literature plays a formative role in cultural identity. China provides an eminent case in point. Chinese civilization enjoys the longest continuing literary tradition in the world. The longevity and enduring influence of Chinese literature may be attributed to two causes: first, the unity of the written language, which was standardized by the early third century BCE, despite a large number of vastly different dialects across the country; and second, the reverence in which writing is held and the great care with which it is preserved in a predominantly civilian society, led by scholar-officials who are not only well-versed in literature but also knowledgable about its most important authors, editors, and commentators.

American students are amazed that even the most ancient works of Chinese literature are preserved in the written and spoken language of modern times. To give an example, the *Book of Songs* (*Shijing*) is the first Chinese anthology of songs, odes, and hymns, compiled in the sixth century BCE. Some verses from this collection are not only familiar to Chinese people today but have become common expressions used on a daily basis. Numerous phrases and sayings drawn from poetry, fiction, drama, and essays in subsequent ages have similarly been interwoven into the language. All great literature enriches and elevates the language in which it is written (one needs only consider Shakespeare in English), but for the two reasons mentioned above, China presents a particularly illuminating example of how literature, more than any other form of writing, embodies the values and captures the essence of a culture. Literature is highly respected in Chinese civilization not because it records history but because it *is* history.

Given the profound interconnection between literature and cultural identity, it is important for anyone seeking to understand China to read the great works of Chinese literature. But how can we make the best use of translations? It is a well-known fact that literature in translation does not sell in the United States. The contrast with the Chinese-speaking world cannot be starker. In mainland China, Hong Kong, and Taiwan, translations of literature written in English and other languages consistently make the best-seller lists. This phenomenon is not new but has existed since the early twentieth century, when China embarked on a national project of wholesale modernization. Through translation, classical writers such as Cervantes, Shakespeare, and Goethe, and contemporary writers such as Gabriel García Márquez, Italo Calvino, Milan Kundera, and Haruki Murakami have exerted seminal influences on Chinese writers. In comparison, literature in translation occupies a minuscule niche in the American market. With a few exceptions—perhaps memoirs about the Cultural Revolution and fiction by 2000 Nobel laureate Gao Xingjian—translations of Chinese literature are read primarily in the classroom.

Nevertheless, the use of translation in the classroom bodes well for the future of Chinese literature in the United States. Enrollments in Chinese-language classes at the college level have been rising nationwide in recent years, and more and more high schools now offer Chinese as an elective. This growth corresponds to the fact that China has become the world's third-largest economy, behind the United States and Japan, and China is the world's leading market for production and consumption. The impact of the large selloff on the Shanghai stock market in February 2007 was felt worldwide. Politically, China is a permanent member of the United Nations Security Council, and its role in the recent intermittent nuclear negotiations with North Korea and its controversial antisatellite weapon testing in January 2007 demonstrate that China plays an increasingly prominent role in international politics. The lavish opening ceremony at the 2008 summer Olympics in Beijing showcased China's rise in the world.

Although language classes do not necessarily focus on literature, it is common for students who study the language to either advance to literature classes or get some exposure to literature as a window on society and culture. For American students who wish to prepare themselves for the world of the future, in which China is to be a major player, translations provide a feasible way to understand the nation's history and culture, because proficiency typically takes much longer to achieve for the Chinese language than for European languages. Thus, at some American universities, getting a minor in Chinese does not require years of study of the language; it may be achieved by taking only courses on Chinese literature in translation. The teaching of Chinese literature in translation is also promoted by such educational programs as the Asian Studies Development Program offered by the East-West Center in Honolulu, which has been successful in introducing American college teachers to Chinese culture and other Asian traditions. Faculty in the humanities and social sciences, including such disciplines as comparative literature, creative writing, history, philosophy, political science, and art history, find it pedagogically enriching and intellectually stimulating to incorporate samples of Chinese literature into their courses.

All of the factors mentioned above give a fairly good indication that Chinese literature in translation is, and will be, an integral part of American higher education in an increasingly globalized world. Having taught Chinese literature in translation for more than two decades, I believe this is an invaluable learning experience for both students and teachers who do not read Chinese. Reading Chinese literature in translation does not, and need not, duplicate the experience of reading the original; nevertheless, it is both pedagogically practical and intellectually rewarding. Rather than seeing translation as an inevitable veiling or distortion of the original, it should be seen as an opening up of a new vista. Once we get over what we "lose" in reading translations, we can begin to appreciate what we "gain" in the process, even in the case of poetry. The conventional wisdom, which holds that poetry is what is lost in translation, must be counterbalanced with what is gained. Granted, a translation cannot recreate the musicality and complex prosody of a poem in Chinese, which is a tonal language; but we gain a variety of readings of the work in question, especially cross-cultural and pluralist readings.

CROSS-CULTURAL READING

Reading Chinese literature in translation offers a cross-cultural context that facilitates comparative and contrastive readings. Identifying commonality goes hand in hand with recognizing uniqueness. For instance, both Chinese and Western literary traditions began with oral poetry, but the contrast between the Homeric epics and the *Book of Songs* cannot be more striking: the dramatic plot, elaborate figurative language, and highly individualized heroes of the Greek epics differ sharply from the short Chinese lyrics (many of which are folk songs) that employ four-syllable lines in refrains to paint vignettes of men and women, from kings to peasants, in realistic scenes. When it comes to the universal theme of love, readers of English may be surprised to find that courtly love is virtually absent in classical Chinese poetry. Although lovesickness is a recurrent theme in both traditions, the idealization of the lover and the lofty, often religious imagery that define the courtly love tradition are foreign to China.

Chinese poetry in translation also lends itself to cross-cultural readings in another context: twentieth-century American poetry. Ezra Pound's seminal translations and imagist poetics in the 1910s catapulted Chinese poetry into the consciousness of poets and general readers alike in the English-speaking world. In 1977, Kenneth Rexroth (1905–1982) declared that Chinese poetry had replaced French poetry as the most important influence on American poets (209), and its popularity has continued to this day. Many American poets have translated Chinese poetry, whether they read Chinese or not, and even more have written poems inspired by it. For students in creative writing programs, Chinese poetry in translation is standard reading. It is no exaggeration to say that Chinese poetry has become part of the American poetic tradition. Depending on the class, Chinese poetry can be read side by side with American poetry to shed light on imagism, modernism, the San Francisco renaissance, and contemporary ecopoetry.

Chinese fiction in translation lends itself to meaningful comparisons too. In China, as in Europe, the term "fiction" encompasses such a wide range of narrative prose that it is not always easy to define the category. Generally speaking, fiction in China evolved from shorter narratives to longer ones; it began with pithy sketches as early as the second century, grew into longer "tales of the marvelous" in the Tang dynasty (618–908), and developed into full-length novels from the fourteenth century onward.

There are some noteworthy differences between Chinese and European literatures. For instance, traditional Chinese fiction draws heavily on oral traditions; the same is true of Chinese drama. Stories told by professional storytellers at the marketplace and in urban entertainment districts in the Song dynasty (960–1279) are important predecessors of fiction, which explains some of the common formal features of Chinese fiction, such as the use of stock expressions and episodic structures. Also unlike its European counterpart, poetry is fully integrated into Chinese fiction.

But there are also interesting parallels between the traditions. In both China and Europe, the flourishing of the novel was accompanied by such developments as a money economy, urban culture, an entertainment industry, the printing press, and rising literacy (Ropp 311). Also as in European literature, history and religion play major roles in Chinese fiction, informing both subject matter and philosophical orientations. Traditional Chinese fiction is typically based on history and often molds the way readers come to view history. *Romance of the Three Kingdoms,* probably the most famous historical novel in Chinese, is set against the background of the fall of the Han dynasty in 220 CE and the formation of the Three Kingdoms competing for dominion over China. It is a story as much about political intrigue, military strategy, ambition, and statecraft as it is about loyalty, friendship, fate, and free will. For centuries the protagonists of this work have served as role models for Chinese people, and political leaders in particular look to this novel for moral lessons.

In *Water Margin* (or *All Men Are Brothers*), which takes place in the Northern Song dynasty (960–1127), 108 men and women are driven by individual circumstances to Mount Liang, where they form a brotherhood of Robin Hood–like bandits. The novel depicts the undeserved suffering of the heroes, often at the hands of the ruthless and corrupt ruling class, and their quest for revenge. The story—with its themes of valor and righteousness, its challenge to political authority, and the eventual triumph of justice—is immensely appealing to Chinese readers, despite its gore and violence.

The historical Buddhist pilgrimage that Master Xuanzang (602–664) took in 627–46 is immortalized in the sixteenth-century novel *Journey to the West* (or *Monkey* for the abridged version). Unlike the two novels mentioned earlier, *Journey to the West* is filled with supernatural characters and fantastic adventures. The pious Xuanzang journeys from the Chinese capital, Changan, to India to bring back Buddhist scriptures. He is accompanied and protected by three supernatural disciples, each with distinct strengths and flaws. Of Xuanzang's three disciples, the dazzling wit, irrepressible creativity, and charismatic leadership of Monkey easily make him the most beloved character in the novel, even though his penchant for mischief and impatience with dogma often get him into trouble. It is no wonder that the story is a perennial favorite of Chinese children and has been made into many versions of animation and film in modern times.

Some of the Buddhist ideas that run through *Journey to the West,* such as karma and retribution, also underscore *The Golden Lotus* (or *The Plum in the Golden Vase*). Ostensibly a spin-off of an episode from *Water Margin,* the novel focuses in vivid detail on the decadent world of money and sex, bribery and murder, in which the protagonist, a wealthy merchant, lives with his concubines. The depravity and excess in which the main characters indulge lead to their inevitable downfall. A masterpiece of realism and satire, the novel is traditionally banned; its graphic depictions of sex make it forbidden reading, especially for younger readers and women.

Finally, one must mention what many consider to be the greatest novel ever written in Chinese: *Dream of the Red Chamber* (also *Story of the Stone*). The male protagonist is a stone in Heaven that wants to experience what it is like to be human. To fulfill this desire, the stone is incarnated as a handsome young man named Precious Jade, born into the aristocratic Jia family. The female protagonist is a flower in Heaven that is watered by the stone. To reciprocate the stone's kindness in watering it, the flower is incarnated as Ebony Jade, the beautiful, talented, but obstinate and frail cousin of Precious Jade. The novel is essentially a tale of love between the two, and it represents the pinnacle of Chinese fiction, with its all-encompassing vision of humanity and masterful language. The remarkable range of human experience depicted in the book reveals great depth of emotive and psychological truth; transcendent ideals are juxtaposed with social consciousness; engrossing prose is interwoven with elegant poetry; realism is rich with allegorical meaning. Offering a panoramic view of the human condition, *Dream of the Red Chamber* is at once Confucian, Buddhist, and Daoist—the three pillars of Chinese civilization.

PLURALIST READING

Pluralist reading means reading multiple translations of the same work. This method of reading works best for poetry, not only because of its manageable length but more importantly because the unique linguistic and formal features of Chinese poetry generate a great deal of ambiguity. Thus, Chinese poetry allows a remarkable degree of freedom in translation. Chinese poetry is more fluid than European languages in that it is uninflected and does not require the use of tense, number, case, mood, or gender. The subject of the sentence, and sometimes even the verb, can be omitted in Chinese. According to James J. Y. Liu, these linguistic characteristics create a "sense of timelessness and universality" in Chinese poetry (40).

Structurally, a Chinese poem is often built on parallelism between the two lines of a couplet, at the levels of word, image, and meaning. To give an example, here is a couplet from "A Rejoinder with Ziyou: Thinking of the Past at Mian Pool" by the great poet, calligrapher, and painter Su Shi (1037–1101). Here is a word-for-word transliteration of the two seven-character lines of a couplet:

1	2	3	4	5	6	7
old	monk	already	dead	complete	new	tower
rotten	wall	no	chance	see	old	inscription

The two words occupying the same position in the line are supposed to match each other in terms of sameness or contrast. In the case of sameness, we see parallelism between "old" and "rotten" (both are adjectives with similar meanings), "monk" and "wall" (both are nouns), and "complete" and "see" (both are verbs). With regard to contrast, parallelism exists between "monk" and "wall" (animate versus inanimate being), "already" and "no" (affirmative versus negative), and "new" and "old." The prescribed use of parallelism in several major forms of Chinese poetry creates in the reader both a sense of anticipation and a sense of surprise.

Written in 1061, "A Rejoinder with Ziyou" is a response to (literally "in harmony with") an earlier piece by the poet's younger brother Ziyou. Ziyou's poem alludes to the Su brothers' first visit to a monastery. At the request of their host, the old monk, the Su brothers inscribed poems on the wall. Years later, Su Shi pays another visit to the monastery, only to find that the old monk has passed away and a new tower has been built where the old walls stood. Gone too are the poems the brothers left behind on their first visit. The couplet under discussion is marked by repetition of the notion of decay ("old" and "rotten") and the contrast between the past and the present (old and new, being and nonbeing). Through these devices, the poem expresses the Buddhist notion of impermanence as the defining feature of life. Buddhism describes impermanence as the inescapable cycle of birth (literally, "completion"), growth, decay (literally, "rotting"), and emptiness. Two of these four words appear in Su's couplet.

Thanks to the popularity of Chinese poetry in the English-speaking world, there is no shortage of translations to choose from. Important collections such as *Book of Songs* and *Songs of the South (Chuci)* are easy to find, and many major poets—such as Tao Yuanming (or Tao Qian, 365–427), Wang Wei (701–761), Li Po (Li Bo or Li Bai, 701–762), Tu Fu (Du Fu, 712–770), Po Chü-I (Bai Juyi, 772–846), Li Shangyin (813–858), and Su Shi—are readily available in anthologies and single-author collections. To be candid, I have not found an anthology that meets all of my needs and expectations by itself, but I have come to see that as an advantage rather than disadvantage. Reading multiple translations of a Chinese poem reveals what readers of only the original or a single translation may overlook. Differences between translations may be subtle or substantial, but when read side by side, they can be mutually complementary and illuminating.

To give an example, here is "Seeing Someone Off" by Tang poet Wang Wei:

> Dismounting, I offer you wine
> And ask, "Where are you bound?"
> You say, "I've found no fame or favors;
> I must return to rest in the South Mountain."
> You leave, and I ask no more—
> White clouds drift on and on.
> (Lo, 96)

The phrase "found no fame or favors" (translation number 1) in the third line is rendered differently by three other translators:

(2) I cannot go where I want to go (Payne, 153)
(3) nothing goes right! (Watson, 202)
(4) At odds with the world (Yip, 247)

All four translations of the line use plain, even colloquial contemporary English. We can therefore assume that collectively they give a good indication of the original language: the poem presents a pithy conversation between the poet and his departing friend, with little commentary or overt emotion.

In translation (1), the combination of "fame" and "favors" may cause contemporary English readers to pause, because they are much more used to the phrase "fame and fortune." Here, the word "favors" evokes authority, particularly political authority; it refers to favorable treatment from the political establishment, perhaps from the emperor himself. In the context of traditional Chinese society, political "favors" go hand in hand with success and stature ("fame") in the world. In comparison, the other translations are more general and less specific, although there are subtle differences among them. Translations (2) and (3) both suggest frustration and disappointment as a result of unfulfilled aspirations, whereas (4) implies loneliness and alienation in an indifferent or incompatible world. In the classroom, we don't have to make a final judgment regarding which translation is the most accurate vis-à-vis the original, but we can certainly make an aesthetic judgment. Read side by side, the different renditions give us an idea of why the friend has decided to retire to the South Mountain, which illustrates the typical choice for a Chinese scholar-official when his career is not going well.

In another example of pluralist reading, a poem by Li Po, one of the greatest Chinese poets, is rendered here in three ways:

(1)   FAREWELLING MENG HAO-JAN AT YELLOW CRANE TOWER
At the Yellow Crane Tower there comes
farewell to Meng Hao-jan; it is the
sweetest time of spring; he goes east
to Yangchow, I watching the sail
of his boat going ever further
and further, until at last it vanishes
in the clear blue sky, yet my heart
runs with the Yangtse waters
flowing, ever flowing
(Alley, 19)

(2)   TO SEE MENG HAO-JAN OFF AT YANG-CHOU
My old friend takes off from the Yellow Crane Tower,
In smoke-flower third month down to Yang-chou.
A lone sail, a distant shade, lost in the blue horizon.
Only the long Yangtze is seen flowing into the sky.
(Yip, 238)

(3)   FAREWELL
And so, dear friend, at Brown Crane Tower you,
        Bidding the West adieu,
    'Mid April mists and blossoms go,

> Till in the vast blue-green
> Your lonely sail's far shade no more is seen,
> Only on the sky's verge the River's flow.
> (Turner, 117)

There are considerable differences among these translations, a fact that should stimulate a good discussion. First, we note that even the forms of the poem look quite different. The number of lines varies from one translation to another. The four end-stopped lines in translation (2) contrast sharply with the nine flowing lines (with enjambment) in translation (1) and the six highly irregular, indented lines in translation (3). In terms of language, both translations (1) and (2) use third-person pronouns to refer to the friend leaving, whereas translation (3) addresses the friend in the second person. The uncommon use of "farewell" as a verb in the title of translation (1) gives the poem an archaic flavor, though the language in the rest of the poem is contemporary and colloquial, similar to that of translations (2) and (3). To go further, we can compare the three translations of the same image:

(1) the sweetest time of spring
(2) in smoke-flower third month
(3) April mists and blossoms

Translations (2) and (3) give concrete images of flowers as metonyms of spring, whereas translation (1) names the season but does not give any tangible detail about it; "sweetest" suggests a sensory experience, but vaguely. Comparing translations (2) and (3), we arrive at the conclusion that the "third month" probably refers to the Chinese lunar calendar, in which the third month corresponds roughly to April. "Mists and blossoms" evoke the moist, flower-scented air of spring; the image is far more sensual than "smoke-flower," which conjures a distant view of flowers that seem to be veiled in hazy spring air.

In the second half of the poem, translation (1) compares the poet's feeling to the ever-flowing river, which is absent in translations (2) and (3). Translation (1) is also more explicit, whereas translations (2) and (3) are more suggestive. The comparison in translation (1) describes the sadness of the first-person speaker in parting with his friend; the feeling lingers on, just as the river flows on. This interpretation differs from what is intimated in translations (2) and (3), in both of which the speaker stands on the bank long after the boat has sailed off. The river and the sky merge, and the pale hull of the boat is barely visible on the horizon. Both interpretations of the image are valid and mutually enhance one another.

In addition to the opportunity for a comparative and "composite" reading, access to multiple translations of a poem allows students to create their own translations based on those they have read. A follow-up discussion of the choices they make in rendering a Chinese poem in English can be just as interesting as a discussion of the original poem itself.

Finally, there are English translations that provide transliterations of original poems. It is advisable to use a word-for-word transliteration of a Chinese poem whenever possible, because this method can definitely enrich the interpretation of multiple translations, making interpretation even more effective and enjoyable. Transliterations of Chinese characters also give students a sense of the original form and help them to better understand the vast differences between the two languages.

CONTEXTUAL KNOWLEDGE

Reading Chinese literature across the linguistic divide allows us to compare and contrast the two cultures involved. To enable such a reading, a certain amount of contextual knowledge is not only desirable but absolutely necessary. Fortunately, much of the contextual knowledge about Chinese literature is readily available in English, in the vast scholarship on the history, recurrent themes, salient features, and major works of all genres. Perhaps the most fundamental contextual knowledge to give students is the traditional role and function of literature in China. As I have done in this chapter until now, I shall once again limit my remarks to two major genres: poetry and fiction. Poetry is the oldest and most revered form of literature in China. As such, it holds the keys to understanding Chinese culture and society. Its importance was established early on by Confucius (551–479 BCE), who viewed poetry as not only as a form of self-expression but also a means of social intercourse and moral cultivation. The poetry collection *Book of Songs* is the leading text in the Confucian canon, which constitutes the foundation of classical education. Thus, the institutionalization of Confucianism in the second century BCE also meant the institutionalization of poetry. The Music Bureau of the Han dynasty, for example, was a government agency charged with collecting contemporary ballads in the empire to inform the emperor of how people viewed the government and its policies. More importantly, poetry was incorporated into the civil service examination system, which was in place from the seventh century until its abolition in 1905, shortly before the fall of the last dynasty, the Qing (1644–1911).

In contrast to poetry throughout most of its history in the West, poetry in China is more than an art pursued by individual talents. It is a form of knowledge and a practical skill required for government officials—imagine if all our legislators and governors had to be poets in order to hold elected office!—as well as a common vehicle of interpersonal and communal communications in a wide range of forms (e.g., epistles, diaries, dedications, and inscriptions at famous sites). Poetry is written for every imaginable social or personal occasion; with calligraphic flourishes, its ubiquitous presence is seen on stone, wood, bronze, and silk, as well as paper.

The great majority of Chinese poets were government officials, commonly referred to as "scholar-officials," who went in and out of reclusion as their political careers rose and fell, and quite a few emperors and princes were accomplished poets. Throughout Chinese history, poetry has paved the way to success or downfall. Li Po, for example, was appointed to the imperial academy because the emperor was a fan of his poetry, but he was also kicked out of the academy because his poetry incurred jealousy and resentment in the court. Poetry is intimately tied to the fate of the scholar-official; it has led to exile, prison, and even execution, and it has also literally saved lives.

Confucian China subscribes to a cyclical view of time and human affairs, which is immortalized in the opening lines of *Romance of the Three Kingdoms:* "When it comes to affairs under Heaven, there is bound to be division after a long period of unity; there is bound to be unity after a long period of division." Man is supposed to model himself after Heaven and embody the innate virtues that Heaven has endowed upon him: humaneness, righteousness, propriety, wisdom, loyalty, filial piety, and so on.

In contrast to the Confucian view, the Daoist view is "amoral" in that morality is not the solution to the turmoil in the world but rather the root of it. Instead of moral cultivation, Daoism advocates a return to nature, of which humans are naturally a part, together with abandonment of artifice and "ingenuity." This indigenous philosophy rejects all human constructs, including government and knowledge, but the imported Buddhist system seeks to transcend desire, which is viewed as the cause of all suffering in the world. Insofar as the Daoist rejects human "interference" with nature or the Way, the Buddhist renounces all forms of human attachment, which is, like all other phenomena, impermanent and therefore illusory.

Confucianism, Daoism, and Buddhism form the three pillars of Chinese civilization. The Confucian devotes himself to moral cultivation, which prepares him for public service. The Daoist embodies spontaneity, harmony with nature, and spiritual freedom. The Buddhist seeks enlightenment and practices compassion for all sentient beings. For millennia these three philosophical traditions have informed the Chinese way of life, and they figure prominently in Chinese literature. The different visions they represent sometimes lead to inner conflict, but more often they complement one another in the journey of life. In *Dream of the Red Chamber,* Precious Jade rebels against his Confucian father and, disillusioned upon the death of Ebony Jade, renounces his family and becomes a monk.

Most poets in traditional China were Confucian scholar-officials, so when they became frustrated with politics, Daoism and Buddhism struck a deep chord with them. In contrast to the Confucian emphasis on poetry as moral education and social discourse, Daoism sees poetry as expressing oneness with nature, and Buddhism sees poetry as a form of meditation and quietude. Also unlike Confucianism, both Daoism and Buddhism harbor a distrust of language, and the ideal poetry is one that approaches silence. It is these two philosophies that led to the emergence of landscape poetry and pastoral poetry in the fourth and fifth centuries. This development followed a renewed interest in Daoism and widespread acceptance of Buddhism among the elites, against the background of incessant political turmoil and violent social upheaval as depicted in *Romance of the Three Kingdoms.* Nature poetry reached its peak in the seventh and eighth centuries, which coincided with the development of Chan (or Zen in Japanese) Buddhism, a Chinese-originated sect that integrated Daoist elements into Buddhism.

This brief summary of contextual knowledge helps explain some of the recurrent themes and motifs in Chinese poetry. As Confucian scholar-officials, poets commented on history past and present, with a view to advising or admonishing the ruler. In attendance at court and various state functions, they wrote—or were asked to write—celebratory or memorial poems. For friends and colleagues who traveled either from post to post or in exile for some offence, they wrote wistful farewell poems. Travel is a major theme in Chinese poetry, because scholar-officials were one of the most mobile groups in traditional society; they were assigned to a post for a limited term and had to travel from one post to the next, often under harsh conditions. Poets wrote about homesickness, scenic sights, and the hardships of their journeys.

When poets withdrew from public service, whether voluntarily or involuntarily, they tended to represent themselves as hermits or recluses, and they wrote about nature and their life within it. Playing the zither, walking alone in the forest, visiting a Buddhist monastery or a Daoist master in a mountain retreat, and, above all, drinking wine to the heart's content were all activities associated with this lifestyle. The figures of fisherman and woodcutter appear often in landscape poetry (as well as landscape painting). Contrary to modern perceptions, fishermen and woodcutters in Chinese culture are symbolic of a simple, nonmaterialistic life in harmony with nature. Together with the hermit-poet, fishermen and woodcutters are associated with Daoist freedom from worldly concerns and Buddhist detachment from the world of "red dust."

When it comes to interpersonal communications, poets addressed numerous poems to their families and relatives, friends and colleagues, patrons and superiors, and even the emperor. Of the five cardinal relationships in Confucianism, poets write more about friendship and brotherly love than about love between man and woman. In contrast with Western poetry, romantic love is not a ubiquitous or dominant theme. This is partly because of the strict moral code that governed gender relations, which viewed marriage as based on familial duty rather than love. Although this does not mean that love is absent from Chinese poetry, it is often depicted in terms of absence rather than fulfillment, expressed through images of pining, reminiscence, and grief.

It is not uncommon for male poets to assume female personae, such as the abandoned wife, the lonely court lady who waits for the emperor in vain, or the soldier's bride whose husband is fighting at the frontier. These recurrent personae in Chinese poetry are conventional types rather than individualized characters, and there is a long exegetical tradition of interpreting the relationship between man and woman in a poem as an allegory of the relationship between the emperor and the subject. This tradition of reading love poems as political allegories is anchored in the Confucian idea of loyalty, and it further shifts the focus away from romantic love in real life. Candid expressions of love are relegated to genres of folk origin. Besides ballads, the song lyric (ci) is closely associated with love. Derived from courtesan songs in pleasure quarters, the song lyric lent itself to romantic subject matter. Although its thematic range broadened considerably when scholar-officials appropriated the form, the song lyric has remained the favorite vehicle for expressing love.

Poetry clearly enjoys high status and is held in great esteem in Chinese society and culture, but not all genres are valued equally. Fiction in traditional China is neither taken seriously nor treated with respect. If poetry is at the top of the cultural hierarchy, fiction is near the bottom. Literally meaning "small talk," fiction—both the short story and the novel—is held in low regard because, unlike historiography, philosophy, or poetry, it supposedly deals with street gossips and fanciful nonsense. This is one reason why fiction writers used to publish their work under pseudonyms, because making their true identities known would have adversely affected their career or standing in a Confucian society.

READING MODERNITY

The status of fiction began to change, however, at the end of the nineteenth century, when a leading young intellectual named Liang Qichao (1873–1929) advocated the use of fiction as an instrument for social reform. A similar kind of reconceptualization also took place in poetry around the same time. Indeed, the turn of the century witnessed radical transformations of Chinese literature as a whole.

Thus far in our discussion we have focused on Chinese literature before the twentieth century, which is commonly referred to as "traditional," "classical," or "premodern." Whether poetry, fiction, drama, or essay, works from ancient times to the 1910s form a largely homogeneous tradition, in which new developments were gradual and incremental. However, the shift from traditional to modern literature was abrupt and dramatic. Beginning with the Literary Revolution, led by Hu Shi (1891–1962) in 1917, and continuing in the wholesale cultural reform known as the May Fourth Movement (1919–25), the modern vernacular replaced classical Chinese as the medium of new poetry, fiction, and drama, and modern forms that were borrowed from other traditions replaced well-established indigenous forms. In fiction, Lu Xun (1881–1936), Mao Dun (1896–1981), Lao She (1899–1966), Shen Congwen (1902–1988), Ba Jin (1904–2005), Ding Ling (1904–1986), and Xiao Hong (1911–1942) were among the most accomplished authors. In the modern "spoken drama," which differs from the operatic drama of the past, Tian Han (1898–1968), Ding Xilin

(1893–1974), Hong Shen (1894–1955), and Cao Yu (1910–1996) made significant contributions. In poetry, Hu Shi, Guo Moruo (1892–1978), Xu Zhimo (1897–1931), and Wen Yiduo (1899–1946) were some of the leading pioneers.

It is noteworthy that many early modern writers studied abroad, and most were prolific translators of foreign literature. A host of European movements—including romanticism, realism, naturalism, symbolism, expressionism, and surrealism—were introduced into China. This trend has continued throughout the twentieth century and beyond to include modernism and postmodernism. Translations of world literature have now inspired generations of Chinese writers. Proficiency in foreign languages has also made it possible for some Chinese writers to write original works in a language other than their mother tongue. From the 1930s to the 1970s, Lin Yutang (1895–1976) published almost thirty books in English, including several novels about China. More recently, Ha Jin (b. 1956) has gained international renown for his fiction in English.

Concomitant with the radical changes in literary form and medium is the cultural status of literature. The longstanding hierarchy of genres was virtually turned upside down. Whereas fiction used to be viewed as an inferior genre, it became elevated as a powerful means of reforming the nation and educating the citizenry. Whereas poetry used to be the unchallenged pinnacle of Chinese literary culture, it was pushed to the margins, having lost its moral, social, and political functions.

Chinese literature of the twentieth century is inextricably related to the ideal of revolution, whether it is the "literary revolution" that ushered in modern poetry in 1917, the "revolutionary literature" advocated by leftist writers in the 1920s and 1930s, the "second poetry revolution" led by Ji Xian (b. 1913) in Taiwan in the 1950s, or the political "proletarian revolution" under Mao Zedong (1893–1976), from the 1940s through the Cultural Revolution (1966–76). Ironically, literary innovations often arise in reaction against political constraints. For example, modernism in postwar Taiwan flourished under the White Terror, and literature in mainland China in the early 1980s was a profound critique of the Cultural Revolution. In both cases, experimental works of lasting value were written, whether modernist poetry and fiction from Taiwan or "Misty Poetry" and "root-seeking" fiction from China.

The body of modern Chinese literature in English translation has been growing since the 1980s. Anthologies are typically organized by genre (poetry, fiction, drama), region (mainland China, Taiwan, Hong Kong), period (modern, post-Mao, contemporary), and gender (women authors). Similarly, more and more single-author collections have appeared in recent years. This boom in publishing corresponds to the fast-growing number of courses on modern Chinese literature and culture on American college campuses. These developments suggest a gradual shift of interest among English readers from classical to modern and contemporary Chinese literature. In addition to the rising enrollments in Chinese-language classes and China's increasing international visibility and clout, noted at the beginning of the chapter, recent film adaptations have also given a considerable boost to the reception of Chinese literature. To give a few examples, *Red Sorghum, Raise the Red Lantern, To Live, Farewell, My Concubine,* and, most recently, *Lust, Caution* are all based on stories by twentieth-century Chinese writers, including Mo Yan (b. 1955), Su Tong (b. 1963), Yu Hua (b. 1960), Li Bihua (Lillian Lee, b. 1950), and Eileen Chang (1920–1995).

Since 1949, Chinese literature has come primarily from mainland China (where simplified characters are used) and from Taiwan and Hong Kong (where traditional characters continue to be the norm). In recent decades we have witnessed the dramatic growth of a global sinophone community, as literature in Chinese is being written in every corner of the world. A prominent representative of this trend is Gao Xingjian (b. 1940), a naturalized French citizen who left his native China in 1987 but has continued to publish works in Chinese from France.

Despite the significant differences between them, modern Chinese literature is inseparable from traditional Chinese literature in terms of language, aesthetic sensibility, and philosophical orientation. Theirs is a relation of continuity and rebellion, inheritance and disenfranchisement. After all, modernity is defined, first and foremost, by what has come before it.

WORKS CITED

Li Po. *Li Pai: 200 Selected Poems.* Translated by Rewi Alley. Hong Kong: Joint Publishing Co., 1980.

Liu, James J. Y. *The Art of Chinese Poetry.* Chicago: University of Chicago Press, 1962.

Lo, Irving Y., and Wu-chi Liu, eds. *Sunflower Splendor: Three Thousand Years of Chinese Poetry.* Garden City, NY: Anchor Books, 1975.

Payne, Robert, ed. *The White Pony: An Anthology of Chinese Poetry.* New York: John Day Co., 1947.

Rexroth, Kenneth. "Chinese Poetry and the American Imagination." Transcript of a speech given at a conference, New York, April 1977, quoted in Eliot Weinberger, ed., *The New Directions of Classical Chinese Poetry,* 209–12. New York: New Directions, 2003.

Ropp, Paul S. "The Distinctive Art of Chinese Fiction." In *Heritage of China: Contemporary Perspectives on Chinese Civilization,* edited by Paul S. Ropp, 309–34. Berkeley: University of California Press, 1990.

Turner, John A., John J. Deeney, and Kenneth K. B. Li, eds. *A Golden Treasury of Chinese Poetry.* Translated by John A. Turner. Hong Kong: Chinese University of Hong Kong Press, 1976.

Watson, Burton, ed. and trans. *The Columbia Book of Chinese Poetry: From the Early Times to the 13th Century.* New York: Columbia University Press, *1984.*

Yip, Wai-lim, ed. and trans. *Chinese Poetry: An Anthology of Major Modes and Genres.* Durham, NC: Duke University Press, 1997.

FOR FURTHER READING

Cai, Zong-Qi. *How to Read Traditional Chinese Poetry: A Guided Anthology.* New York: Columbia University Press, 2008.

Chen, Xiaomei. *Acting the Right Part: Political Theater and Popular Drama in Contemporary China.* Honolulu: University of Hawaii Press, 2002.

———, ed. *Reading the Right Text: An Anthology of Contemporary Chinese Drama.* Honolulu: University of Hawaii Press, 2003.

Dooling, Amy D. *Women's Literary Feminism in Twentieth-Century China.* New York: Palgrave Macmillan, 2005.

———, and Kristina Torgeson, eds. *Writing Women in Modern China: An Anthology of Literature by Chinese Women from the Early Twentieth Century.* New York: Columbia University Press, 1998.

Duke, Michael S., ed. *Contemporary Chinese Literature: An Anthology of Post-Mao Fiction and Poetry.* Armonk, NY: M. E. Sharpe, 1985.

Gu, Ming Dong. *Chinese Theories of Fiction: A Non-Western Narrative System.* Albany: State University of New York Press, 2006.

Gunn, Edward M., ed. *Twentieth-Century Chinese Drama: An Anthology.* Bloomington: Indiana University Press, 1983.

Hegel, Robert. *The Novel in Seventeenth-Century China.* New York: Columbia University Press, 1981.

Hsia, C. T. *The Classic Chinese Novel.* New York: Columbia University Press, 1968.

———. *A History of Modern Chinese Fiction.* New Haven, CT: Yale University Press, 1961.

Lau, Joseph S. M., C. T. Hsia, and Leo Ou-fan Lee, eds. *Modern Chinese Stories and Novellas, 1919–1949.* New York: Columbia University Press, 1981.

Levy, Dore J. *Ideal and Actual in The Story of the Stone.* New York: Columbia University Press, 1999.

Li, Wai-yee. *Enchantment and Disenchantment: Love and Illusion in Chinese Literature.* Princeton, NJ: Princeton University Press, 1993.

Lin Shuen-fu, and Stephen Owen, eds. *The Vitality of the Lyric Voice: Shih Poetry from the Late Han to the T'ang.* Princeton, NJ: Princeton University Press, 1986.

Link, Perry, ed. *Roses and Thorns: The Second Blooming of the Hundred Flowers in Chinese Fiction, 1979–80.* Berkeley: University of California Press, 1986.

Ma, Y. W., and Joseph S. M. Lau, eds. *Traditional Chinese Stories: Themes and Variations.* New York: Columbia University Press, 1978.

Owen, Stephen. "Poetry in the Chinese Tradition." In *Heritage of China: Contemporary Perspectives on Chinese Civilization,* edited by Paul S. Ropp, 294–308. Berkeley: University of California Press, 1990.

———, and Kang-i Sun Chang, eds. *Cambridge History of Chinese Literature.* Cambridge, UK: Cambridge University Press, 2010.

Plaks, Andrew H. *The Four Masterworks of the Ming Novel: Ssu Ta Ch'i-Shu.* Princeton, NJ: Princeton University Press, 1987.

Ralston, David L. *How to Read the Chinese Novel.* Princeton, NJ: Princeton University Press, 1990.

Van Crevel, Maghiel. *Chinese Poetry in Times of Mind, Mayhem and Money.* Leiden, the Netherlands: Brill, 2008.

———. *Language Shattered: Contemporary Chinese Poetry and Duoduo.* Leiden, the Netherlands: Research School of Asian, African, and Amerindian Studies, 1996.

Wang, David Der-wei. *Fictional Realism in 20th Century China: Mao Dun, Lao She, Shen Congwen.* New York: Columbia University Press, 1992.

———. *The Monster That Is History: Violence, History, and Fictional Writing in 20th Century China.* Stanford, CA: Stanford University Press, 2004.

———, and Jeanne Tai, eds. *Running Wild: New Chinese Writers.* New York: Columbia University Press, 1994.

Yeh, Michelle, ed. and trans. *Anthology of Modern Chinese Poetry.* 2nd ed. New Haven, CT: Yale University Press, 1994.

———. *Modern Chinese Poetry: Theory and Practice since 1917.* New Haven, CT: Yale University Press, 1991.

———, and N. G. D. Malmqvist, eds. *Frontier Taiwan: An Anthology of Modern Chinese Poetry.* New York: Columbia University Press, 2000.

Identity and Relationships in the Context of Latin America

Kathleen Ross

Latin America is a vast region of the world comprising several distinct geographical areas (Mesoamerica, Central America, South America, and the Caribbean) where the legacies of Spanish, Portuguese, French, English, and Dutch colonial rule have combined with surviving indigenous languages and cultures to create a complex group of some two dozen or more independent nations and dependent territories. Numerous definitions of the term "Latin America" (originally coined in the nineteenth century) are commonly accepted. Some include countries and territories where French, English, Dutch and other languages (such as Kreyol or Papiamentu) are spoken; some exclude all but Romance (Latinate) languages; some include only Spanish- and Portuguese-speaking places. For the purposes of this chapter, Spanish America might be a more accurate description of the object of study, because only texts translated from Spanish will be discussed. Undoubtedly, however, many of the concepts to be examined here that deal with identity and relationships in Spanish-speaking countries can be extended, in whole or in part, to other locations in the region as well.

Before commencing this focus on issues of identity and relationships and their specific importance to Latin American literature, a caveat is in order. Not only is Latin America a conglomeration of geographical and political components that sometimes differ greatly from each other; in addition, each country exhibits cultural, linguistic, racial, religious, and linguistic variations among its own people. To be sure, there exist myths of national identity, built up over centuries, that present simplified and often homogenized versions of a country's inhabitants and customs. Many Latin Americans, just like people from any other global region, hold these stereotypes about themselves and others to be true. This chapter, nonetheless, will strive to highlight cultural differences often erased by national myths, by considering texts that address identity and relationships from both dominant and marginal perspectives. However, a short essay of this scope can only begin to scratch the surface of the multiplicity of human experiences that make up present-day Latin America. The reader, then, should take this essay very much in the spirit of an opening for future inquiry rather than a conclusive pronouncement of truth.

Generally speaking, in Latin America family structures and interpersonal relationships are central to a person's daily life to a greater degree than in North America. Although important patterns of internal and external migration exist—particularly with regard to people from poor countries relocating to the region's richer nations or to North America—people who are not forced to leave their homes for political or economic reasons are likely to stay in the same town or city where they were born and where their family members live. Young people of both sexes often live at home until they marry or otherwise leave to form their own families. Although many variations on these themes exist, it can be stated confidently that individuality, self-reliance, mobility, and autonomy—characteristics all greatly prized in North American culture and particularly in the United States—are not key values in Latin America. There, the maintenance of intimate friendships, close family ties, intergenerational continuity, and clan loyalty are cardinal tenets as a person moves through life. One's identity is thus defined collectively as well as individually, as is the case all over the world; but in Latin America the individual aspect does not automatically predominate.

As many literary texts illustrate, this concept of group identity can have negative consequences for those in subordinate positions (such as racial, ethnic, and religious minorities, or women, lesbians, and gay men), because their traditional place in the collective can be upheld as part of a natural order. Strong family and community relationships, then, provide opportunities both for individual support and individual constraint. Again, while this dilemma can be seen as part of the human condition everywhere, the emphasis placed on family in Latin America affects identity and relationships in a way that is specific to the region and that is often reflected in its literature.

Some of the best-known works of Latin American literature that have been translated into English provide evidence for these cultural generalizations. Gabriel García Márquez's *One Hundred Years of Solitude,* for example, delves into the life of Macondo, an imaginary Colombian town, and the complex history of several generations of the Buendía family. García Márquez's works tell stories of places where a person is defined by his or her family's history, and where sometimes (such as in his short novel *Chronicle of a Death Foretold*) tragedy results from that linking of personal fate with collective identity. In the works of Isabel Allende, notably *The House of the Spirits,* several generations of women in one family fulfill their destiny in Chilean society through relationships sometimes communicated in magical ways, despite the harmful disruptions of political turmoil. Laura Esquivel's *Like Water for Chocolate* likewise portrays the warmth of family life in Mexico while illustrating the changing roles of women within a conservative society.

Other texts often taught in English translation discuss identity and relationships from minority points of view. This is the case with Rigoberta Menchú's memoir *I, Rigoberta Menchú,* in which the story of an indigenous Guatemalan family and its surrounding community, decimated by political violence, is recounted. Menchú's narration sheds light on daily life among the Maya-Quiché people, on their intergenerational relationships, and on the struggle to maintain their culture as a dynamic process amid poverty and deprived material conditions. Although indigenous people, themselves diverse in tribe and language, make up the majority of Guatemala's population, their collective identity is one of historic oppression. In Manuel Puig's *Kiss of the Spider Woman,* the homosexual protagonist Molina voices both the pain of isolation from the mainstream and a fascination with the popular culture of the cinema, in which relationships are often idealized. Valentin, his cell mate, represents the political dissident who nevertheless takes part in homophobic oppression. Here Puig presents a picture of how problematic and complex identities can become when one does not conform to traditional roles.

This chapter will focus on several texts not often taught in U.S. classrooms, although excellent English translations are available. They present interesting challenges to the translator, and discussion of those technical difficulties could be included in their teaching, thus enriching the classroom experience of English-language students. The works discussed here also represent a range of literary genres, offering the instructor an opportunity to explore with students the varying approaches that must be employed in the translation of poetry, fiction, and memoir. Finally, they are texts that reflect the cultures of different parts of Latin America, each with its own historical and social conditions informing identity, family, and relationships among its inhabitants.

FAMILY ALBUM, CLARIBEL ALEGRÍA

Claribel Alegría (b. Managua, Nicaragua, 1924) is a prolific, prize-winning author of poetry, fiction, and nonfiction prose. Many of her works have been translated into English and published by small presses, from which they are readily available for classroom use. Alegría grew up in El Salvador, although for the last few decades she has once more made her home in Nicaragua. Her work reflects her deep knowledge and experience of Central American culture, history and politics, and it often centers on themes of social justice. Gender roles also figure prominently in her writing, as women question the traditions that both bind them to others and limit their freedom. These issues of self and other are both present in the text to be examined here.

Family Album (*Album familiar*), a collection of three novellas, was originally published as a complete volume in Spanish in 1986, although each text had been published separately at earlier dates. Its English version, translated by Amanda Hopkinson, was first published in London in 1990, then in the United States in 1991. A note on the copyright page of the U.S. version indicates that editors at Curbstone Press adapted the translation slightly to conform to American English, with the help of Alegría's husband and frequent collaborator, Darwin Flakoll (now deceased). The existence of different U.S. and U.K. translations raises the issue of multiple possible versions of a literary text rendered into the same target language—a good topic for classroom discussion. In this case, one could ask: Should a translation inflected by British usage be adapted for an American audience? Why or why not? It could be noted that this is also an issue for translations of English texts into Spanish, because a translator from Spain may produce a very different version from a translator from Argentina or Mexico.

All three novellas in *Family Album* treat themes of identity and relationships, but the title piece is perhaps most useful for the classroom. It is set in August 1979, when Sandinista rebels successfully overthrew the regime of Nicaraguan dictator Anastasio Somoza. Ximena, the protagonist, is a Salvadoran woman married to a Frenchman and living in Paris. Her dead father was Nicaraguan, and her cousin from that side—Armando, a former Sandinista now living in exile in Paris—comes to tell her the news of the successful revolution. Through their conversation and shared recollections of life in Central America, Alegría skillfully intertwines Ximena's thoughts on her personal situation with commentary on larger social issues. The novella also features some complex shifts of time and place; Ximena's inner communication with her long-dead indigenous nanny; many colorful stories of her large, eccentric Salvadoran family; and the strange, perhaps unexplainable disappearance of faces from an album of family photographs.

Ximena's identity as a Central American woman, wealthy in her poor country of origin but merely middle class in Paris, gets thrown into question by political events that force her to take stock and decide what will give her life meaning. She has escaped the confining structures of a traditional small town in El Salvador, but life in Paris with a husband who finds her native culture somewhat inferior to his own has its own limitations. She finds herself longing for relationships not only with individuals but also with a larger patriotic project, a national identification through her Nicaraguan father that will contribute to social justice and liberation from fear. These are themes to which students of any background can relate, but the many specifically Central American details with which Alegría infuses the narrative will require English readers to enter a different, foreign world.

Translating those details poses a challenge for the translator, and Amanda Hopkinson's solutions to particular problems can be brought out when teaching the text. For example, *Family Album* includes four short footnotes either explaining words that the translator has left in Spanish or identifying historical figures named in the story. One of the words left untranslated is *latifundista,* meaning a major Central American landholder. Students could be asked whether the presence of this word adds to or detracts from their reading experience, whether they think the use of footnotes is the best way to handle such localisms, and in even more general terms, how much a translation should attempt to preserve the foreignness of the original text. When Hopkinson translates the typical Salvadoran baked goods *quesadillas* as "cheese buns" but leaves the French *baguette* as is, what kinds of decisions is she making about her audience and their tolerance for foreign details? Why might she have decided to preserve *latifundista* but to translate *quesadillas,* when both words give the reader insight into aspects of Central American culture?

The novella's reception could also be discussed within the framework of national and personal identity. *Family Album* was originally published in 1982 by EDUCA, a press shared by a consortium of Central American universities whose publications reach readers throughout the region. That 1982 audience was only a few years removed from the events described in the book. Moreover, Alegría was by then a well-known writer with many publications to her credit who was publicly allied with the Sandinista cause, and whose books attracted instant attention. Clearly the English-language reader approaching the text a decade later, whether in the United Kingdom or the United States, would not be able to participate in that sense of historical immediacy or shared cultural experience. How much should the translator try to compensate for such difference in her translation? Should she trust that her readers will fill in gaps of understanding for themselves, or should she make adjustments within the text that will perhaps bring them closer to the Central American experience? Armando, for example, describes for the naive, bourgeois Ximena a method of torture used in Somoza's prisons called *la capucha,* translated as "the hood." The Spanish term alone would have inspired feelings of horror in its 1982 readers. Does the English version necessarily lose some of that emotional impact? Would there have been any other way to bring the English reader closer to "identifying" with Central Americans while reading this work?

Finally, although the distance between present-day students and the events of 1979 is potentially even harder to bridge, the themes of class, race, and gender; personal freedom versus collective ties; differences between poor and rich nations; and political terror and torture in the name of national security all remain pertinent today. Moreover, the Sandinista Daniel Ortega was once again elected president of his country in 2006 and took office in January 2007. Claribel Alegría's *Family Album* offers instructors a timely and excellent vehicle for teaching about Latin American identity and relationships within a social context.

THE FAMILY TREE, MARGO GLANTZ

Margo Glantz's memoir *The Family Tree* (*Las genealogías*) presents a completely different narration of Latin American identity. Glantz (b. Mexico City, 1930) is one of contemporary Mexico's best-known intellectuals. Her extensive body of work includes volumes of literary and theatre criticism, short fiction, and novels. *The Family Tree,* translated by Susan Bassnett, was published in England in 1991; it was the first of Glantz's works to appear in English. (Her novel *The Wake,* translated by Andrew Hurley, was published in 2005.) In Spanish, *Las genealogías* originally appeared in the

Mexico City newspaper *UNOMASUNO* in the form of short pieces, and it has been published several times as a collected volume (1981, 1987, 1998), with each edition adding material to the last. Bassnett's translation follows the 1987 edition.

The Family Tree tells the life stories of Margo Glantz's parents, Elizabeth and Jacob Glantz, including their early years and families of origin in Ukraine, their emigration as a young married couple from the Soviet Union to Mexico in 1925, the family they formed in their new Latin American home, and the lives they led there until old age (Jacob's death in 1982 figures in *The Family Tree,* while Elizabeth's 1997 death provides a definitive end for the 1998 Spanish edition). In recounting her parents' navigation, both literal and figurative, of the transatlantic crossing and a completely new culture and language, Glantz also meditates on her own identity as a Mexican born to Ukrainian Jewish immigrants, her feelings of Jewishness or lack thereof, the Russian part of her soul and how it meshes with a profound commitment to the study of colonial and modern Mexican culture, and the mixture of languages (Russian, Yiddish, Spanish) to which she has been exposed since childhood. Through tape-recorded interviews with her parents, old family photographs, and a trip to the Soviet Union in 1981, Glantz gathers information and then recreates it as a literary form combining history and fiction, biography and autobiography. In its origins, *The Family Tree* can be traced to the *crónica,* a creative form of journalism widely practiced by writers in Latin America since the nineteenth century; but its subsequent reordering into a volume makes it most similar to the English-language memoir, itself a loosely defined type of writing about the self. Here the question of generic boundaries in prose writing and the blurring of "fact" with storytelling across the Americas pose rich topics for classroom discussion.

The Family Tree can appeal to English-language students on several levels, because the narrative or novel of immigration is recognized as an important and integral component of modern North American literature. Students may be surprised to encounter a similar tale told from within a Latin American context, challenging possible stereotypes of a monocultural, Catholic Mexico. The story of a child of immigrants and her own efforts (as well as those of her parents) to integrate cultures and languages will ring true for students who themselves may not be far removed from the immigrant experience. Although Glantz's parents lived and worked in bohemian, artistic circles in the exciting international atmosphere of postrevolutionary Mexico City and were perhaps unusual in their liberalism, at the same time they were small business owners trying to survive despite hard economic conditions and anti-Semitism. Moreover, the horrors of pogroms in Russia and the precariousness of life there in both the city and the countryside do not get glossed over. While the story maintains a tone of humor and irony in the face of pain, the Jewish legacies of persecution, wandering, and forced migration emerge as a tragic backdrop to Margo Glantz's lovely tribute to her parents, sisters, and extended family.

Teaching *The Family Tree* thus offers opportunities for exploring how members of a minority culture establish new roots and identities within the majority culture in Mexico, and how that experience contrasts with the North American immigrant story. Reading Glantz's memoir in translation also presents topics for stimulating discussion related to the translation itself. *The Family Tree* features frequent use of Yiddish and Russian words, almost always accompanied by an explanation within the text, as Glantz's parents tell the stories of their life in Ukraine and the Soviet Union and translate foreign words for their Mexican daughter: "'Byelorussia, yes, White Russia,' my father agrees, '*biely* means white'" (Glantz, *Family Tree*, 9). She in turn interprets broader cultural aspects unfamiliar to her predominantly non-Jewish Mexican readers, such as Jewish religious customs and typical foods, although she can assume a common basis of Mexican cultural knowledge. The translation into English adds yet another layer to the interpretation, and students could be asked if they think the result succeeds in drawing them into both the Russian Jewish and Mexican worlds. How can a translator approach the double strangeness of a minority within a foreign culture without confusing English readers?

One strategy is the addition of explanatory material. Numerous important Mexican cultural figures from throughout the twentieth century make cameo appearances in *Las genealogías,* in relation to Elizabeth's and Jacob's lives as well as to Margo's. Some of these references have been deleted from the English version of the memoir, but the many that remain are listed in a helpful biographical glossary at the back of the book. Students reading the translation could discuss the use of the glossary: does it enhance their reading experience?

Finally, issues regarding the translation of humor, one of the most difficult challenges for any translator, could be fruitfully explored in a reading of *The Family Tree*. Jacob Glantz, a poet and lover of language, makes frequent jokes whose humor relies on wordplay that is often bilingual in nature. One might think such jokes are "untranslatable," but in several instances Bassnett has come up with excellent solutions that effectively communicate Glantz's character and humor. Here students could consider the concept of an "untranslatable" text: Do certain aspects of culture, such as humor, truly resist all efforts at translation? What does "untranslatability" imply for cross-cultural understanding in a larger sense?

"ODE TO THE TOMATO," PABLO NERUDA

The final text to be discussed is Pablo Neruda's "Ode to the Tomato" ("Oda al tomate"). Neruda (Chile, 1904–1973), who won the 1971 Nobel Prize for Literature, was one of Latin America's most renowned poets, and his prolific work has been translated extensively into many languages. The *Elemental Odes* (*Odas elementales*) were published in three volumes from 1954 through 1959. These poems celebrate the quotidian details and objects of life, including flora and fauna, items of clothing, geography, and more abstract concepts such as time, the atom, and laziness. Often their themes are either specifically Chilean (for example, "Ode to the Birds of Chile"), or, like the poem to be discussed here (included in the 1954 volume of *Elemental Odes*), they examine common objects from within a Chilean context.

Although Neruda's *Odes* are not generally considered from the perspectives of identity or relationships, their often intimate, personal voice, combined with the intense identification of the poet with his native country, make them appropriate for such an approach. Moreover, multiple translations of the *Odes* exist in English, giving instructors the opportunity to compare and contrast different versions. The "Oda al tomate" is just one possible text that could be used in the classroom; it is selected here because of its easily accessible theme, its relative importance within the overall project of the *Odes,* and its existence in two readily available published versions by accomplished translators.

Space prevents inclusion of the entire text here. It is composed of eighty-six short lines, many only one word long. The role of the tomato in Chilean cuisine, emblematic of the bounty of December (summer in the Southern Hemisphere), is given a sensuous treatment appealing to sight, smell, texture, and taste. By evoking home cooking, mealtimes, and the atmosphere of a kitchen in a Chilean home at midday in summer, Neruda creates a warm, colorful portrait of natural simplicity and plenty, the richness of the fruit of the earth, and a sense of place revolving around seasonal changes and ingredients. Here the poet's voice is first-person plural, a collective Chilean "we" celebrating freshness and luxury available to even the most humble neighbor.

The translators of two different versions of this ode, Margaret Sayers Peden and Ken Krabbenhoft, have taken two distinctly different approaches to their work. In general terms, Peden's version is more literal, following the Spanish text's form and wording closely, while Krabbenhoft uses a freer hand with both punctuation and word order. That said, there are exceptions to this generalization; for example, the title of Peden's translation is "Ode to Tomatoes," while Krabbenhoft renders a more literal "Ode to the Tomato." But an examination of the first twelve lines, which in Spanish form one sentence punctuated by four commas, will give a good idea of the two translators' sensibilities. Peden's version reads: "The street / filled with tomatoes, / midday, / summer, / light is / halved / like / a / tomato, / its juice / runs / through the streets" (139). Here the number of lines and the punctuation are kept scrupulously close to the Spanish original, and the poem's first line is preserved (*La calle* in Spanish).

Krabbenhoft's version, in contrast, reads: "On the street / at noon, / tomatoes everywhere, / in summer. / Daylight / splits / into a tomato's / equal / halves: / its juice / flows / in the streets" (141). Not only has one sentence been divided into two, but the punctuation has been altered, preserving two commas while changing the third into a period and the fourth into a colon. Krabbenhoft has also added prepositions not in the Spanish to his first, second, and fourth lines, while eliminating the preposition from the third line. Students could consider which version they respond to, and why. Is the more literal version truer to the text? Does its economy work well in English? Or is the division of one sentence into two justified by a more natural English diction?

Further on in the poem, lines twenty-eight through thirty-four describe the violent cutting of the tomato's whole roundness into pieces for a salad. Here the "we" appears for the first time in the ode. Peden renders the lines thusly: "Unfortunately, we must / murder it: / the knife / sinks / into living flesh, / red / viscera" (141). Krabbenhoft's version is somewhat more embellished and interpretive: "All the same, we'll have / to put this one to death: / the knife / sinks into / its living pulp, / it's a bloody / organ" (143). Which version succeeds best in establishing Neruda's tone, intimate but somewhat ironic? Is the literal "red viscera" perhaps less emotionally charged in English than the "bloody organ"? Is one of these versions more faithful than the other, and if so, why?

Finally, the two translations end the ode very differently in the last seven lines. Peden's version reads: "no pit, / no husk, /no leaves or thorns, / the tomato offers / the gift / of fiery color / and cool completeness" (143). Again, the translator has followed Neruda's punctuation and vocabulary as closely as possible. Krabbenhoft forms a new sentence at the end: "free of pits / and peels, / thorns and scales. / It's the tomato's / gift to us, / this fiery color / and undiminished freshness" (145). The "us" in this version is indeed present in the Spanish (*nos entrega*) but absent from Peden's otherwise more literal rendering. Does this change the tone of the translation at its crucial end? How does each version succeed or fail at communicating Neruda's love of the simple things that make Chilean life both unique and universal? By contrasting multiple versions of translated texts in this way, an instructor teaches students that there is no one "right" translation, but rather different approaches. When translations are evaluated, it is important to consider not only which version one subjectively "likes" better but also what the translator was trying to accomplish and if the translation succeeds in maintaining a consistent reading of the original.

The texts examined here represent but three possibilities for teaching about identity and relationships through Latin American literature in translation. They should be considered as points of departure for instructors' explorations in the field. Many more could be suggested, taking into account both better- and lesser-known works, and always keeping in mind the diversity of the region and its peoples.

WORKS CITED

Alegría, Claribel. *Family Album*. Translated by Amanda Hopkinson. Willimantic, CT: Curbstone Press, 1991.

Allende, Isabel. *The House of the Spirits*. Translated by Magda Bogin. New York: Knopf, 1985.

Esquivel, Laura. *Like Water for Chocolate*. Translated by Carol Christensen and Thomas Christensen. New York: Doubleday, 1992.

García Márquez, Gabriel. *Chronicle of a Death Foretold*. Translated by Gregory Rabassa. New York: Knopf, 1983.

————. *One Hundred Years of Solitude.* Translated by Gregory Rabassa. New York: Harper and Row, 1970.

Glantz, Margo. *The Family Tree.* Translated by Susan Bassnett. London: Serpent's Tail, 1991.

————. *The Wake.* Translated by Andrew Hurley. Willimantic, CT: Curbstone Press, 2005.

Menchú, Rigoberta. *I, Rigoberta Menchú: An Indian Woman in Guatemala.* Translated by Ann Wright. Edited by Elizabeth Burgos-Debray. London: Verso, 1984.

Neruda, Pablo. *Odes to Common Things.* Translated by Ken Krabbenhoft. New York: Little, Brown, 1994.

————. *Selected Odes of Pablo Neruda.* Translated by Margaret Sayers Peden. Berkeley: University of California Press, 1990.

Puig, Manuel. *Kiss of the Spider Woman.* Translated by Thomas Colchie. New York: Random House, 1979.

Nordic Exposure: Teaching Scandinavian Literature in Translation

Niels Ingwersen and Susan C. Brantly,
with Thomas A. Dubois and Dick Ringler

Works by Scandinavian authors are taught widely in North America, and some Scandinavian authors are part of the Western canon while being known outside Western culture. Such names as Henrik Ibsen, August Strindberg, Hans Christian Andersen, and Søren Kierkegaard attest to that, as do Sigrid Undset, Knut Hamsun, Selma Lagerlöf, Isak Dinesen (aka Karen Blixen), and Pär Lagerkvist, if to a lesser degree. The same is true of Astrid Lindgren, the author of delightful children's stories, and of the anonymous authors of the Icelandic sagas. College courses on the rise of modern Western drama cannot avoid Ibsen and Strindberg; courses on the advent of feminism are bound to include Ibsen's *A Doll's House* (1879); philosophy courses on existentialism very likely will offer a solid dose of Kierkegaard; and in folklore or children's literature classes, Hans Christian Andersen tends to figure prominently. Most of the students in Scandinavian programs are likely to be found in literature-in-translation courses. Modern-language programs are increasingly offering courses on the tales of Hans Christian Andersen, the rise of modern Western drama (Ibsen and Strindberg), or Finnish folklore (*Kalevala*).[1]

Nevertheless, only a minority of the instructors of these courses know a Scandinavian language, and many instructors of texts in translation have only a scant knowledge of Nordic letters and of countries at the northern tip of Europe. Instructors of those texts should surely be able to address the issue of Nordic identity—or, to be precise, the presence of various Nordic identities—and they should also be familiar with the intricate relationships among Scandinavian literatures and European cultures.

Fortunately, excellent or adequate translations are in print; many of them are annotated scholarly editions. The works of lesser-known authors—

especially recent ones—are often issued by small presses in limited editions, which can present a problem; but even so, a vast array of works is available, even if their availability is constantly fluctuating.

Survey courses are popular, and students generally expect a bird's-eye view of the development of Nordic literatures. The instructor enters a room containing about two hundred undergraduates, most of whom have only a vague notion of what Scandinavia is. During the first few meetings, that instructor must give the students a sense of a most varied geography—fertile hills, majestic mountains, and icy wastes—and of a variety of languages, some of which are closely related, and some of which are not even Indo-European (thus, even the Scandinavianist encounters problems).[2] A history lesson, both political and cultural, is also needed, and that is an absolute necessity. The instructor must put the Nordic countries into the European context for the simple reason that most American students know little about the history of Western civilization. An instructor would be remiss if she or he did not chart the travels of the Vikings, deal with the conversion of the Nordic peoples to Christianity and the ensuing bloody Reformation, or give attention to the (muted) arrival of Renaissance ideas and art. The list of important elements of Scandinavian history could go on and would eventually include the Industrial Revolution, the impact of two world wars, and the emergence of the welfare state. Experienced instructors find that students both need and desire that kind of background.[3]

In such well-enrolled courses it is difficult to deal with the issue of translation in detail, but PowerPoint presentations (or an overhead projector) make it easy to demonstrate that Scandinavian languages and English have a common ground. A detour through the vocabulary of the people of Yorkshire (the settling ground of the Danish Vikings in England) would make that point crystal-clear.

The presentation of the cultural and historical backgrounds of these countries can easily include a discussion of some translation problems. In the abovementioned survey course, the instructor may want to include examples of the beautiful and violent Scandinavian ballads, recorded in the 1500s. Of course, in terms of ideology or ethics, they may seem distant, and the instructor would need to bridge some historical gaps.[4] The ballads frequently refer to fate, often using the Nordic terms *lykke* (Danish and Norwegian) or *lycka* (Swedish), which eventually came to mean "individual happiness." That change in meaning of a single word is loaded with significance. Such older texts are hard to translate, for some words have fallen out of use, and others are obscure. In short, translations of these older texts are approximations constructed via either of two different mechanisms: (1) The translator is impressed with the beauty, the rhythm, the rhymes of the lyrical flow, and thus tries to poetically capture all those elements; but in so doing, he or she removes the poem from the language and meaning of the original. (2) The translator wants to be close to the original and thus produces a pedestrian paraphrase of the text that translates the individual words correctly but loses the lyrical magic of the original.

This tension between a desire to attend to individual words and syntactic structure, on the one hand, and to provide the reader with the effects of the original, on the other, is not limited to medieval ballads. Any student who takes a poetry course in a foreign language knows that she or he is in for problems that might seem nearly insurmountable. The most outstanding nineteenth-century Icelandic poet, Jonas Hallgrímsson, may serve as a case in point.[5]

Here is the first stanza of a drinking song. It is quite literally a *song*, because it was constructed to be sung to a preexisting melody:

Hvað er svo glatt sem góðra vina fundur	A
þá gleðin skín á vonarhýrri brá?	b
eins og á vori laufi skrýðist lundur	A
lifnar og glæðist hugarkætin þá;	b
og meðan þrúgna gullnu tárin glóa	C
og guðaveigar lifga sálaryl	d
þá er það vist, að bestu blómin gróa	C
í brjóstum sem að geta fubdið til	d

Until the nineteenth century, Icelandic verse was generally intended (at least notionally) for oral presentation; consequently, it is very rich in acoustic effects. Some of these are obligatory and are deployed in definite and unvarying patterns. Notice here the structural alliteration (indicated by boldface type), which derives from the traditions of the earliest Germanic oral verse: two of the stressed syllables in every odd-numbered line alliterate with the first stressed syllable in the following even-numbered line. Only much later, under the influence of modern European verse, was end rhyme added to the mix, thus producing in this stanza the rhyme sequence AbAbCdCd, where capital letters indicate disyllabic ("feminine") rhymes, and lower-case letters indicate monosyllabic ("masculine") rhymes.

It is worth discussing with students whether, in approaching this kind of highly formal lyric poetry, there is any point at all in reading a bald prose translation: "What is so cheerful as a meeting of good friends, when joy shines on brows warm with hope? This is the time when mental delight comes to life and catches fire, just as in spring the grove adorns itself with foliage. And as long as the tears of golden grapes are glowing [i.e., as long as the wine is flowing] and divine draughts are inspiring warmth of soul, it's certain that the loveliest flowers are growing in breasts that are able to feel emotion." This prose rendering is perfectly lifeless. There is nothing here to hold one's attention. Everything that makes the poem a poem is gone. Would it not be much better to read a translation that attempts to reproduce the acoustic patterns of the original with some exactitude, while retaining most of its sense, and that also attempts to get across something of its lyric quality (but without employing vocabulary or syntax that sounds bizarre in Modern English)?

Who has such joy as friends who get together,	A
with grateful smiles alight in every face?	b
Like barren twigs that sprout in springtime weather,	A
spirits are blooming now with love and grace,	b
for while the tears of golden grapes are flowing,	C
the godlike draughts inspire our hearts and eyes,	d
it's certain that the brightest flowers are blowing,	C
in breasts that love and feel and sympathize.	d

Through this exercise, the students will experience firsthand the challenges posed by the translation of distant texts such as traditional Icelandic lyric poetry. Let them wrestle with this problem! Not all Nordic poetry poses such severe challenges, and one reason to welcome modernism was that it made life easier for translators; but the problems encountered above will tax anyone who attempts to translate Baroque poetry or the exquisite sonnets of the romanticists.

Most courses may, however, deal with Scandinavian prose narratives or theater. Translation courses of Nordic prose tend to start with the remarkable flourishing of narratives in Iceland in the late Middle Ages. Here again, a history lesson is imperative: why did so many Norwegians leave their native country for Iceland? They came from a monarchial political system, so why did they then establish a republic with an extremely weak central government and no executive branch? Luckily, an abundance of academic editions and numerous scholarly works await the teacher who wishes to teach about the rise of that early form of the novel called the saga.

Many sagas record the violent family feuds of Iceland, in a language that is spare and laconic. The narrators are the next of kin to an excellent reporter, one who observes events at close quarters, reports action, and listens to and records dialogue, but does not interpret or moralize. An illusion of objectivity is created. The discourse is taciturn, and litotes is frequently used. A few lines of the original Old Norse, with translation provided, will help students understand how translators try to convey the specific tone of the originals. In *Hrafnkel's Saga*, Eyvind is being pursued by Hrafnkel and his men, who intend to kill him. Eyvind states that he has no quarrel with Hrafnkel and sees no reason to flee. A young boy responds to that statement: "I have the feeling it's you he wants to see."[6] Students may well respond that the boy could have exhorted Eyvind to flee and warned him that if he did not, he would surely be killed; but the boy's understated words certainly convey that dire meaning to those well-versed in the conventions of saga discourse. That discourse may trouble those students who want the narration to be more "informative," so the instructor must be able to help the students probe behind a seeming neutrality or objectivity in an effort to fathom the mindsets of the characters in the sagas.

Perhaps it is wise to insert a few comments on Nordic folklore at this point. Although most of the canonized texts were recorded during the 1800s, they give glimpses of earlier times. Once again, such texts are often taught by teachers who do not know Nordic cultures; nevertheless, if someone teaches "Beauty and the Beast," it is tempting to include the Scandinavian variants, and it is significant that French versions give elaborate descriptions of exquisite courts, whereas the king in the Norwegian text seems more like a wealthy farmer than a monarch. Nordic folklore also includes plenty of resourceful, independent young women, as well as a plethora of trolls.

One outstanding text that commends attention in this context is the Finnish *Kalevala*, a complex literary epic compiled by Elias Lönnrot (1802–1884).[7] Lönnrot, a romantic intellectual in the mold of the Brothers Grimm, set out to collect the epic songs of his nation, which were still being performed in his day in remote districts of Northen Finland and Karelia. *Kalevala*'s rather meandering plot centers in part on the creation, theft, and final destruction of the *sampo,* a magical item that provides its owner with all the money, flour, salt, or other provisions ever needed. In poem forty-three of the fifty-poem work, our heroes, led by the aged seer Väinämöinen, have left their home of Kaleva and have stolen the *sampo* from the clutches of Louhi, the greedy witch who rules the northern land of Pohjola. They rush homeward with their treasure, but Louhi turns herself into an eagle and pursues them. She battles with Väinämöinen, who manages to cut off all her talons with his oar; but in the end, she carries off the *sampo* with her one remaining digit, her "nameless finger." However, she drops the *sampo* into the White Sea by accident, which is why the White Sea is salty while the Baltic is not.

Teaching *Kalevala* requires giving students much cultural information; without it, they will not be able to understand even the broad outlines of the plot, let alone its nuances. Take, for instance, the "nameless finger." Students often think this term must refer to the middle finger, which is used in obscene gestures in the United States. Alternatively, they often read the finger as some mysterious extra digit that only Louhi has (or that only eagles have). The answer, however, is both simpler and more meaningful. In Finnish, the fingers have names: in some places, the names (beginning with the thumb) translate as "out scrubber," "pan licker," "tall Heikki," "nameless Antti," and "little Matti." In other areas, the same fingers are called "louse squisher," "butter licker," "pitch Pietari," "nameless Matti," and "tar plug." As can be seen from these lists, most fingers are named for jobs they can be used for. The thumb, for instance, is good for scraping cooked-on grease out of a pan that has been used over an open fire. It is also good for squishing lice, a perennial nuisance in all traditional societies. But the finger we call the ring finger seldom has any particular use, except, perhaps, when playing a musical instrument. Thus, in Finnish tradition the ring finger is called the nameless finger. In a traditional farming society, being useless was a supreme evil, and the person who did no work hardly deserved the honor of a name. This is, of course, a wonderful metaphor for what happens in poem forty-three. Louhi manages to steal back the *sampo* with her least likely appendage, but the finger's weakness and unreliability cause her to lose the treasure, thereby depriving the entire world of its benefits. The little detail of the nameless finger holds great import, although students will not appreciate that import without the proper cultural information.

Although *Kalevala* was published at a time when Nordic literature was heading toward a golden age, today most Nordic authors included in the canon of world literature wrote during the nineteenth century. Søren Kierkegaard is, of course, part of that canon. A course on Kierkegaard is bound to attract very good students from a variety of fields. Inadequate translations have luckily been replaced with splendid new ones, but students are nevertheless intrigued with the nuances of Kierkegaard's complicated language, and they often ask the instructor to explain exactly what a given word means in Danish. One example is the word *angst,* which Kierkegaard made well-known. It signifies a fear with a cause that cannot be determined. *Angst* can cause a state of mental dizziness in which sin may be committed, but it also educates the individual. Students are bound to be puzzled by the ambiguity of this concept and to ask about the origin and meanings of the word.[8] And when Kierkegaard writes about *evighed* (eternity), what exactly does he mean? Kierkegaard writes a dense, complex prose filled with allusions to writers and thinkers from antiquity to his own time. He assumed that his audience would share his learned background, and that poses a problem to modern-day readers. Fortunately, a fine annotated translation of Kierkegaard's collected works, recently published, was reissued in 2009.[9]

Courses on Ibsen and Strindberg will naturally draw in students who will never learn Norwegian or Swedish. Luckily, nearly every decade sees new translations of both authors, so there is a wide array of translations available, some in annotated editions. Thus, the instructor has to make a choice: which among this multitude shall I use? It would be wise to explain that choice to the class and to accompany that justification with representative samples from various translations. Because a number of drama students with a good knowledge of stagecraft tend to take such courses, it would be worthwhile to let them perform some crucial scenes that are disturbing to audiences, for example, the last scenes of Strindberg's *The Father* (1887) and Ibsen's *Hedda Gabler* (1890). Nearly all of Strindberg's and Ibsen's plays pose translation problems.

In Strindberg's expressionistic *A Dream Play* (1901), one phrase is repeated: "*Det är synd om människorna.*" That phrase, states Elizabeth Sprigge, "is exceedingly difficult to translate. 'Mankind is pitiable,' or 'pitiful,' 'Human beings are to be pitied,' are all fair versions of the Swedish, but there is also a suggestion of 'it is a shame about human beings.'"[10] Sprigge, a capable translator, admits that it is hard to capture all the nuances of the original, and she suggests that ambiguities are inevitably lost.

In his play *A Doll's House,* Ibsen uses the Norwegian word *vidunderlig* (wonderful), which he uses as both an adjective and a noun, and the superlative *vidunderligst* (most wonderful). The protagonist, Nora, realizes that a crime she has committed—falsifying her father's name in order to save her ill husband's life—may be found out, something she both desires and fears. She hopes that the revelation of her guilt will bring her husband, Helmer, to see her not as a doll, but as a loving woman; yet she naturally dreads the arrival of the police. Nevertheless, that moment of truth would be "wonderful" or a miracle, for she would be liberated from her doll-like existence. Toward the end of the play, Nora understands that her husband is not worthy of her, and she is planning to leave him. He asks if they will ever get together again, and she says that would only happen if *det vidunderligste* (the most wonderful) should happen; but she adds that she no longer believes in *det vidunderligste*. She leaves, and the play ends with Helmer saying, hopefully, *det vidunderligste*. That adjective, therefore, lies at the heart of the play.

The word *vidunderlig* is related to *vidunder* and *under* (wonder or miracle). In daily use, however, that connection hardly comes to mind. The common translation of *vidunderlig* is "wonderful," but because "wonderful" cannot stand alone, "thing" is usually added (e.g., "a wonderful thing is going to happen"). But the word "thing" is not that poetic or descriptive; thus, some translators have paid homage to the "wonder" hidden in the adjective *vidunderlig* by translating the term as "the miracle," or "the greatest miracle," or "the miraculous." Revealing this translation problem to a class can bring the students closer to the text and can result in a lively discussion about the ways in which Ibsen uses a single word. The class can also discuss which translation seems to be the most worthwhile, of course. Consensus is rarely reached.[11]

A Doll's House is taught everywhere. Many courses dealing with that text focus on women writers in Nordic cultures and will require a solid introduction to what in the Nordic countries was once called the "emancipation of women." That chapter of Nordic history tells the story of a rebellion, some defeats, some victories, and some measure of liberation. The work of major nineteenth-century women writers such as Victorian Benedictsson, Amalie Skram, Selma Lagerlöf, and Sigrid Undset is available in translation. Scandinavian prose at the end of the nineteenth century was fully as influential as its drama. Knut Hamsun's *Hunger* (1890) and Jens Peter Jacobsen's *Niels Lyhne* (1880) exist in new and skillful translations. These two novels left a mark on the work of Joyce and Rilke. A word of caution must be offered against the translations of older texts available for free online, however. For example, Ellie Schleussner's 1913 translation of August Strindberg's *By the Open Sea* (1890)—a favorite novel of Franz Kafka—costs nothing to read online, but the language of the translation is so awkward that it can be difficult to convince students that Strindberg was a good writer. Important background information about all these nineteenth-century authors can be found in the Danish, Finnish, Norwegian, and Swedish literary histories published by the University of Nebraska Press.[12]

During the twentieth century, Nordic literature made stunning advances in children's literature, and a broader lesson concerning cultural information can be gained from an examination of that body of texts.[13] In literature intended for children, we tend to depict the world as we would like it to be, pointing up ideals that we would like our children to aspire to in their lives. When one examines Nordic children's literature over time, it becomes clear that these ideals have changed. Nineteenth-century children's books lauded diligence and a sense of duty, but independence gradually became more and more of an ideal, as in North America. In fact, the child characters in Nordic children's books sometimes lead strikingly autonomous and even countercultural lives. One need think no further than Astrid Lindgren's Pippi Longstocking for an example.

In the postwar era, social compassion was presented as the means of rebuilding and improving the lives of all people in Nordic countries. Thorbjørn Egner's *When the Robbers Came to Cardamom Town* (1955) illustrates the ideals of a social-democratic Norway: robbers come and make off with food, but as the story progresses they are gradually won over to goodness. After a little time in prison, they learn to dress well and bathe often, and they recover their former livelihoods as street musicians. Their sense of daring translates into a social good when they fearlessly enter a burning building to save an aging townsman and his new parrot. The criminal is transformed into an active and positive contributor to society through the kindness of the police chief, Bastian, and his warmhearted wife. When one reads a book like Egner's it becomes evident how different postwar Nordic ideals are from those that developed in the United States during the same period. It also becomes clear what an important role cultural ideals play in books, stories, plays, and movies aimed at children. These narratives typically intend to socialize the child to become a constructive citizen who enjoys fellowship with others. It should be noted that concepts often valorized in American culture—such as ambition, competitiveness, and aggression—are viewed less positively in Nordic cultures.

When you mention children's literature and Scandinavia in the same breath, Hans Christian Andersen is bound to come to mind. By all means include some Andersen tales in a children's literature course, but do not forget that Andersen detested being considered an author who wrote for children only. Some of his best and darkest tales have more in common with Kafka and Hawthorne than with sweet Doctor Seuss stories; they are complex and ambiguous, and they often veer toward the tragic. Consequently, the instructor who teaches a course on the tales of Andersen will have to make it clear to students who flock to such a class with erroneous expectations that they are in for a course that will not be an easy ramble through a landscape of happy stories.

Once again, the instructor will have to choose a translation, and once again the students can be made aware of how that selection has taken place. One example of a recent translation juxtaposed against an earlier one will be most illuminating. A more recent translation of Andersen's "The Tinderbox" starts as follows: "A soldier came marching along the road: left, right! left, right!" However, the 1846 translation reads: "Once upon a time, a soldier came marching along on the highway." The first translation is very close to Andersen's language and captures its lively oral quality, whereas the older translation veers away from Andersen's style in order to push the tale in the direction of the popular, but somewhat bookish, style of the traditional fairy tale.[14] The newer translation, in all its brevity, suggests Andersen's attempt to create a language that sounded like the vernacular of his day. Here a parallel may be drawn to Mark Twain and the other frontier writers who wrestled with the American literary idiom, turning it away from the polish of eastern cities and pushing it in the direction of the spoken language of the rest of nineteenth-century America.

The instructor who teaches Andersen's tales has a wealth of opportunities to switch to language lessons, for the translator who attempts to render Andersen's whimsical imitations of nineteenth-century spoken language is bound to encounter headaches. One example will have to suffice: "The Shadow" (1843).[15] It is a complicated story that has attracted hundreds of pages of analysis, but a simplified version of the plot is as follows: a scholar from the north is visiting a southern European town, and he becomes preoccupied with a house across the street. One night, in jest, he tells his shadow to investigate what goes on inside that house. His shadow leaves but, to the scholar's annoyance, does not return. Years later, back in the north, the shadow visits the scholar with the purpose of severing their master-servant relationship, and the scholar—who is a decent man—easily and naively gives the shadow his freedom. Andersen relates those events with an elegant use of Danish second-person-singular pronouns.

Initially the scholar addresses the shadow with the informal *du,* whereas the shadow addresses his master with the formal *De.* When the shadow returns, he asks whether the scholar will refrain from using *du* and instead switch to *De.* The scholar agrees; thus, they are now on equal terms. As the plot moves on, the scholar is doing poorly, for no one reads his Romantic writings on "the true, the good, and the beautiful." The shadow then suggests, seemingly generously, that they travel abroad together to a resort. On that trip the good-hearted scholar suggests that since they are old friends, they should say *du* to each other. The shadow agrees to use *du* when addressing the scholar but admits that he himself cannot stand anyone using *du* with him. In short, through the use of pronouns Andersen shows the complete reversal of the relationship between the two.

At the resort a princess falls in love with the shadow, and they and the scholar travel to her country to celebrate the wedding. When the shadow demands that the scholar lie at his feet as a shadow, the scholar has had enough and threatens to expose the shadow for being merely a shadow, but the shadow has the scholar thrown into jail and sorrowfully tells the princess that his poor shadow has lost his mind. When the princess suggests they should do away with that deluded person, the shadow agrees, seemingly with regret. His pained reaction prompts the princess to declare her future spouse to be a noble person, and for the first time she addresses him as *De.* The shadow has now gained absolute power, and he—a cynical, homicidal immoralist—will be the future ruler of the land. Through the shadow one gains a disconcerting glimpse of a ruthless totalitarian power. The plot one expects from a fairy tale has been turned topsy-turvy. The story is chilling, for the victor is evil. One can see why well-meaning souls have tried to censor Andersen.

The instructor teaching this story will have to give some background on the use of formal and informal pronouns in Danish culture. The formal *De*—note the capital *D*—was the most prevalent form of address until about 1970; *du* was used only within the family and among good friends. Children used *du* among themselves, but they most certainly called their teachers *De.*

How can translators deal with that problem? The English *Thee* and *Thou* would be accurate, but because those terms seem antiquated, they will hardly work. Various translators have chosen various solutions: the shadow may say, "Please do not use my first name, please call me *sir*," in order to eliminate the hierarchy that makes him feel inferior to the scholar. A text like this one will require the instructor to deal with not only linguistic matters but also the social and ideological changes that took place during the nineteenth century. The century that led up to the Industrial Revolution and to the introduction of parliamentary governments saw much social upheaval as the masses became restless and rebellious. Put very briefly, one might say that the plot of "The Shadow" reflects this moment, when servants tired of their humble role and desired to remove their masters or even take their place. The story provides grim insights into the totalitarian mind, one that ruthlessly eliminates all opposition.

Karen Blixen, known in the United States as Isak Dinesen, is another Dane who enjoys an international reputation, and her works appear with frequency in English department courses. Her case is a special one with regard to translation. Although Danish was her mother tongue, Blixen/Dinesen wrote most of her works in English first, recasting them into Danish later. Susan Hardy Aiken has gone so far as to suggest that Isak Dinesen and Karen Blixen are two distinct but deeply intertextual writers.[16] After the success of *Seven Gothic Tales* (1934), Dinesen auditioned and rejected two Danish translators before deciding to take on the task herself. Elias Bredsdorff compared the English and Danish versions of *Seven Gothic Tales* and concluded that the Danish version was an improvement over the English.[17]

The Danish title of "The Invincible Slave-Owners" ("De standhaftige Slaveejere") in *Winter's Tales* (1942) invokes Hans Christian Andersen's "The Steadfast Tin Soldier" ("Den standhaftige Tinsoldat," 1838), which leads to a number of interpretive possibilities that are regrettably lost in the English. The most puzzling difference occurs in "The Pearls." The English story places Jensine and Alexander at the same window: "From the window the husband and wife looked down into the street."[18] The Danish version has them standing at separate windows. One of the interpretive conundrums of this tale is the question of whether husband and wife are united or alienated from each other at the end of the story. This different positioning of the characters invites two different readings, even though the two versions are supposed to tell the same story. The last volume of tales published before Dinesen's death, *Anecdotes of Destiny* (1958), contains even lengthier discrepancies between English and Danish, especially in "The Diver." Some illuminating passages on the nature of storytelling are absent from the English, which may well affect the way the story is read.[19]

When we come to twentieth-century and contemporary Nordic texts, many of which are being translated and used in classrooms, we have to mention the important Danish novelist Peter Høeg, whose novel *Smilla's Sense of Snow* (1992) became quite well-known and provides an excellent opportunity for discussing the cultural diversity of the Nordic countries. Whereas Høeg looks at the relationship of the Danes to the Inuit of Greenland, Kjerstin Ekman's *Blackwater* (1993) examines Swedish attitudes toward the Sámi. Both novels take the genre of the mystery/thriller to new literary heights. Norwegian writer Jostein Gaarder and Swedish author Per Olof Enquist have enjoyed literary success in the United States as well. Enquist's *The Royal Physician's Visit* (1999) is a brilliant historical novel that provides insight into the difficulties of establishing enlightenment ideas in 1700s Denmark.

In the novel *Out Stealing Horses* (2003), Norwegian author Per Petterson provides links to American literature when he includes references to *David Copperfield* (1849–50), just as J. D. Salinger did in *Catcher in the Rye*. The sixty-seven-year-old narrator, who loves to read Dickens, ardently hopes that his life will reach the satisfying culmination of his becoming a Dickensian hero, but he realizes that life rarely conforms to the consoling bildungsroman paradigm so popular in the Western world during the early nineteenth century. Modern texts such as those by Petterson move from a reassuring world into one filled with ambiguities.

What Petterson's novel and numerous other texts emphasize is the fact that when the first-person-singular narrator gained prominence in the late nineteenth century in Scandinavia—as in Knut Hamsun's *Hunger*—authors created voices of striking individuality. It is that unique (and, in Petterson's case, colloquial) voice that translators must try to capture in their renditions. When teaching *Out Stealing Horses,* instructors can show students how Petterson's work is indebted to Hamsun's, even as Petterson's colloquial narrative voice differs from it. They can draw parallels with the American tradition of returning to the wilderness to show the distinctiveness of northern European traditions in this regard, in which nature is perceived as a space of possible peace and forgiveness rather than as space wasted without the presence of modern technology. They can also highlight the way in which the text's colloquial voice suggests a loner rather than someone who is lonely, as in the example below, and they can ask whether the translation lets the reader know that the text comes from *elsewhere:*

> But I was not quite with him in my thoughts, and I wonder whether that is how we get to be after living alone for a long time, that in the middle of a train of thought we start talking out loud, that the difference between talking and not talking is slowly wiped out, that the unending, inner conversation we carry on with ourselves merges with the one we have with the few people we still see, and when you live alone for too long the line which divides the one from the other becomes vague, and you do not notice when you cross that line. Is this how my future looks?[20]

A major contemporary Norwegian writer who could be discussed alongside Petterson is Dag Solstad. His novel *Shyness and Dignity* (1994), obviously influenced by Hamsun and Strindberg, describes a day in the life of a teacher, Elias Rukla, who is experiencing an existential crisis. The introspective brooding of the narrator, both comic and bitterly sad, evokes another kind of solitude: that of a modern, middle-class person whose safe life is nonetheless filled with despair. While the theme of the novel may seem familiar to students, the extraordinary syntax, which alternates short sentences with pages-long monologues and stretches the limits of what is permissible in English, will force a discussion of the original language. This discussion can start with the fact that the title was translated in French as *Honte et dignité* and German as *Scham und würde* (i.e., *Shame and Dignity*). In modern novels like those of Petterson and Solstad, the issue of translation is unavoidable and can lead to a new awareness of the ways in which linguistic and cultural distances can be perceived and bridged, but not erased.

Three of the Nordic countries—Denmark, Norway, and Sweden (together called Scandinavia)—speak languages that are very similar; thus, those who speak Norwegian will be able to read and understand Danish and Swedish. Icelandic and Faroese are Nordic languages, but they are not immediately understood by Scandinavians. Finnish is a non-Indo-European language unrelated to the Nordic languages, but a Swedish-speaking minority is present in Finland. The Sámi, who live in northern Norway, Sweden, and Finland, and the Inuit, the inhabitants of Greenland, speak non-Indo-European languages as well. The Scandinavian countries may seem to be fairly similar culturally, but these facts should dispel the myth that the Nordic countries are homogeneous. They do, however, share a sense of special identity that makes them feel separate from their neighboring countries (England, Germany, and Russia).

Students who take courses in translated literature from the Nordic countries may feel they are traveling into tantalizing worlds that they find attractive even though they barely understand them. Little by little, as work after work is discussed, a few students may follow the example of James Joyce, who found Ibsen's work so intriguing that he taught himself to read Dano-Norwegian.

NOTES

1. Some enrollment numbers from the Department of Scandinavian Studies at the University of Wisconsin–Madison may illustrate my points.

	Spring 96	Fall 96	Spring 97	Fall 97	Spring 98	Fall 98	Spring 99
Literature in Translation	136	185	236	244	269	250	340
Literature in Nordic Language	94	131	126	157	120	127	103

	Fall 99	Spring 00	Fall 00	Spring 01	Fall 01	Spring 02	Fall 02
Literature in Translation	336	520	615	772	693	768	728
Literature in Nordic Language	138	111	141	104	149	200	144

	Spring 03	Fall 03	Spring 04	Fall 04	Spring 05	Fall 05	Spring 06
Literature in Translation	831	619	739	428	572	380	598
Literature in Nordic Language	131	173	156	166	178	193	135

The figure reflects enrollments from the 1996–97 academic year through the 2005–6 academic year. The top row lists the courses for which knowledge of a Nordic language is not required, mainly literature-in-translation courses. The bottom row lists the courses for which the student must acquire or know a Nordic language. The increase of enrollments in literature-in-translation courses that started in 1999 and peaked during the next few years was caused by the initiation of a video distance-learning course (The Tales of Hans Christian Andersen) that was shown on Wisconsin Public Television and that permitted an enrollment of four hundred students each semester. The decrease during the last two years was caused by a retirement that forced the department to cancel the course as a distance-learning venture. The Tales of Hans Christian Andersen is presently taught as a regular course by other instructors.

2. Consequently, I asked three colleagues to contribute to areas that lie outside my expertise. In the ensuing endnotes, I identify the sections written by those colleagues.

3. For good surveys of the history and literature of Nordic countries, see Knut Helle, *The Cambridge History of Scandinavia* (Cambridge, UK: Cambridge University Press, 2003); Horn Frederik Winkel, *History of the Literature of the Scandinavian North from the Most Ancient Times to the Present* (Honolulu: University Press of the Pacific, 2002); Daisy L. Neijmann, *Histories of Scandinavian Literature*, vol. 5, *A History of Icelandic Literature* (Lincoln: University of Nebraska Press, 2007); and Sven Hakon Rossel and Anne C. Ulmer, *A History of Scandinavian Literature, 1870–1980* (Minneapolis: University of Minnesota Press, 1982).

4. See Larry E. Syndergaard, *English Translations of the Scandinavian Medieval Ballads* (Turku, Finland: Nordic Institute of Folklore, 1995); he provides an exhaustive annotated list of Nordic ballads translated into English.

5. Dick Ringler is the author of this chapter's section on Jónas Hallgrímson. See Ringler, *Bard of Iceland* (Madison: University of Wisconsin Press, 2002). Translation issues pertaining to poetry are discussed in the section on prosody, 361–84.

6. Herman Pálsson, trans., *Hrafnkel's Saga* (New York: Penguin Classics, 1971), 65. See Pálsson's "Note on the Translation," 32–33.

7. This chapter's section on the *Kalevala* is written by Thomas A. DuBois. The problems of providing a new translation of the *Kalevala* are discussed by Keith Bosley, trans., *The Kalevala* (Oxford: Oxford University Press, 1989), 30–33.

8. The term appears in the title of Kierkegaard's *Begrebet angest* (1844), which originally was translated as *The Concept of Dread*. More recently the translation of the term has been revised, e.g., *The Concept of Anxiety*.

9. Howard V. Hong and Edna H. Hong, eds., *Kierkegaard's Writings*, 26 vols. (Princeton, NJ: Princeton University Press, 2009).

10. August Strindberg, *Six Plays of Strindberg*, trans. Elisabeth Sprigge (New York: Anchor Books, 1955), 190.

11. A long list of translations could be supplied, but in this note we only discuss four representative instances. The first piece of dialogue in each translation reflects Nora's expectations, expressed towards the end of act 2; the second expresses her spouse's hope as the play closes:

(1) "You see, something miraculous is going to happen"; "a miracle of miracles," James W. McFarlane, ed., *The Oxford Ibsen* (Oxford: Oxford University Press, 1961), 5:256, 286.

(2) "A miracle is about to happen"; "The greatest miracle of all?" *A Doll's House*, trans. Nicholas Rudall (Chicago: Ivan R. Dee, 1999), 80, 119.

(3) "We're going to see—a miracle"; "The greatest miracle of all?" *The League of Youth, A Doll's House, The Lady from the Sea,* trans. Peter Watts (New York: Penguin Books, 1965), 201, 231.

(4) "It is the wonderful thing—it's about to happen, you see"; "It is the most wonderful thing of all," *Six Plays by Ibsen,* trans. Eva le Gallienne (New York: The Modern Library, 1932), 53, 82.
Instructors should consult James McFarlane, ed., *The Oxford Ibsen,* 8 vols. (Oxford: Oxford University Press, 1960–77). This edition includes all of Ibsen's works and offers extensive introductions and notes.

12. The series titled A History of Scandinavian Literatures provides the most recent and comprehensive background information available for all eras of Scandinavian literature. The series includes: Sven H. Rossel, ed., *A History of Danish Literature* (Lincoln: University of Nebraska Press, 1992); Harald S. Naess, ed., *A History of Norwegian Literature* (Lincoln: University of Nebraska Press, 1993); Lars G. Warme, ed., *A History of Swedish Literature* (Lincoln: University of Nebraska Press, 1996); and George C. Schoolfield, ed., *A History of Finland's Literature* (Lincoln: University of Nebraska Press, 1998).

13. This chapter's section on children's literature is written by Tom DuBois.

14. The poor translation is the first one rendered in English. See Hans Christian Andersen, *Tales,* trans. Charles Bonner (London: Grant and Griffith, 1848), 272. The accurate translation is taken from *Hans Christian Andersen's Fairy Tales,* ed. Jackie Wullschlager, trans. Tiina Nunnally (New York: Viking Books, 2004), 5. In that volume, Nunnally's "Translator's Note" (xlix–liv) discusses the task of translating Andersen's texts. See the same issue discussed in *Tales and Stories by Hans Christian Andersen,* trans. Patricia L. Conroy and Sven H. Rossel (Seattle: University of Washington Press, 1980), "Translators' Preface," ix–xiii.

15. *Hans Christian Andersen's Fairy Tales,* 223–34; *The Shadow and Other Tales,* ed. Niels Ingwersen (Madison: Wisconsin Introductions to Scandinavia, 1982), 21–33; *The Annotated Hans Christian Andersen,* ed. Maria Tatar (New York: W.W. Norton, 2008), 263–79.

16. Susan Hardy Aiken, *Isak Dinesen and the Engendering of Narrative* (Chicago: University of Chicago Press, 1990), xxiv.

17. Elias Bredsdorff, "Isak Dinesen v. Karen Blixen," *Facets of European Modernism,* ed. Janet Garton (Norwich, UK: University of East Anglia, 1985), 292.

18. Isak Dinesen, *Winter's Tales* (New York: Vintage Books, 1991), 124.

19. Susan C. Brantly, *Understanding Isak Dinesen* (Columbia, SC: University of South Carolina Press, 2002), 184–85. Most significant linguistic differences between Dinesen's English and Danish texts have been pointed out in this study.

20. Per Petterson, *Out Stealing Horses,* trans. Anne Born (Saint Paul, MN: Graywolf Press, 2007), 155.

POWER STRUGGLES

Translations from South Asia:
The Power of Babel

Christi A. Merrill

South Asia's historical multilinguality has become synonymous with ethnic diversity, making linguistic identity an integral part of ethnic identity in the twentieth century's nationalist struggles. As a result, linguistic identity has become as much of a cause for violent division and a rallying call for unity as religious identification has. Today, for example, we see ongoing civil war between Sinhalese speakers and Tamil speakers in Sri Lanka. In the 1970s, the resentment of the Bengali-speaking population of East Pakistan toward Urdu as the national language led in part to the formation of a separate Bengali-speaking state, Bangladesh. Before then, the region's newfound independence from the British empire resulted not only in the formation of two separate nation-states—Pakistan and India—in 1947, but also in the institutionalization of two separate national languages, Urdu and Hindi, written in scripts associated with Arabic and Sanskrit, respectively.

In the decades leading up to independence and partition, it was not clear that Urdu and Hindi should be considered separate, and nationalist leaders such as Mohandas K. Gandhi urged for the adoption of a less sectarian language called Hindustani. Gandhi wanted Hindustani to be written in the more neutral roman letters that did not declare a division between an Islamicized Urdu and a Hinduized Hindi. Even if this impossible compromise could have been worked out, nationalist leaders also had to contend with the fact that speakers of Dravidian languages, such as Tamil, in southern India felt alienated by the prospect of designating an Indo-Aryan language to represent the diversity of Indian speakers. Leaders decided in the end to promote Hindi as the national language in gradual increments but to recognize Tamil, English, Urdu, and eleven other viable idioms as official languages of India. In the intervening years of much contentious struggle, eight languages have been added to the number recognized by the Indian constitution. In practice, however, English has continued to be the de facto language of governance and business for the elite in many South Asian countries, serving to bridge linguistic gaps both intranationally as well as internationally among the many languages in use in South Asia.

Rather than bemoaning such a situation, many scholars and activists see such daily acts of translation as an opportunity to rethink the terms of such exchanges. G. N. Devy argues that the subcontinent's long-standing multi-linguality promotes what he calls a "translating consciousness" that allows individual speakers to maintain fluid boundaries among the various formal language systems in which they are fluent, and thus to move easily from one register or dialect to another without signaling the move as a transgression of fixed linguistic categories (135). Meenakshi Mukherjee likewise suggests that "translations have always been a vital part of Indian literary culture even when the word 'translation' or any of its Indian language equivalents— *anuvad, tarjuma, bhashantar,* or *vivartanam*—were not evoked to describe the activity.... Translations, adaptations, abridgements and recreations were overlapping activities and it was not considered important to mark their separate jurisdictions" (187). Both Mukherjee and Devy insist that tradition-ally, such works have not been judged on their ability to replicate a prior text; instead, in Devy's words, they were evaluated on the basis of their "capacity to transform, to translate, to restate, to revitalize the original" (147). At its best, such an approach promotes a flexible heterogeneity that might serve as a model for challenging us to rethink the ways we demarcate difference in the rhetoric of nationalist-minded or even globalized identitarian politics.

For a theorist such as Tejaswini Niranjana, the issue is not the relationship of the original to its derivative per se but rather the hierarchies of relation that are part of the received rhetoric of translation in English. She is especially criti-cal of translation projects that apply such an approach in order to "fix" South Asian literature to make it seem derivative of European examples, therefore depicting South Asian culture as chronically lagging behind. While the his-tory of translation into English is rife with images of the translator slavishly following in the footsteps of the author, the hierarchical implications of such spatialized imagery is especially potent in the context of relations between European and South Asian cultures. Niranjana, like so many theorists of postcoloniality, cites Thomas Macauley's infamous 1835 "Minute on Indian Education" that was part of the debate about the official language of administration and instruction in the Indian colony, in which Macauley insisted that he could find not a single Orientalist "who could deny that a single shelf of a good European library was worth the whole native literature of India and Arabia" (31). Until that time, Persian had remained the official language of administration, as it had been since the rise to power of the Mughal empire. The assumption by Macauley and other British administrators was that one imperial language must replace another, and because there was no single indigenous South Asian language worthy of being designated as hegemonic, English had to be used.

James Joyce's modernist, multilingual experiments in *Finnegan's Wake* prove that savvy readers recognize the aesthetic and political power of such mixing, as does Salman Rushdie's postmodern mixing of Hindustani with his English prose. It is the assumption of monolinguality, and its implicit post-lapsarian, post-fall-of-the-Tower-of-Babel fear of multilinguality, that Devy in particular is resisting with his call for "translating consciousness." While Niranjana urges a strategy of reading translation that challenges the implicit Hegelian conception of history based on a teleological, hierarchical model of civilization, Devy's proposition offers a means for rethinking the postlapsarian narratives written into our approaches to multilinguality today.

In their introduction to *Postcolonial Translation: Theory and Practice*, Susan Bassnett and Harish Trivedi likewise argue for a new approach to the reading of translated literature, one that accounts for what they see as "the asymmetrical power relationship between the various local 'vernaculars' (i.e. the language of the slaves, etymologically speaking) and the one master-language of our post-colonial world, English" (13). They use as an example Tulsi Das (1523–1623), regarded as "the greatest poet ever in Hindi for having (re-)written" Valmiki's Sanskrit *Ramayana*, to challenge our own assumptions about what is valuable in translated work (10). They claim that Tulsi Das's *Ramcaritmanas* rates as highly in Hindi as "Shakespeare and the Authorised Version of the Bible put together in English"; thus, this work of recreation succeeded in releasing the epic from "the monopolistic custody of Sanskrit pundits" and therefore in conferring a new status onto the vernacular itself (10). (See Lutgendorf's English version, for one example.) Translation in this context must be understood as a strategy for renegotiating political power between the languages involved. Sujit Mukherjee goes so far as to suggest that "almost every one of the new (or modern) Indo-Aryan languages which emerged between the tenth and fifteenth centuries tested its new-found prowess at a crucial stage of its development by translating and adapting the *Mahabharata* and the *Ramayana*" (126).

Sheldon Pollock has argued that these reworkings of Sanskrit epics into local languages across South and South East Asia—from kingdoms in present-day Afghanistan to Indonesia, Sri Lanka to Cambodia—"gave voice to imperial politics not as an actual, material force, but as an aesthetic practice" in a thriving premodern cultural economy he has called "the Sanskrit cosmopolis" (15). He suggests that the relationship between vernacular and cosmopolitan language was mutually dependent—the local languages invoked Sanskrit's status through its "poetry of politics," and Sanskrit in turn was transformed and renewed through these various translations—which thus challenges European-based accounts of the adversarial relationship between classical and vernacular languages. In Pollock's version of the history of the Sanskrit cosmopolis, a text such as the *Ramayana* cannot be said to exist primarily in a single, timeless form but must instead be understood as a series of ongoing conversations that make preceding versions relevant to local, contemporary concerns. Paula Richman's edited volume, *Many Ramayanas: The Diversity of a Narrative Tradition in South Asia,* makes this point with particular eloquence and in rigorous detail: essays by scholars such as A. K. Ramanujan, V. Narayana Rao, and Clinton Seeley show how contemporary versions in Tamil, Telugu, or Bengali might focus on scenes depicting the unfair treatment of women in the epic or offer a more complex and even sympathetic portrait of the villain, Ravana, who fights Rama. The volume offers a more complex scholarly approach to reading a multilingual, multiform text such as the *Ramayana* and allows us to think about the connections between translating and storytelling.

Significantly, one of the common Sanskrit-based words for translation, *anuvad,* might be rendered as "telling in turn." In contrast with the spatial imagery of *trans-latus* as a carrying across, figuring translation as a telling allows us to engage critically with a text as it is performed in many times and places. Rather than comparing the translation to a single original figured as central and authoritative, reading the translated work as a telling should allow readers to pay more attention to the political tensions being reflected in any of a number of versions—concerns with caste discrimination in Tulsi Das's *Ramcaritmanas,* for example, or issues of gender inequities in the oral Telugu tales Rao refers to in his essay in Richman's volume.

The *Ramayana* is but one example. Romila Thapar has traced the process of retelling to particularly vivid effect in a monograph comparing versions of the story of Shakuntala as it appears in various forms over the millennia, from an appearance in the grand epic, the *Mahabharata,* just before the common era, to a fully realized treatment in a courtly drama from the fourth century. The story tells of a king who falls in love with a semi-immortal beauty while wandering in the forest on a hunting trip. Shakuntala has been left in the care of an elderly ascetic to be raised in his hermitage, but in her guilelessness she is soon convinced to agree to a temporary marriage with the king. A year later, when she presents the offspring of this happy idyll before King Duhshanta at court, he claims not to recognize her. Thapar makes clear how historical attitudes toward women and nature influence the setting of the narrative as much as the generic framing. In the version in the *Mahabharata,* for instance, the tale is told within a larger narrative to show that even a figure as powerful as a king might be taught a lesson: after humiliating her by accusing her of "speaking like a whore" (in the translation by J. A. B. van Buitenen, which Thapar includes) (31), a disembodied voice warns him in the end not to abandon the seed he planted in her womb, for "Shakuntala has spoken the truth" (33). Thapar then goes on to show how the celebrated dramatist Kalidas enhanced the tension between the characters arising from the difference in their social stations, by having the various characters speak in different languages (as was the tradition in courtly the-ater): the male, high-caste men speak in Sanskrit (literally "well-wrought" or "artificial"), while the women and low-caste members of the cast speak in Prakrit ("natural"). Although Thapar never uses Devy's phrase, "translat-ing consciousness," she makes clear that in Kalidas's version, "language is a marker of status and identity," and the expectation was that an educated person had command of a number of languages; elite Sanskrit speakers of that time were assumed to be conversant in the local idiom (Prakrit) as well as the cosmopolitan language (78–79). She includes Barbara Stoler Miller's translation of Kalidas's play into English in its entirely to show how we might read the text closely to understand historical tensions in gender and class hierarchies, even when we read an English translation that cannot convey a similar effect of multilinguality. Rather than being seen as a sign of chaotic backwardness, multilinguality is a sign of power and learning. In subsequent chapters Thapar makes such a lesson more pointed by warning that these many adaptations "take on another dimension when one form is singled out as representative" (196), as when in 1789 the British Orientalist William Jones rendered Kalidas's play into a cloyingly elitist version in a bid to (in Thapar's words) "understand the high culture of the colony which they were governing, to better control it" (198). These comparisons invite English speakers to consider the limitations of a monolingual tradition that is ill-equipped to represent the complex tension between the Sanskrit and Prakrit elements of this literary work, for example.

A more contemporary text that contends with these issues of multilinguality is Saadat Hasan Manto's exceedingly popular 1953 Urdu short story, "Toba Tek Singh." The story takes place just after the violent partition of the subcontinent into the separate nations of India and Pakistan in 1947. The story features a Sikh man named Bishen Singh, who is so traumatized by the event that he dwells in an insane asylum in Pakistan, unable to understand why his homeland is suddenly divided and his home in former India is now in Pakistan and thus can no longer be his home. Significantly, Singh can only mumble a mixture of Hindustani, Panjabi, and English, in phrases so jumbled they all sound like "gibberish" or "babble" (depending on whose translation you read). Thus, the very effort to divide one language from another forces readers to consider the effect of dividing India and Pakistan. At the same time, the way each of the English-language translators handles this "babble" allows readers to think more self-consciously about demands for a monolinguality that banishes all other languages from one's domain. That is, the various translations of "Toba Tek Singh"—by Haldane, Hassan, Naqvi, Trivedi, Assaduddin, Murphy, Pritchett, and others—help English-language readers think about the ways in which this story's babble challenges fall-of-the-Tower-of-Babel narratives written into our own literary histories of translated material. Why do we expect to understand every word of a translation? Does a word-for-word translation of nonsense help us make sense of a situation that makes no sense? Even the line between common sense and nonsense is called into question in this story.

In the introduction to the Katha Press volume *Translating Partition*, Ravikant and Tarun K. Saint write that the story deploys the motif of madness subversively so as to invert "the wide ranging consensus about the Partition as an outbreak of collective madness," which sees such an event as exceptional. The story then leads readers to question "the consequent and facile exculpation of blame for the Partition" (xvi). Their volume brings together an interesting range of translated fiction, critical commentaries on the stories, and insightful overviews of the historical event of partition, making it eminently usable in an undergraduate English-language classroom—whether in Asia, Africa,

America, or Europe. For instance, M. Asaduddin's elegant version of "Toba Tek Singh" subtly calls into question the simplistic binaries that trap translation projects as inevitably as the protagonist of "Toba Tek Singh" is trapped in the no-man's land between India and Pakistan. Asaduddin's narrator does not name Bishen Singh's talk as babble or make any effort to simplify the confusing multilinguality; rather, the mix of languages is allowed to speak for itself in an English that tests fixed borders: "If they asked him anything, he would either stay silent, or sometimes blurt out, 'Opar di gurgur di annexe di bay dhiana di mung di daal of the laltain'" (67). Such a strategy works to call into question the very limits we as readers might unconsciously set for English. As with many of the translations published by Katha, Asaduddin's writing creates a vital, viable South Asian English and in the process announces a new relationship between English and the South Asian vernaculars—a relationship that sees the two linguistic traditions as mutually enhancing.

Not only in *Translating Partition*—one of Katha's series of classroom texts—but in all the press's publications, Katha writers and editors distinguish themselves as being particularly attentive to the ideological import of their smallest stylistic choices. Since its founding in 1988, Katha has brought together scholars (such as G. N. Devy), creative writers, translators (such as M. Asaduddin), editors, primary and secondary school teachers, and social activists committed to combining community activism and literary translation to link South Asia's diverse storytelling cultures across languages. Katha (literally "story") began with the founding of a prize for the best stories in each of the regional languages of India. Each year the winning stories are translated into English and collected in a volume titled *Katha Prize Stories,* with the aim of promoting domestic appreciation of Indian literature across language barriers. Remarkably, the organization equally recognizes the achievements of both the stories' authors and their translators. With each Katha prize, for example, both author and translator are honored in the annual ceremony in Delhi, and both are invited to take part in the ongoing work of Katha. The organization has thus put itself at the center of a vibrant cultural community working for social change in a region that in the past decade has moved beyond its national borders, and has extended across media as well. Besides an innovative publishing arm and a National Institute of Translation, Katha also runs adult learning centers, children's learning centers, schools on wheels, teacher training programs, two magazines for children, and a cable television network. (For their latest projects, see Katha's Web site: www.katha.org.) These efforts are intended to minimize and even undermine the divisive violence associated with South Asia's fraught multilinguality, and thus to work toward a more complex unity based on an empowered translating consciousness.

WORKS CONSULTED

Bassnett, Susan, and Harish Trivedi, eds. *Postcolonial Translation: Theory and Practice.* London: Routledge, 1999.

Bhattacharya, Rimli and Geeta Dharmarajan, eds. *Katha Prize Stories.* Vol. 1. New Delhi: Katha, 1998.

Devy, G. N. *In Another Tongue: Essays on Indian English Literature.* Frankfurt, Germany: Peter Lang, 1993.

Lutgendorf, Philip, trans. "*Ramcaritmanas:* From Book Five. The Beautiful Book." In *The Norton Anthology of World Masterpieces,* edited by Maynard Mack, 1:2316–32. New York: W.W. Norton and Co., 1995.

Manto, Saadat Hasan. "Toba Tek Singh." Translated by Frances W. Pritchett. February 2005. http://www.columbia.edu/itc/mealac/pritchett/00urdu/tobateksingh/translation.html?.

———. "Toba Tek Singh." Translated by Harish Trivedi. In *Breakthrough: Modern Hindi and Urdu Short Stories,* edited by Sukrita Paul Kumar, 215–20. Shimla: Indian Institute of Advanced Studies, 1993.

———. "Toba Tek Singh." Translated by Jai Ratan. In *Modern Urdu Short Stories,* 22–27. New Delhi: Allied Publishing Ltd., 1987.

———. "Toba Tek Singh." Translated by Khalid Hasan. In *Kingdom's End and Other Stories,* 11–18. London and New York: Verso, 1987.

———. "Toba Tek Singh." Translated by Madan Gupta. In *Saadat Hasan Manto: Selected Stories,* 151–55. New Delhi: Cosmo Publications, 1997.

———. "Toba Tek Singh." Translated by M. Asaduddin. In *Translating Partition,* edited by Ravikant and Tarun K. Saint, 63–72. New Delhi: Katha Press, 2001.

———. "Toba Tek Singh." Translated by Richard McGill Murphy. *Words without Borders,* September 2003. http://wordswithoutborders.org/article/toba-tek-singh/.

———. "Toba Tek Singh." Translated by Robert B. Haldane. *Journal of South Asian Literature* 6 (1970): 20–23.

———. "Toba Tek Singh." Translated by Tahira Naqvi. In *Another Lonely Voice: The Life and Works of Saadat Hasan Manto,* 281–88. Lahore: Vanguard, 1985.

Mukherjee, Meenakshi. *The Perishable Empire: Essays on Indian Writing in English.* Delhi: Oxford University Press, 2000.

Mukherjee, Sujit. *Translation as Discovery.* Hyderabad: Orient Longman, 1994.

Niranjana, Tejaswini. *Siting Translation: History, Post-structuralism, and the Colonial Context.* Berkeley: University of California Press, 1992.

Pollock, Sheldon. "Cosmopolitan and Vernacular in History." *Public Culture* 12 (2000): 591–625.

Ravikant and Tarun K. Saint, eds. *Translating Partition.* New Delhi: Katha Press, 2001.

Richman, Paula, ed. *Many Ramayanas: The Diversity of a Narrative Tradition in South Asia.* Berkeley: University of California Press, 1991.

Thapar, Romila. *Śakuntalā: Texts, Readings, Histories.* Delhi: Kali for Women, 1999.

African Europhone Literature in Translation: Language, Pedagogy, and Power Differentials

Paul Bandia

African literature is channeled and received in the West mainly through translations. As a literature often grounded in languages and cultures without literary capital, it has made its way into the international literary space mainly through its writing and translation in global European languages. Vernacular-language writing is on the increase, enhanced by writing practices in more widespread, locally derived lingua francas such as Swahili and pidgins, but such writing is often destined for local consumption, and it relies heavily on translation to become known beyond its ethnic and linguistic boundaries. Circumscribed for the most part within the landscapes of its specific ethnic traditions, African literature has yet to gain the kind of international recognition enjoyed by its European-language counterpart. Hence, the reading and teaching of African literature in institutions of higher education across the world (including Africa, for that matter) is highly dependent upon translation. The significance of translation is compounded by the fact that even the creative writing of African literature in European languages has recourse to translation practices in representing African sociocultural realities and worldviews. Therefore, by its very nature, African literature cannot be fully understood without a reading and teaching practice that explores both the writing-as-translation strategies used by creative writers and the interlingual translation processes involved in the translating of intercultural writing from non-Western societies.

COMING TO AMERICA

To understand the significance of translation in the teaching of African literature in North America, a brief history of the emergence of this literature in American universities and the polemics concerned with its critical framework is in order. African literature made its way into the curricula of American universities as a consequence of the civil rights movement and the black studies movement, which thrived on campuses in the mid-1960s. There was a general outcry against the Eurocentric bias of university programs and a call for the representation of other cultural viewpoints, to reflect the diverse ethnocultural makeup of the university community and society at large. African literature was therefore typically introduced into American universities as part of various black studies programs, to meet the demands of African Americans who had expressed an increasing desire to explore the literary and cultural heritage of African Americans and the history of black people in general. Given the conditions of contestation under which African literature was adopted in American academia, and given the fact that African literature was appended to black studies programs, there was a need to make this literature available to American students in English (whether in original or translated versions), in order to reach a diverse population of students from a variety of disciplines. For ease of use, African anglophone literature was quickly adopted and was eventually followed by English translations of francophone and lusophone works.

The label "African literature" is increasingly becoming a misnomer, as it does not reflect the fact that African practices of writing in European languages vary according to colonial histories. Moreover, today there are many European-language translations of works initially written in indigenous or national languages. Although these works often gain recognition in global European languages, it has become common practice to emphasize their national character by using labels such as Nigerian, Senegalese, or Cameroonian literature. This balkanization of African literature reflects the deep-seated feeling that the cultures from which the writers draw their inspiration are clearly distinct and vary widely from one ethnolinguistic group or region to another. The splitting up of African literature along national lines makes it even more necessary to read it as translation, in order to highlight its specific national provenance. Through a reading-as-translation strategy, students will become aware of the differences in cultural background between a Nigerian novel and a Kenyan novel, for example, even though both novels are written in English.

When African literature entered American universities, it usually did not have a department of its own, so it was assigned to a variety of departments, often in minor or optional courses taken by students with some interest in

Africa. These courses were offered not only in literature programs but across a wide range of disciplines, such as economics, history, anthropology, sociology, fine arts, and the sciences. It quickly became obvious that for some, African literature was viewed not as literature but rather as a means to become familiar with African culture. This attitude was encouraged and sustained by literary critics and academics who approached African literary criticism from a mainly anthropological standpoint. For these Eurocentric critics and academics, African literature provided a window into an exotic, premodern world, giving them a glimpse of what their own world was like before modernity and the age of reason and rationalism. Through this literature, Africa became a sounding board for Western notions of reason, technological advancement, and civilization; issues of language, translation, and literary aesthetics were of secondary importance. Delivered in English translations or African English writing, the literature merely served as a way to satisfy the need for exotica.

Even when African literature began to gain respect as a legitimate discipline in the 1970s and 1980s, the debate was still raging over how to read African literature or practice its literary criticism. In the context of African literary criticism, the term "anthropology" had become a dirty word because of a new awareness of how colonial anthropologists had treated Africans and the realization that African literature had been exoticized in the West. African literary criticism became bogged down by endless debates about whether to establish separate criteria for judging African literature or whether to apply Western critical frameworks. At the core of this debate was the fact that the generalizability of Western theoretical criticism had been questioned, and the real issue was to ascertain the options left for a Western reader of non-Western literature. Could a Western reader "read the other, the African, as if from an authentically African point of view, interpreting Africa in African terms, perceiving rather than projecting?" (Miller 1).

TRANSLATING AFRICAN LITERATURE

The fascination of American critics and the general public with African literature in English, coupled with African literature's acceptance in university programs in the mid-1960s, led to more demands for this literature and gave rise to a small but vibrant publishing industry for English translations of African literature from other colonial languages. Given the political climate in which African literature was introduced in American universities, there was an urgent need to make the literature available to students and teachers, which included not only texts created and written originally in English but also English translations of some major texts originally written in European languages, particularly in French. Hence, by 1968 there were a great number of English translations of African novels in French. The irony is that even though African francophone fiction was generally seen as a poor cousin of metropolitan French literature (and was often subsumed under the label "French literature"), African francophone literature was often taught in English translations in order to reach a wider, more varied clientele. Even some Ph.D. theses consisted in carrying out annotated translations (sometimes with commentaries) of francophone novels into English (see Huannou). There was therefore an unavoidable presence of translation in the teaching of this foreign literature, which unfortunately was hardly acknowledged because of the monolingual practice of teaching foreign literatures in English as if they were original English-language texts.

TRANSLATION AS LITERARY CRITICISM

The issue of African literary criticism is directly related to the need to read works of African europhone literature as translations, or at least as transcultural texts, rather than monolingual English-language texts. A reading-as-translation approach would indeed enable Western readers to delve beyond superficial content-oriented reading and deep into those linguistic, cultural, and literary aesthetic qualities of the text that would allow one to perceive the text rather than project his or her Western sensitivities or preconceptions onto it. A reading-as-translation strategy would thus reveal facts about the linguistic innovations, oral artistry, cultural aesthetics, and historical contexts that inform African European-language fiction. This allows the Western student of African literature to see that there is more, for instance, to Chinua Achebe's *Things Fall Apart* than a nativist desire to reminisce on a pristine precolonial era, or to Ferdinand Oyono's *Houseboy* than a comic or burlesque interaction between a local indigenous servant and his European masters.

In the years following independence and decolonization, many African writers and critics voiced their concern about what they saw as a Eurocentric reading practice of their works. For instance, Chinua Achebe denounced the attitude of some Western critics who sometimes acted as if they had a better understanding of Africa than African writers did, and he advised Westerners to adopt some measure of humility "appropriate to [their] limited experience of the African world" (Achebe 1975, 6). Moreover, he further recommended that "the word *universal* [be] banned altogether from discussions of African literature until such time as people cease to use it as a synonym for the narrow, self-serving parochialism of Europe," with "Europe" here understood as including America (Achebe 1975, 6, 9). The francophone critic and novelist Jean-Pierre Makouta M'Boukou reprimanded those Western critics who refused to acknowledge the distance between themselves, their life-world, and African culture, and who would read African literature mainly from the standpoint of their own cultural context (9). Disappointed with Western critical readings of African literature, the Nobel laureate Wole Soyinka delivered this sobering comment: "We black Africans have been blandly invited to submit ourselves to a second epoch of colonisation—this time by a universal-humanoid abstraction defined and conducted by individuals whose theories and prescriptions are derived from the apprehension of *their* world and *their* history, *their* social neuroses and *their* value systems" (x). These comments and complaints reveal the power differentials involved in the reading and dissemination of African literature, particularly in the West, where there is a perception that African writers are mere producers of a raw material to be processed and refined by the more sophisticated Western critic, in much the same way that Africa has been a source of raw material for the more technologically advanced Euro-American industries.

Much time has passed since comments such as those cited above were made, and in the interim there has been a great deal of progress with respect to the reading and criticism of African literature. A general consensus has been reached that readers should be able to conceptualize Africa and its cultures by contextualizing African texts within an African critical framework. Western readers must therefore be willing to turn to models elaborated by Africans themselves for the reading of their literature. As Christopher Miller argued in the early 1990s, many works are now available to readers who want to inform themselves about such strategies, such as those by African critic and philosopher V. Y. Mudimbe. "All of the disciplines in the humanities are in the process of decolonization," Miller said, "and as the process moves forward, it becomes both possible and imperative for readers to supplant Eurocentrism with Afrocentrism, while remaining attentive to *eccentric* strategies that operate in new, overdetermined spaces" (3).

However, the fact that a fair amount of decolonizing has accompanied the reading of African literature in American schools in recent times—due in part to the availability of abundant critical material produced by African critics and scholars, the presence of many African academics and professors of African literature in American universities, and other "gatekeepers" such as the African Literature Association—does not diminish the gravity or seriousness of the power struggles involved. Witness the continued practice of presenting African literature to generations of American students as original, monolingual English texts rather than as translations from a source African language and culture or from another European colonial language. For example, how can francophone literature be taught in English in a way that accounts for its literary qualities without dwelling on the fact of translation? The fundamental differences between francophone and anglophone African literature have been established (see Gérard), and although writers from both linguistic persuasions often depend on a similar oral narrative tradition for their inspiration, the role of translation at the two interfaces—namely orality-writing and French-English—must be explored in order to highlight the specific character of francophone literature in English translation and to ensure a more complete and representative act of reading.

In his quest for a responsible reading of African literature by Westerners, Miller falls back—courageously, I might add—on anthropology. He bases his hypothesis on the belief that Westerners simply do not know enough about Africa, and "no responsible Western reading of African literature can take place in the vacuum of a 'direct' and unmediated relationship with the text" (4). In his view, "What the literary text says is necessary but not sufficient; other texts must be brought into the dialogical exercise of a good reading" (4). Bringing other texts to bear on the reading process calls for a dialogical exercise that places the non-Western text within its historical, sociological, political, and anthropological context. This allows for a hybrid approach that takes into account the complexity of cultural issues in the foreign text and their translations into Western language. Although this dialogical approach deals generally with the process of reading non-Western texts, it can be appropriated to address the specific issues constellated by reading these texts as English translations grounded in non-Western cultures and linguistic practices. The framework is reminiscent of the basic instructions or guidelines for any literary or cultural translation activity. Any translator worthy of the title knows that texts must be contextualized in terms of their historical, political, and cultural background before an adequate linguistic transfer can be achieved. Emily Apter has suggested that translation studies be viewed as providing a new approach to comparative literary criticism. In a similar way, Western critics of African or non-Western literature might well look to recent developments in translation studies, especially postcolonial translation theory, to enhance their critical framework with a translation dimension.

African texts make reading-as-translation necessary, but they also help with that process by the use of paratextual devices and other interpretive cues that impose a kind of sight-translation activity upon the reader. In other words, the non-African reader is bound to engage in a kind of mental translation process as he or she reads along. Furthermore, it should be said that some of the culture-specific information in the novels may not be accessible to African readers who may not be from the author's ethnolinguistic group. This leads one to believe that there is already a translation process going on in the crafting of the African novel, which a reading-as-translation approach should bring out in the teaching of this literature. Kwame Anthony Appiah has referred to the use of paratextual strategies as "thick translation" (817), a term that highlights the kind of anthropological rhetoric that has always accompanied African creative writing. As readers cannot always be presumed to be local, various modes of address are used—such as footnotes, character-to-character explanations, parentheses, and interlinear translation of vernacular language items—to provide the necessary cultural information to a reader presumed to be alien to the author's world. As Miller argues convincingly, the ideas of "difference" and "otherness" are always present in African europhone literature. He states, "Every time an author uses a phrase like 'here in Africa,' a *non-Africa* is revealed to be at play in the writing and reading process. A degree of 'otherness' is inscribed in any text which addresses itself to a world that is construed as outside" (6). Texts are therefore nothing if not "inscribed" and are inevitably affected by their historical and cultural situation, Miller says, making difference and otherness inescapable armatures of reading and writing (10).

Although I have argued elsewhere that "thick translation" as a writing device could prove detrimental or cumbersome to the reading process and could turn African literature into anthropological or exotic artifacts (Bandia 2006), this strategy may seem rather useful as a way to force the reading of African literary texts as translation. Using such anthropological rhetorical devices in a classroom in order to unearth the necessary cultural information can engage students in a kind of "pragmatic essentialism" (Spivak 186), whereby the reader-as-translator is called upon to pay particular attention to the language, oral artistry, and narrative aesthetics embedded in the cultural context of the literary text. "Thick translation" practice can therefore encourage the reading of African literature not merely as an original writing in a global language but rather as active or passive translations from an African narrative tradition. It is important to elucidate the relationship between colonial-language writing and its traditional antecedent; this can be achieved by exploring parallels between postcolonial writing and translation, which can indeed lead the reader to transparent translations of the African difference. It is productive to read the African past to understand its present. The African text can then be read on its own terms without projecting colonial-type anthropological otherness or difference onto it. Translated into political terms, such projections become "colonial *inscription*" (Miller 14) or "manifest Orientalism" (Said 206).

African writers have used numerous strategies to force the reader to apprehend the indigenous subtexts of their works and negotiate the tensions between African cultural aesthetics and European linguistic expression. These strategies, which often seek to overcome the impediments of expressing African sociocultural reality in alien colonial languages, enable the teacher of African europhone literature to draw the attention of the American student to the translated nature of this literature by revealing the tensions and plurilinguistic dimensions of the African text. Some authors practice literary heteroglossia or hybridity by deliberately writing in indigenous languages or other locally derived vernaculars within the European-language text. In Achebe's *Things Fall Apart,* when a character says, "He is Okonkwo *kpom-kwem,* exact, perfect" (227), the reader can surmise that the Ibo expression *kpom-kwem* means "exact" or "perfect." Achebe uses an interlinear translation strategy to explain the Ibo expression for the benefit of the non-Ibo reader. Yet, in addition to its aesthetic value, the Ibo expression calls the reader's attention to the fact of translation by evoking the overall language culture that informs Achebe's English-language fiction. There are also several statements or expressions written in what seems to be standard English but which can only be understood in terms of the related African culture.

In Gabriel Okara's novel *The Voice,* which he claims to have crafted through a deliberate literal translation process from his native Ijaw language, characters bid each other goodnight with the statement "may we live to see tomorrow" (51), echoing a bygone era when it was dangerous to travel at night for fear of wild animals. To grasp the full meaning of such a culture-specific expression, it should be understood as a translation from an alien culture into the English-language novel. This also holds true for expressions such as "her husband's senior wife" (Achebe 1958, 123), which alludes to the practice of polygamy, and "to be found at home" (Achebe 1958, 122), an expression translated from the Ibo that refers to a young bride who has been proven a virgin on her wedding night. The cultural specificity of these expressions, as well as many other aesthetic devices used by African writers, point to the need to highlight the role played by translation in the writing of European-language fiction. Instructors must be aware of this link between translation and intercultural writing if they hope to uncover the full range of signification in the African literary text.

Teaching Ferdinand Oyono's *Houseboy* in English can be particularly tricky from a linguistic standpoint, as it is an English translation of a French original, which sometimes represents discourses from indigenous languages or other locally derived vernaculars. These native expressions undergo a double transposition process as they are first captured in French and then translated into English. The reader of the English version of the novel should be made aware of the translational itinerary of some African dialectal forms, which have been transposed into French and then into English. For instance, in *Houseboy* one of the illiterate characters makes the following statement: "Man . . . Panther-Eye beat like Gullet. Him kick me bam! Go like dynamite. Panther-Eye no joke" (25). This statement was originally written in French by Oyono (in *Une vie de boy*) in what he describes as "*français petit nègre*" (broken French): "Movié (mon vieux! en petit nègre!)! Zeuil-de-Panthère cogner comme Gosier-d'Oiseau! Lui donner moi coup de pied qui en a fait comme soufat'soud. . . . Zeuil y en a pas rire" (40). Oyono's attempt to capture the illiterate character's approximate French is meant to enhance the humor of the novel, which can only be fully apprehended in its French colonial context. The English translation fails to reflect this historical reality; it is merely the translator's own creation of what he assumes to be the English equivalent of broken French. While the French vernacular mimics the basic French spoken by an illiterate in colonial Africa, the English translation does not. In fact, the "broken English" used here is not recognizable as African and does not resemble any form of nonstandard English used in West Africa, including pidgin English. The reader of *Houseboy* must therefore be made aware of the translational trajectory of the novel in order to appreciate the author's deliberate practice of literary heteroglossia to achieve humor. The movement of language from the popular French spoken by the natives via Oyono's rendition in fiction into its English version can only be revealed through a reading-as-translation process.

READING BETWEEN THE LINES:
THE LANGUAGE OF AFRICAN LITERATURE

Besides the social and political reasons behind the emergence of African literature in North America, it can also be argued that interest in African literature might have developed out of sheer intellectual curiosity for an alien or remote language culture. Unlike European colonial powers such as Great Britain, France, and Portugal, the United States never had colonies in Africa. This fact, coupled with an element of geographical distance, must have piqued American intellectual curiosity for the African continent to such an extent that this curiosity could not be assuaged by the presence in America of people of African heritage brought to this continent as slaves. From a cultural standpoint, Africa remained an enigma, a distant otherness, more so for Americans than for the European subjects of former colonial powers. African literature thus became for some a means to grasp the heart and soul of Africa, to under-stand the continent's social, cultural, and political realities. This intellectual curiosity was also attributable to a desire for difference or an anthropological otherness, a movement away from a familiar literary discourse and toward a different literary ecology, which often led to an excessive reading of exotica in the literature. A major area of curiosity for the American intellectual was the African writer's seemingly exotic use of the colonial language.

Language use is a major factor in defining African europhone literature and should therefore draw considerable attention in the reading process. I have argued elsewhere (Bandia 1993, 1996) that the African writer's peculiar use of the European language can be attributed to the writing of orality, either consciously or unconsciously, as a form of translating from a real or imaginary "metatext of culture" (Tymoczko 24). This fact must be accounted for in any reading of African literature, which implies a kind of back-translation if the reader wants to decipher the linguistic innovations practiced by the African writer. Hence, translation again becomes part of the reading process in order to highlight the fact that the African writer's apparent non-Western use of the colonial language is heavily grounded in the oral narrative tradition.

Furthermore, literary heteroglossia and plurilingualism are part and par-cel of postcolonial writing, even if the literature is expressed in a dominant global language like English. Besides reflecting the multilingual experience of postcolonial writers, plurilingual writing is also a way for these authors to assert their identities and resist the hegemony of the dominant Western language. The coexistence in postcolonial writing of indigenous languages, locally derived hybrid forms such as pidgins and creoles, and the colonial language points to an unequal, diglossic relationship between the dominant colonial language and the other languages in the text. Postcolonial writers often use devices such as translation, paraphrase, gloss, footnotes, and explanation to reveal the message conveyed by these "minor" languages to the reader of the dominant language. This dimension of resistance and subversion in postcolonial plurilingual writing has been explored by many critics who point to a counterhegemonic discourse with the imperial or colonial language. For instance, in her reading of the north African francophone novel, Samia Mehrez points out that the plurilingual practice that brings together different symbolic representations of the colonizing and the colonized world in the postcolonial text calls for a more global or pluralistic reading practice that goes beyond the usual normative reading of monolingual literature. In her view, "So long as the institutions that form the reader have not changed, the works of francophone North African writers will resist and defy colonial and imperialist monolingualism which continues to believe that it can read the world through its own dominant language" (136–37).

Therefore, teaching or reading such postcolonial texts in English (or French, for that matter) as if they were written exclusively in the global language may overlook the tensions inherent to the heteroglossia at work in the text. Studying them as translated texts is likely to reveal these tensions and show how the reading of such texts involves a constant movement between languages in order to piece together the cultural information necessary to understand them not as simple language games but as aesthetic forms of resistance and contestation.

The writing of national literatures in nonindigenous languages, as African writers have done, has moved the issue of multilingualism in literature to the forefront of contemporary literary criticism. There has been a growing interest in the relation between literary criticism and cultural history, and the expansion of fields such as cultural studies have drawn attention to issues of transnationalism and transculturality. These developments make it even more necessary to read foreign texts as "foreign," or as translations, to avoid unnecessary domesticating through projections onto the Other or self-reflexivity.

WORKS CITED

Achebe, Chinua. *Arrow of God*. London: Heinemann, 1964.

―――. "Colonialist Criticism." In *Morning Yet on Creation Day*, 3–18. London: Heinemann, 1975.

―――. *Things Fall Apart*. London: Heinemann, 1958.

Appiah, Kwame Anthony. "Thick Translation." *Callaloo* 16 (1993): 808–19.

Apter, Emily. *The Translation Zone: A New Comparative Literature*. Princeton, NJ: Princeton University Press, 2006.

Bandia, Paul. "African Europhone Literature and Writing as Translation: Some Ethical Issues." In *Translating Others*, edited by Theo Hermans, 1:349–62. Manchester, UK: St. Jerome Publishing, 2006.

―――. "Code-Switching and Code-Mixing in African Creative Writing: Some Insights for Translation Studies." *TTR* 9 (1996): 139–54.

―――. "Translation as Culture Transfer: Evidence from African Creative Writing." *TTR* 6 (1993): 55–78.

Gérard, Albert S., ed. *European-Language Writing in Sub-Saharan Africa*. 2 vols. Budapest: Akadémiai Kiado, 1986.

Huannou, Adrien. *La critique et l'enseignement de la littérature africaine aux États-Unis d'Amérique*. Paris: Harmattan, 1993.

Makouta M'Boukou, Jean-Pierre. *Introduction à l'étude du roman négro-africain de langue française*. Abidjan: Les nouvelles Editions Africaines, 1980.

Mehrez, Samia. "Translation and the Postcolonial Experience: The Francophone North African Text." In *Rethinking Translation*, edited by Lawrence Venuti, 120–38. London: Routledge, 1992.

Miller, Christopher. *Theories of African Francophone Literature and Anthropology in Africa*. Chicago: University of Chicago Press, 1990.

Okara, Gabriel. *The Voice*. London: Heinemann, 1964.

Oyono, Ferdinand. *Houseboy*. London: Heinemann, 1966.

―――. *Une vie de boy*. Paris: Julliard, 1956.

Said, Edward W. *Orientalism*. New York: Random House, 1979.

Soyinka, Wole. *Myth, Literature and the African World*. Cambridge, UK: Cambridge University Press, 1976.

Spivak, Gayatri Chakravorty. "The Politics of Translation." In *Outside in the Teaching Machine*, edited by Gayatri Chakravorty Spivak, 179–200. London: Routledge, 1993.

Tymoczko, Maria. "Post-colonial Writing and Literary Translation." In *Post-colonial Translation: Theory and Practice*, edited by Susan Bassnett and Harish Trivedi, 19–40. London: Routledge, 1999.

The North-South Translation Border: Transnationality in the New South American Writing

Kelly Washbourne

Llegamos a pensar que América Latina era un invento de los departa-
mentos de español de las universidades norteamericanas. (We wound
up believing that Latin America had been dreamed up by the Spanish
departments of North American universities.)
Alberto Fuguet and Sergio Gómez

A transnational, "migrant" knowledge of the world
is most urgently needed.
Homi Bhabha

Write for a stranger born in a distant country
hundreds of years from now.
Mary Oliver

To what extent can a transnational writer be said to represent his or her
country? Are notions of representation and national identity in literature
giving way to aesthetic "islands" that transcend nationhood? What role,
whether hegemonic or counterhegemonic, does translation perform in an era
of globalized, intercultural identities, particularly because strict nationalisms
framed much of our current thinking about the craft? The reexamination
of the canon of magical realist writers by two contemporary younger generations of writers (the so-called "McOndo" and "Crack" groups) who are
gaining entrée into the academy and into English translation, often embrac-
ing United States values and effacing or complicating their national origins,
prompts these questions and more. Let us briefly consider these issues for

thé classroom. We will proceed through translation's part in the acquisition and containment mechanisms of the border; the advent, continuity and resistance of the Crack and McOndo groups; changing demographics and their implications for publication practices; language politics and the redrawn maps of center and margin in North American Spanish-language writings and their translations; the reception of these young generations; national and international (transnational) writers' "translatability" and subject matter; and, finally, a meditation on reading in translation.

Delisle and Woodsworth note that "one of the oldest meanings of translation is 'to pass contraband'" (222), a violation of borders. An agency of this "borderland," translation selectively polices the inflow or outflow, volume, and type of narratives on offer. Mignolo and Schiwy (23) have taken to calling this *translanguaging*, the "border thinking" that breaks with the equation of language with nation, and they argue that a transnational English can become the vehicle for subalternity (22). Recent works such as Silva Gruesz's *Ambassadors of Culture: The Transamerican Origins of Latino Writing* are questioning monolithic views of literary history, while Bakhtin had already challenged the conceptual nationality of the novel, claiming that national languages are "interanimated"; thus, notions of nation and canon, as Cohen and Dever observe, are made problematic as well: "From a Bakhtinian perspective, it is simultaneously perverse and yet understandable that a novel would signify the coherence of national identity; it is a genre that dwells at borders whose policing is crucial to the nationalist project" (6). The border is the symbol of the reductive politics of imagining the Third World, whereby "the nearer the border, the more anxious the containment and policing of cultural representativity becomes" (Molloy 194). Historically, all too often it was those Spanish American works that conformed to restrictive preconceptions that were admitted into English; thus, ironically, translation rendered works accessible only to distance them as folkloristic amusements. Molloy's criticism of the consumption of magical realism as partaking of "a regional, ethnicized commodity, a form of . . . essentialized primitivism," and ultimately as a mode of representation, not production (195), is telling.

In the context of this border crossing and policing, a few recent developments in literary production, distribution, and reception should be borne in mind. Resistance to reader expectations of myth and magic has risen among Spanish-language writers in this hemisphere in the wake of the Boom, most programmatically among the McOndo and Crack groups. These are loose affiliations of writers born, for the most part, in the 1960s. Alberto Fuguet, Edmundo Paz Soldán, and Sergio Gómez are often associated with McOndo; Mexican writers Jorge Volpi, Pedro Angel Palou, Eloy Urroz, Cristina Rivera Garza, and Ignacio Padilla, with Crack, whose name plays on the Boom. Both groups are more imbued with a mass-media savviness and alternate literacies than with an exclusively "high-culture" literary tradition. The McOndo group—whose name (in)famously embraces the multiple signifiers of condos, McDonald's, and Macintosh, while making sport of García Márquez's fabulous Macondo—is abandoning strict geographies of north and south, English and Spanish, in forming identity. Heirs to Manuel Puig, McOndo has embraced "pop culture, rock, movies from the 1980s and other audiovisual forms, and bourgeois rituals of the 1990s" as their cultural imaginary (Amar Sánchez, "Literature in the Margins"). Crack, for its part, has expressed a devotion to transcending the frivolity of certain recent Spanish American works and to contributing not only to the Mexican tradition but to world literature (Carbajal 123). Their mass-culture orientation may be part of what despatializes these writers' narratives. For them, the inhabited/imagined city is, as Amar Sánchez contends, a nonplace: "Cable has replaced the city. Nothing can be seen or imagined in the city unless it is *through* a mediating form" ("Deserted Cities" 213). They thus are twice translating across different signifying systems: re-mediating a mediated worldview. In Edmundo Paz Soldán's view, critics' contentions that the young writers are not Spanish American enough ring false: "We, according to them, are not authentic Latin American writers, since we are so sold-out to American popular culture. The problem, however, is that it is getting increasingly hard to define what is authentically Latin American; we reject any sort of essentialist claim." Paz Soldán disconnects the contemporary Latin American writer from the long-assumed role of spokesperson for nation, for local reality. In this conception, then, as Michael Cronin has described, the contemporary writer becomes a universal *flâneur;* in a word, a *translator* (141–45).

A representative collection of the new writing in this vein now being taught and read is *A Whistler in the Nightworld: Short Fiction from the Latin Americas* (the imaginational plural is instructive: physical geography moves to the second order of importance). Editor Thomas Colchie notes (xvii) that U.S. publishers are now more willing to bring out works in both English and Spanish. This in fact happened with the simultaneous release of Fuguet's *Las películas de mi vida* and *The Movies of My Life* at HarperCollins. Other works of fiction have even begun appearing in single-volume bilingual format, notably in the Vintage Español imprint. Publishing houses in the United States—such as Planeta Editores, which has produced many streetwise novels from Colombia's new writers—are *not translating* and yet, or thereby, they are finding a large audience in Spanish in the United States. Demographics—a burgeoning Spanish-speaking population, including U.S. writers writing in Spanish and what Mike Davis in his book *Magical Urbanism* calls the "Latin Americanization" of the populace—in some measure is moving nontranslated works into the space where once only translations existed to expand readership (and a critical mass of readership is almost an obligatory stop to academic canonization).

The demographic growth of Spanish-preferring bilinguals coincides with a parallel phenomenon—the U.S. Latino/a writer who chooses English and relegates Spanish to an "ornamental role," a mere "token of cultural filiation," in Perez Firmat's phrasing (141). This same author recounts that "the ranks of crossover writers have even swelled with bilingual Latin Americans who have switched to English . . . in search of larger audiences. Some recent Latin American novels—Carlos Fuentes's *Gringo viejo* (1986) comes to mind—read as if they had been written to be translated. Like that of *House of Mist* [Maria Luisa Bombal's miscarried self-transcreation], the prose of *Gringo viejo* carries a foretaste of the English-language movie script it was destined to become." One wonders what will become of the erstwhile stigma of writing for translation within the new translational consciousness.

Bilingual "secret sharers," McOndo and Crack writers are breaking down the distances between U.S. academies and their home countries; many are professors here, and at least one—Eloy Urroz—was born in the United States. Padilla (Colchie xvii) marks this shift: "The current homeland of Latin American literature is literature itself." Fuguet calls this multinational fusion a "Free Trade Area of the Americas (FTAA) sensibility" ("Magical Neoliberalism" 68). The act of Englishing, then, to use the Romantics' vernacular, takes on a different air for works like Paz Soldán's *Turing's Delirium,* a Bolivian cyberthriller researched in English and centered on fictional antiglobalization hackers. In this work, one senses English not as a latent fluency just below the surface but as a *tension,* an international, technological dialect. Even a main character calques his Spanish and compulsively code-switches. In an interview with Paz Soldán, Claudia M. Milian Arias quotes a review of the writer's first translated work in English, *The Matter of Desire,* a reading that underscores the asymmetricality of this effect in translation: "[T]he multicultural nature of the world Paz Soldán portrays is more poignant in the Spanish version of the novel, in which some of the characters break into English phrases as they attempt to explain a concept, make a point or describe new technology. In this agile English translation, the bilingual world is accented in reverse, but the Spanish phrases sprinkled among the English don't work as well or ring as genuine" (Milian Arias 144).

Thus we begin to suspect that it is the uneasy coexistence of two languages, two cultures, and two traditions that provides the most teachable instances of these generations' writings in the classroom. Works in this vein make problematic Evan-Zohar's well-known contention that marginal literatures need translation, while central ones do not, because the latter are part of the international canon (48); and, as we will see below, his idea that translations are selected due to vacuums in the target literary system becomes problematic as well. The McOndo group is dispersed and intercontinental, which poses a challenge to those who see the canon in the traditional terms of a stabilizing, shared consciousness. The realities of "center" and "margin" are shown to be far more complex to identify; Szegedy-Maszák (63) notes the displacement and potentially problematic and contingent appropriability inherent in any translation: "A work can realize its aesthetic potential within an interpretive community that shares its mother tongue with that work, taking the term mother tongue in a broad cultural and historical sense and granting that *communities are temporary, shifting, constantly embattled, disintegrating, multiple, and intersecting.* Translation means the canonicity of a work has been de(con)structed" (emphasis mine).

Let us consider an example: Cristina Garcia's *Bordering Fires: The Vintage Book of Contemporary Mexican and Chicano/a Literature* (Random House, 2006; forthcoming in Spanish). This collection juxtaposes Mexican writer Xavier Villaurrutia writing about the United States ("L.A. Nocturne: The Angels") and a Chicano writer, Rudolfo Anaya, writing on a border crosser ("B. Traven is Alive and Well in Cuernavaca"). The anthology effaces the border not only geographically but also translationally: the linguistic provenance of the works is elided, relegated to the credits, revealing a virtual community where once had been necessarily separate (and unequal) realms—the Mexican and the Mexican American. In Garcia's anthology, Crack writer Ignacio Padilla appears as a Chicano alongside writers working in English (Rubén Martínez and Ana Castillo). Arguably we have a case where translation made visible would have been a reminder, a reinforcement, of border checkpoints, of difference. *Bordering Fires* would have been a ludicrous if not impossible project only ten years ago; now it feels, and is, pioneering, border-crashing. Now, readerships of Spanish American and U.S. Latino/a writing are interrelated, each conditioning and extending the other. The mutually countervailing forces that contextualize the task of today's translator, according to Snell-Hornby—globalism and tribalism—prove unstable.

In this light, a critic might be prompted to reason thus: If the exoticizing magical realism stands at one pole of literary importation, what is gained by "smuggling"—translating—foreign writing steeped in the United States's own worldview and indices of class and "progress," the markers of status, self-consciously echoing them back into our own canon? Does translating globalized North American perspectives back to North American readers short-shrift the very act of reading *differently,* i.e., the imperative that translation of works from outside our national boundaries, aesthetics, or ethos supplement and enrich? Are these instances of a self-translation by proxy, a masquerading "*cultural back-translation*"? The truth of Grasso's declaration—"Translation can help to spread narratives that are already appealing for the target audience" (204)—is evidenced by many precedents, most notably the Pablo Neruda that has washed up on United States shores. A selective recreation, our Neruda is not the declamatory bard holding forth on human dignity before a crowd of rapt miners, but largely a depoliticized, lovelorn scribbler of odes. Even Neruda's compatriot, Nicanor Parra, was co-opted into being an honorary Beat writer through translation in the 1970s, excising the Chileanness—and the local polemics (including resonances against Neruda) that had shaped his "anti-poems."

A response may be twofold: first, the more these McOndo and Crack works appear North American, the more their threat to the North American canon may be mitigated by unflattering labels that assert North American precedence or dominance while advertising palatability ("the South American Burroughs," "the Latino Salinger") or by these works' relegation to Spanish American literature courses rather than presenting them to a wider audience in comparative literature survey courses and anthologies, for example. Second, it is arguably the very affinity of these writers for North American culture that creates *homologies*—structural similarities (Hermans 133; the term is Bourdieu's) between the two systems; hence they are translated *because* we are at home with them, in the way we have been at home with a homogenizing, undifferentiated representation of Third World writing. "American literature is tailored to be meaningful for American people," Stephen Kinzer writes. But the issue is no longer inaccessibility but the *hyperaccessibility* of world literature—in Owen's damning phrase, works "written to travel well" (31). Damrosch argues: "Non-Western works from earlier periods have often been excluded from world literature courses on the grounds that they are too difficult.... Now the converse fear is expressed: that contemporary world literature isn't worth the effort it doesn't require" (18–19).

Pedro Angel Palou, author of the Crack Manifesto, rejects the for-export mentality of what he calls "Made In Latin America" writers (Carbajal 124), and indeed, the Crack writers strive to produce challenging works even as they embrace North American pop references. It remains to be seen whether these generations will be burdened by their penchant for foreign cultural capital, as the Boom writers were:

> Critics eventually came to see the Boom as a locus of privilege or elitism. The problem with the Boom for many critics was that it essentially took place in Europe [in its promotion, translation, and publication]. This led to a critical perception that the coming of age of the Latin American novel was a part of a process of that novel's Europeanization, of its "catching up" with the sophistication of European (or North American) modernist narrative. Before long, a key and often repeated criticism made against many literary critics (and indeed, many literary writers) was that of Eurocentrism—the reading of Latin American culture through a European lens.... This led ultimately to a whole trend in literary criticism in which the contextual specificity of Latin America came to be seen as paramount. (Swanson 120–21)

So how does global reach affect writers' loyalties to, and concepts of, audience and subject matter? What happens to national identities in an era of hybrid loyalties and the advent of the already-translated text? Do Spanish American writers have to write about Spanish America? Consider Jorge Volpi's prize-winning *En busca de Klingsor* (*In Search of Klingsor*) and Ignacio Padilla's *Amphitryon* (*Shadow without a Name*); both deal with Nazism. Carbajal (127) notes that the Crack group "strives for the universal, while 'McOndo' registers the 'new' Latin America, complete with North American influences." Can a translation be expected to "represent" Latin America if, following Vargas Llosa's contention, such constructions are reductive even in the original (Carbajal 129)? Writers in Spanish America struggled for centuries to transcend regionalism, and indeed writers who are inextricably bound to their nationality, whether for reasons of language or culture or both, are legion, though there have always been world citizens from these countries. For instance, one can read Jorge Luis Borges profitably, if selectively, without exclusive reference to Argentinean reality. We should be clear that the immediate context in which writing has been received in Spanish America has been national, not pan-American, production; even schoolchildren in the Americas are far more likely to study their respective national literary antecedents in great depth than Spanish American ones.

The acknowledged godfather of these younger writers' form of universalism is a Chilean quickly gaining legendary status: Roberto Bolaño (1953–2003). Bolaño is being read and translated feverishly into many languages. Like his younger cosmopolitan protégés, Bolaño lived many years abroad—in Mexico—and those of the Crack movement have identified his *Los detectives salvajes* (*The Savage Detectives*) as a masterpiece. One of his translators, Natasha Wimmer, remarks that Bolaño "is not really from any one place, but is a sort of international, post-nationalist writer with strong emotional ties to Chile, Mexico, and Spain" (Rohter). In a *New York Times* article introducing his masterpiece, *2666*, Larry Rohter draws a contrast important for our purposes here: "Bolaño . . . differs from the generation of writers preceding him in that his national identity is fluid. Whereas Gabriel García Márquez of Colombia, Mario Vargas Llosa of Peru and Carlos Fuentes of Mexico all identify closely with their native lands in their important works, Bolaño makes his protagonists move from country to country."

Bolaño's sameness-in-difference may play into publishers' shrewd interest in "branding" a new writer to replace García Márquez, as Pollack notes (346–55). In *The Savage Detectives* the critic finds an appeal to an "adolescent" road-narrative idealism that is perhaps "even more fantastic than García Márquez's inventions" (360). She further argues that the "geography" of his persona plays a part in conditioning his reception: "Bolaño's creative genius, compelling biography, personal experience of the Pinochet coup, and untimely death . . . as well as the labeling of some of his works as Southern Cone dictatorship novels, all contributed to 'produce' a Bolaño well suited for U.S. reception and consumption" (355).

Casanova is categorical in her view of a writer's access to modernity, to the "real time of international life" (93), arguing that it is open only to "those writers on the peripheries of the world of letters who, in their openness to international experience, seek to end what they see as their exile from litera- ture. 'National' writers, by contrast, whether they live in central or outlying countries, are united in ignoring world competition (and therefore literary time) and in considering only the local norms and limits assigned to liter- ary practice by their homelands" (94). This interpretation may be reductive; surely it is the fate of many who aspire to be international and, thereby failing, are merely national. Many of these generational writers under discussion strive for both, as Padilla asserts in analyzing the Crack Manifesto ("McOndo y el Crack," 142):

> Si bien se abogaba ahí por la literatura difícil, no se demonizaba al mer- cado editorial, si por un lado se invitaba a la ruptura con las tendencias recientes de la literatura en español, se defendía a ultranza la continuidad de la tradición de la gran novela hispano-americana, si por una parte se esgrimía el derecho del escritor a sentirse parte de la humanidad y deslindarse de los localismos, no por ello se dejaba de hablar desde un sentido profundamente latinoamericano ni se renunciaba a escribir sobre América Latina. (Though we advocated difficult literature, we did not demonize the publishing trade; if on the one hand, we encouraged a break with recent trends in Spanish-language literature, on the other we fought tooth and nail for furthering the tradition of the great Spanish American novel; if on the one hand we upheld the writer's right to feel a part of humanity and to distance himself from local realities, we did not thereby speak any less from a deep Latin Americanness nor did we refuse to write about Latin America.)

Another question asserts itself: given the worldwide diffusion of English, and alternate and "contestatory" Englishes, the very fact of a translation's Americanness (or Britishness) cannot be uncoupled from the political, economic, and social realms—and, it should be remembered, neither is the classroom outside the economy of book production. The magical realist vein itself, long characterized as inextricable from the postcolonial condi- tion, now has been exported to England and elsewhere around the world. The cumulative effect of translations, the extent to which whole genres are translated, transformed, and presumably enriched (viz. the Argentinean contribution to the Anglo-American detective story), show translation not as a random exchange of authors but as a critical tool in shaping canons, and the prime mover of, if not exactly Goethe's *Weltliteratur,* then of some kind of international canon perpetually in the making.

In "Atlas of the Difficult World: The Problem of Global Poetry," John Palattella (56) describes how the "non-English language poet [who wants recognition is] compelled to write verse that is easily translatable into English" and thus "must betray a local idiom and extinguish traditional sources of inspiration." The author, drawing on Stephen Owen's identification of a trend that finds poets engaging "in the peculiar act of imagining a world poetry and placing themselves within it"—an imaginary community and an inauthentic act—concludes that this renders the non-English poet "at once world poetry's culprit and its victim." The contemporary work jockeys for space in the world marketplace of ideas and commodities—but only if it can make it there; once there, a Bolivian thriller competes with an American one, with the traditional canon in university curricula, and with its own country's literary traditions. Market demands and academic agendas, moreover, may well accelerate synchronous (contemporary) translation more toward a state of simultaneous (instant) translation, whereby writers are translated long before they have proven their staying power. Translation clearly will play a role in establishing these groups writing against reductive expectations; translators of stature, in many cases ones that helped canonize the Boom writers, are already giving their imprimatur. Gregory Rabassa has published a McOndoan work, Colombian Jorge Franco's edgy, magicless *Rosario Tijeras,* in English.

For translations to be read *as* translations, students must be sensitized to a translation's migratory situatedness (contextuality), the "*from*" and the "*into,*" and in the case of these writers, the "*between.*" Naive readings of translation place emphasis on how well a translation represents the source, not on what interpretive strategies it takes, what other representations are possible, or what linguistic and cultural interstices can be revealed. Many Spanish American works hold little interest for a U.S. reading public, due less to unserviceable translations than to narrow expectations and the misapprehension of what ends a translation should serve. Donald Hall's remarks serve as good "talking points" in the classroom, in that they represent the view of translation as a distracting adulteration of a "pure" source: "I deplore the practice of writing about poets known only in translation because the practice derives from and perpetuates the notion that there is some noumenal poem inside the skin of language—or that a poem is 'information,' for heaven's sake. I believe that we do not know a lyric poem except through the mouth and the muscles of the leg, and that translation will always be inadequate to tongue and limb. The prevalence or popularity of translations—the notion of their sufficiency—leads to slackening of exact language" (Renner 1).

Hall's is a Trojan horse of an argument: it plays on our sympathetic recognition of poetry as visceral, yet it dismisses the possibility that translators can recreate it "bodily," as if translators and their production were the disembodied wraiths of literature. Readers of translations, as always, inherit through this well-aired view the idea of translation as insufficient, but not because the translation hews to the surface of a source text—its "skin"—but because readers rely on a translation as a *whole picture.* The fallacy at the argument's core is that the art of translation itself is demonized if translation users do not read translations critically. To be blithely monolingual is not the same as to read uncritically. Yet note the fretfulness of Hall's assessment that translations are cribs, and leaning on them erodes the standards of "exact language." He continues: "Translations of Homer and Gilgamesh are approximations only—but story translates as phonemes, and dictional textures do not. And . . . when I read Dryden's *Aeneid* I read late seventeenth century England more than I read Augustan Rome."

Rather than shifting focus to *what it is that seventeenth-century England has read* in Dryden—translation as criticism and reflection of the ethos of one's age—translation is once again reduced to an impossible formula: $B \neq A$, therefore $B < A$. What of the new multilingual, multicultural sensibilities informing contemporary writing? What of intercultural intertextualities, cultural lacunae, the comparative inequivalency of genre across cultures? Because whole genres can have a different relevance in the receiver culture, are reader expectations of the language of a novel the same as those for poetry, the same across languages? What of notions of power as set forth by theorist Peter Fawcett, which center on the use of language to *include* or *exclude* the reader—decisions about how accessibly a text may be rendered, and the agents of power involved in the published version of a text? What of the particularly relevant modern phenomenon of the author who rewrites via translation, collaborating with the translator to produce a new "tongue and limb"? Or the self-translator, once a rarity and quickly becoming commonplace in these generations? What of considerations of the hierarchical relationships between languages in the United States and the effects of translation on these relationships? Poey (34–37) argues that seamless Boom novels are dissociated from the low status of Spanish or bilinguality of Latino/a literature. In short, then, students should be prompted to study translation's role in uncovering "the consequences of interpretation of other cultures; the problems springing from the rebirth of xenophobia and racism; the understanding of the exotic, not in terms of false imaginary constructions, but as an historic reality in itself which must be respected *disregarding hierarchical cultural boundaries*. It could be said that translation is a provisional way to encounter the strangeness of languages, to paraphrase Benjamin" (Alvarez and Vidal 3, emphasis mine).

The globalizing forces at work compel fresh approaches to understanding how "selves" and "others" are represented in the marketplace and in the classroom. These young generations we have been discussing offer a glimpse into new and productive problems for teachers of literature to pose.

WORKS CITED

Alvarez, Román, and M. Carmen-Africa Vidal. "Translating: A Political Act." In *Translation, Power, Subversion,* edited by R. Alvarez and M. Vidal, 1–9. Clevedon: Multilingual Matters Ltd., 1996.

Amar Sánchez, Ana María. "Deserted Cities: Pop and Disenchantment in Turn-of-the-Century Latin American Narrative." In *Latin American Literature and Mass Media,* edited by Edmundo Paz-Soldán and Debra A. Castillo, 201–21. New York: Garland, 2001.

———. "Literature in the Margins: A New Canon for the XXI Century?" November 1, 2006. http://www.lehman.cuny.edu/ciberletras/v15/amar.html.

Bolaño, Roberto. *Los detectives salvajes.* Barcelona : Editorial Anagrama, 1998.

———. *The Savage Dectives.* Translated by Natasha Wimmer. New York: Farrar, Straus and Giroux, 2008.

———. *2666.* Barcelona: Editorial Anagrama, 2004.

Bourdieu, Pierre. *Language and Symbolic Power.* Translated by G. Raymond and M. Adamson. Cambridge, UK: Polity Press, 1991.

Carbajal, Brent J. "The Packaging of Contemporary Latin American Literature: 'La Generación del Crack' and 'McOndo.'" *Confluencia* (2005): 122–32.

Casanova, Pascale. *The World Republic of Letters.* Translated by M. B. DeBevoise. Cambridge, MA: Harvard University Press, 2004.

Cohen, Margaret, and Carolyn Dever, eds. "Introduction." In *The Literary Channel: The Inter-national Invention of the Novel,* 1–34. Princeton, NJ: Princeton University Press, 2002.

Colchie, Thomas, ed. *A Whistler in the Nightworld: Short Fiction from the Latin Americas.* New York: Plume, 2002.

Cronin, Michael. *Across the Lines: Travel, Language, Translation.* Cork, Ireland: Cork University Press, 2000.

Damrosch, David. *What is World Literature?* Princeton, NJ: Princeton University Press, 2003.

Davis, Mike. *Magical Urbanism: Latinos Reinvent The U.S. City.* New York: Verso, 2000.

Delisle, Jean, and Judith Woodsworth, eds. *Translators Through History.* Philadelphia: J. Benjamins, 1995.

Evan-Zohar, Itamar. "The Position of Translated Literature within the Literary Polysystem." *Poetics Today* 11 (1990): 45–51.

Franco, Jorge. *Rosario Tijeras: A Novel.* Translated by Gregory Rabassa. New York: Seven Stories Press, 2004.

Fuguet, Alberto. "Magical Neoliberalism." *Foreign Policy* (2001): 67–73.

———. *The Movies of My Life.* Translated by Ezra E. Fitz. New York: HarperCollins, 2003.

———, and Sergio Gómez, eds. *McOndo.* Barcelona: Grijalbo Mondadori, 1996.

Garcia, Cristina, ed. *Bordering Fires: The Book of Contemporary Mexican and Chicano/a Literature.* New York: Vintage Books, 2006.

Grasso, Daniele Emanuele. "Translation Serving Global Narratives: The Case of 'Poverty' in Niger." *IATIS Yearbook* (2005): 198–215.

Hermans, Theo. *Translation in Systems: Descriptive and System-Oriented Approaches Explained.* Manchester, UK: St. Jerome Publishing, 1999.

Kinzer, Stephen. "America Yawns at Foreign Fiction." *New York Times,* July 26, 2003. http://www.nytimes.com/2003/07/26/books/america-yawns-at-foreign-fiction.html.

Mignolo, Walter D., and Freya Schiwy. "Double Translation: Transculturation and the Colonial Difference." In *Translation and Ethnography: The Anthropological Challenge of Intercultural Understanding,* edited by Tullio Maranhão and Bernhard Streck, 3–29. Tucson: University of Arizona Press, 2003.

Milian Arias, Claudi M. "McOndo and Latinidad: An Interview with Edmundo Paz Soldán." *Studies in Latin American Popular Culture* 24 (2005): 139–49.

Molloy, Sylvia. "Latin America in the U.S. Imaginary: Postcolonialism, Translation, and the Magic Realist Imperative." In *Ideologies of Hispanism,* edited by Mabel Moraña, 189–200. Nashville, TN: Vanderbilt University Press, 2005.

Owen, Stephen. "What is World Poetry?" *New Republic* 19 (1990): 28–32.

Padilla, Ignacio. "McOndo y el Crack: dos experiencias grupales." In *Palabra de América,* 136–47. Barcelona: Fundación José Manuel Lara, 2004.

————. *Shadow without a Name.* Translated by Peter Bush and Anne McLean. New York: Farrar, Straus and Giroux, 2003.

Palattella, John. "Atlas of the Difficult World: The Problem of Global Poetry." *Lingua Franca* (1999): 52–58.

Paz Soldán, Edmundo. "Between Tradition and Innovation: The New Latin American Narrative." *World Literature Today* (2004): 16–19.

————. "McOndo: Latin American Fiction Today." ABC National Radio. September 25, 2006. http://www.abc.net.au/rn/perspective/stories/2006/1748231.htm.

————. *The Matter of Desire.* Translated by Lisa Carter. Boston: Houghton Mifflin, 2003.

Perez Firmat, Gustavo. *Tongue Ties: Logo-eroticism in Anglo-Hispanic Literature.* New York: Palgrave Macmillan, 2003.

Poey, Delia. *Latino American Literature in the Classroom: The Politics of Transformation.* Gainesville: University Press of Florida, 2002.

Pollack, Sarah. "Latin America Translated (Again): Roberto Bolaño's *The Savage Detectives* in the United States." *Comparative Literature* 61, no. 3 (2009): 346–65.

Renner, B. "An Interview with Donald Hall." *elimae,* December 1996–January 1997. http://www.elimae.com/interviews/hall.html.

Rohter, Larry. "A Writer Whose Posthumous Novel Crowns an Illustrious Career." *New York Times,* August 9, 2005. *http://www.nytimes.com/2005/08/09/books/09bola.html.*

Santiago, Fabiola. "Professor's Homecoming is a Puzzle." *Miami Herald,* April 15, 2004.

Silva Gruesz, Kirsten. *Ambassadors of Culture: The Transamerican Origins of Latino Writing.* Princeton, NJ: Princeton University Press, 2002.

Snell-Hornby, Mary. "Communicating in the Global Village: On Language, Translation and Cultural Identity." In *Translation in the Global Village,* edited by Christina Schaffner, 11–28. Bristol, UK: Multlingual Matters, 2000.

Swanson, Philip. *Latin American Fiction: A Short Introduction.* Oxford: Blackwell, 2005.

Szegedy-Maszák, Mihály. *Literary Canons: National and International.* Budapest: Akadémiai Kiadó, 2001.

Volpi, Jorge. *In Search of Klingsor.* Translated by Kristina Cordero. New York: Scribner, 2002.

BELIEFS AND VALUES

Translating Eastern Europe and Russia

Brian James Baer

Although eastern Europe may appear to be a simple geographic designation, its borders have always been difficult to define.[1] As a cultural unity, the concept of eastern Europe is even more problematic; for, as Larry Wolff notes, "It was not a natural distinction, or even an innocent one, for it was produced as a work of cultural creation, of intellectual artifice, of ideological self-interest and self-promotion" on the part of the militarily more powerful and economically more developed nations of western Europe (4). Robert Pynsent and S. I. Kanikova assert that an internalized eastern European identity, to the extent such a thing exists, derives from a common feeling that "Europe" was something "outside" these nations, compounded by "some sense of a period of suffering or some 'national trauma'" (ix). And while Milan Kundera insists that such national trauma has been integral to the experience of the "small nations" of eastern Europe, which "have rarely been the subjects of history but almost always its objects" (2007, 32), it is no less true of imperial Russia. In fact, Russians have experienced the sense of being "outside" Europe with particular acuteness.

Born in the Enlightenment and reinforced by the Cold War, the cultural construction of eastern Europe represented a conceptual remapping of Europe, a shift from the North/South division that organized Renaissance thinking to the East/West division that persists to this day, occasionally complicated by the assertion of a third cultural zone: central Europe (Kundera 1984). Moreover, the region historically designated as eastern Europe is rife with its own internal contradictions and rivalries. For example, it is home to various religious confessions. In addition to Catholics and Orthodox Christians (whose competition resulted in the creation of Eastern Rite Catholics, or Uniates, during the Counter-Reformation), eastern Europe has for centuries been home to Muslims in the south (Albania, Kosovo, Bosnia-Herzegovina, Bulgaria, the northern Caucasus), Protestants in the Baltic states (Lutherans) and the Czech lands (Moravian Brothers), and of course Ashkenazi Jews, concentrated in the Pale of Settlement, which covered large parts of present-day Lithuania, Poland, Belarus, Moldova, Ukraine, and a portion of western Russia.

And while the region is home to virtually all of the Slavic languages (with the exception of Sorbian, spoken in southwest Germany), other languages are also spoken there: Romanian, a romance language; Hungarian and Estonian, which, like Finnish, belong to the Finno-Ugric sub-group of the Altaic language family; as well as Albanian, Latvian, Lithuanian, Yiddish, Romani, and German, spoken in centuries-old communities in Hungary, Romania, and Russia (Volga and Black Sea Germans). Moreover, the Slavic languages spoken in eastern Europe are themselves divided into three linguistic groups: West Slavic (Polish, Czech, Slovak), East Slavic (Russian, Belarussian, and Ukrainian), and South Slavic (Bulgarian, Serbian, Croatian, Macedonian, Slovenian, and now Bosnian). Some of these Slavic languages make use of the Cyrillic alphabet, while others use the roman, which generally corresponds to the religious/cultural distinction between Orthodoxy and Catholicism, respectively.[2] And so, while the traditionally Orthodox Serbs use the Cyrillic script and the traditionally Catholic Croats use the roman, Serbian and Croatian are mutually comprehensible to such a degree that they have at different times been considered one language (Serbo-Croatian). The political break-up of Yugoslavia, however, resulted in the break-up of Serbo-Croatian, as well as the appearance of Bosnian as an independent language for the newly independent state of Bosnia and Herzegovina.

The complex history of colonization in the region has done much to politicize these linguistic and cultural differences, producing layers of resentment. As Pynsent and Kanikova point out, "Slovaks felt oppressed by Hungarians and Hungarians by Vienna; or Roumanians felt they were oppressed by Greeks and Greeks by Turks" (vii).[3] Moreover, shifting imperial boundaries have resulted in a complex mingling of languages, ethnicities, and religious confessions across national boundaries, which challenges any simple, unified notion of national identity. At least four great multinational empires have left their mark on modern eastern European identity: the Mongol empire, the Commonwealth of Poland and Lithuania, the Russian (then Soviet) empire, and the Austro-Hungarian Empire (and its offspring, the multinational state of Yugoslavia). Some historians assert that Mongol domination of Moscovy continues to be felt today in Russians' preference for strong centralized government, while colonization by the Poles has left an indelible mark on the language, religion, and customs of western Ukraine, sharply distinguishing it from the eastern half of the country, which remains largely Russian-speaking.

Of shorter duration, but arguably more traumatic, were the invasion and occupation of large portions of eastern Europe by the armies of Napoleon and Hitler. The construction of communism as a bulwark against fascism forced the suppression of the complicated and tragic history of Nazi occupation in many parts of eastern Europe, a history that has become the subject of some of the most powerful literature of the new postcommunist eastern Europe. The experience of communism also ostensibly united eastern Europe, although there, too, significant differences obtained. In Russia, for example, communism replaced an autocratic monarchy, whereas in Czechoslovakia it replaced one of Europe's most vibrant democracies. In any case, the censorship that accompanied communist rule in eastern Europe and Russia resulted in twin phenomena: on the one hand was Aesopian language, and on the other was émigré literature, with its own traditions, thematics, and even aesthetic modes.

The tendency to "imagine" eastern Europe as the less-developed other of the West has greatly influenced both the choice of texts for translation and the approach taken to the translation of literary texts from that region. In the late eighteenth and early nineteenth centuries, for example, Russian literary works translated into English were selected largely for their exotic depictions of Russian life and customs. In other words, works were chosen less for their literary or aesthetic merit, and more for the local color they offered (May 2000, 1205). This changed significantly only in the first decades of the twentieth century, when Russian literature in the popular translations of Constance Garnett came to exert an enormous influence on English literary tastes. For example, by tempering the stylistic barbarisms of Dostoevsky, she facilitated his belated acceptance by English audiences. Joseph Brodsky complained, however, that Americans for the most part cannot tell the difference between Tolstoy and Dostoevsky as stylists because they both appear in the style of Garnett, their prolific translator (Remnick 98–99). Be that as it may, the sprawling prose works of "Tolstoevsky" continue to inform the Western view of Russia and of Russian literature, thanks in no small part to Garnett, while the short lyric

works of arguably the most central figure in Russian literature for Russians—
Alexander Pushkin—have never found a broad readership in English, despite
the (in)famous efforts of Vladimir Nabokov.[4]

Naked political concerns, of course, stand alongside the tendency to
fetishize the exoticism or cultural otherness of Russia and eastern Europe
in shaping translations of literature. During the Soviet period, for example,
Western sympathy and support for dissident writers led to the speedy
translation of "anti-Soviet" literary works such as Boris Pasternak's *Doctor
Zhivago* and Alexander Solzhenitsyn's *Gulag Archipelago*. As a consequence,
the first translations of these works were riddled with inaccuracies and
infelicities. Translators also took enormous liberties with the early novels
of Czech author Milan Kundera, which were translated—often before they
were published in Czech—as depictions of life under communism rather
than as works of universal literary value. This led Kundera to carefully vet
later translations or to take the work of translation (into French) upon himself. (Of course, there are notable exceptions, writers from eastern Europe
who have successfully transcended the small context of their country—or
region—of origin and entered the ranks of world literature, such as Danilo
Kis, Witold Gombrowicz, and Wislawa Szymborska.)

The tendency to construct Russia and eastern Europe as both the political and cultural other of the West—and of the Anglo-American West, in
particular—makes it especially important to resist the temptation to teach
its literature in translation as if it were an eyewitness account of the culture.
Instead, as Rachel May argues, literature in translation should be understood
not as being *about* the source culture—a simple and "true" reflection—but
rather as being *of* that culture, that is, a complicated product of a complex,
contested, and evolving culture, or even configuration of cultures. It is therefore
important to present this literature in such a way as to expose for discussion
three interrelated issues: cultural prejudice, (literary) authority, and the notion
of truth in literature, i.e., the idea that literature does not offer a transparent
window onto a culture (May 1994, 142–43). This can be done in a variety of
ways, May suggests, ranging from offering students a selection of translated
passages for comparison to discussing translators' prefaces and their use of
scholarly apparatus. A comparison of author's notes and translator's notes, for
example, raises the question of assumed background knowledge, which may
be very different for the reader of the work in translation and for the reader
of the text in the original language of publication. To demonstrate this, and

in order to help focus the attention of readers of Russian and eastern European literature(s) in translation on these issues from *within* translated texts themselves, I will discuss three distinctive features of Russian language and literature that offer special insight into the cultural imagination of the region: key words, proper names, and the use of foreign words.

Key words. In many ways the sense of economic—and in some cases political and cultural—backwardness that was associated with Russia and various nations of eastern Europe has led nationalists there to define themselves against the West and to turn their perceived "weaknesses"—industrial underdevelopment and an overreliance on agriculture—into virtues, i.e., a spiritual relationship to the soil and a closeness to peasant or folk culture. Russia, in particular, engaged in a mutually defining relationship with the West, alternately celebrating and decrying those non-Western characteristics of its culture—specifically, emotionality, irrationality, moral passion, and lack of personal agency (Wierzbiczka 395). Three key words, in particular, express or embody these characteristics: *dusha* (soul), *sud'ba* (fate), and *toska* (yearning).

The importance of "soul" in Russian culture has been compared to its importance in African American culture, for in both instances it is invoked as a way to define these cultures against the dominant cultural values of the West and to "justif[y] the margins" (Peterson 749). Soulfulness attests to the importance of emotional connection between people and implies a rejection of cold rationalism. And while *sud'ba* and *toska* may find ostensible English equivalents in "fate" and "yearning," the Russian inflection of these terms is lost if they are not understood in relation to the deep-seated belief that human beings have only very limited control over the events in their lives, which produces "a tendency to fatalism, resignation, submissiveness" (Wierzbicka 395). A comparative study of Russian and American reactions to Anton Chekhov's play *Uncle Vanya* revealed the very different cultural frameworks readers bring to a text. Americans, for example, criticized the characters again and again for their passivity and lack of initiative, something the Russian readers failed to "see." At the same time, the American readers noted the emotional openness of Chekhov's characters (Pshenitsyn). A discussion of these cultural values—with the understanding that they are often contested within Russian culture itself—can help readers better understand characters' motivations and judgments, that is, the options available to them, on the one hand, and the complicated and unpredictable ways culture shapes individual identities, on the other.

Proper names. Although linguistic differences are often invoked—and, one might argue, exaggerated—by eastern European ethnic or religious groups to support calls for political independence, the major languages of eastern Europe share some general features. For example, the Slavic languages as well as Hungarian and Estonian are heavily inflected (that is, suffixes or declensions indicate the part of speech a noun or noun phrase plays in a clause, not word order), which means that word order is much freer than in a noninflected language such as English. Moreover, every noun in these languages possesses a grammatical gender (masculine, feminine, and neuter), which, while obligatory and unchanging, may be exploited by writers to artistic effect.

Nouns are also subject to various degrees of diminutization through suffixing. This is especially true of proper names, which helps to explain why one of the most common complaints voiced by English readers of Russian literature in translation concerns the difficulty of keeping track of characters' names. This complaint is amply justified not only by the plethora of names, nicknames, and diminutized forms in Russian, but also by the fact that these various Russian names often bear little resemblance to one another. For instance, Shura and Sasha are common nicknames for Aleksandr and Aleksandra. Moreover, the sociolinguist Valentina Zaitseva maintains that the use of name forms in Russian is largely governed by the central cultural opposition of *svoi* versus *chuzhoi* (ours, our own vs. alien, someone else's), which in the Russian cultural imagination is gendered feminine and masculine, respectively. The association of the feminine with discursive intimacy and familiarity, Zaitseva contends, corresponds to the opposition of motherland (*rodina*) and fatherland (*otechestvo* or *otchizna*), or of unofficial and official society, which is another reflection of the deep structural opposition of *svoi/chuzhoi* (ours/theirs). The profound influence of this opposition on Russian culture is demonstrated by the fact that the distinction between a formal "you" (*vy*) and an informal "you" (*ty*), which was adopted during Peter's reforms from French (*tu/vous*), quickly took hold in Russian culture, whereas the distinction in English, represented by the singular and familiar "thou" and the plural and formal "you," is now defunct. This, however, has not stopped translators from resurrecting "thou" to represent the Russian distinction.[5]

In official settings Russians commonly make use of a person's first name and patronymic, the latter formed from the father's first name with the appropriate masculine or feminine suffix to indicate "son of" (*ovich/evich*) or "daughter of" (*ovna/evna*). In familiar, unofficial discourse one encounters far greater variation in Slavic name forms and modes of address. In addition to a shortened first name (typically with a grammatically feminine ending), which expresses in a more or less emotionally neutral form closeness or familiarity, such as Iura for Iurii, there are any number of forms derived from the use of "emotionally loaded" suffixes that indicate "subjective assessment" (i.e., Iurochka, Iurik, Iurka, and Iurashka). The sheer number of expressive suffixes, each with its own pragmatic meaning (caressing, diminutive, familiar/vulgar, teasing, scornful, pejorative, and contemptuous), makes any simple "tripartite division of names . . . into full first names, nicknames, and affectionate nicknames" unthinkable (Wierzbicka 237). The choice of one derivational form of name will depend on the speakers' mood and "the specific attitude that they wish to convey at that particular moment, rather than on any stable and rigid personal and interpersonal conventions (as is usually the case in English)" (238).

Therefore, the use of a certain form of name or the switch from one form to another in Russian literature is often artistically motivated, to a greater or lesser degree.[6] For example, in Fyodor Dostoevsky's novel *The Brothers Karamazov* (1880), two of the brothers, Alesha and Misha, are always referred to by a short forename, while the third brother, Ivan, the cold rationalist, is only referred to by his full name—he is never Vania, let alone Vaniuskka (Wierzbicka 259). Or in the novel *The Death of Achilles* (2006), Boris Akunin offers an early indication that there is something rotten at the highest echelons of the Russian government when the governor general of Moscow addresses Pyotr Parmyonovich Khutinsky, the head of the secret police, with an affectionate diminutive, as "my Petrusha" (9). Readers of translations should be aware that some translators reduce the variety of suffixed forms (Garnett) or use English suffixes (Greenall) to allow the English reader to follow the characters more easily, although it has become more common today to preserve the full panoply of Russian forms in order to respect the emotional subtleties associated with them (e.g., Monas, Bromfield, Pevear and Volokhonsky).

The second issue readers need to be made aware of is the use of allegorically inflected names (referred to in Russian as *govoriashchie imena,* or "talking names"), a very common feature of Russian literature, which can be found in almost every major literary movement. Talking names have been deployed to great comic and satirical effect in the naturalist works of Nikolai Gogol and Fyodor Dostoevsky, as well as in the postmodern works of Viktor Pelevin and Vladimir Sorokin. However, allegorical names have also been used with great seriousness, perhaps nowhere more so than in Dostoevsky's psychological detective novel *Crime and Punishment* (1866). As Monas notes: "The family names are allegorically significant; I think some of the first names and patronymics are, too" (viii). Dostoevsky's use of talking names—for example, Raskolnikov refers to *raskol*, or "schism," and Razumikhin refers to "intellect," "reason"—offers an allegorical reading of Russian history and in particular of the cultural divide, or schism, created by the reforms of Peter the Great, suggesting that the real object of investigation is nothing less than Russian national identity itself.

The translation of talking names, however, presents innumerable challenges. Therefore, rather than translate a name into English, translators will typically explain the allegorical meaning behind a character's name in a preface or footnote. For example, in their translation of Maxim Gorky's play *Down and Out* (1902), George Rapall Noyes and Alexander Kaun note in the list of characters that the name Kostylev "suggests *kostyl*, 'crutch'," the name Medvedev "suggests *medved*, 'bear'," and the name Bubnov is "possibly suggestive of *buben*, 'tambourine'" (626). Sydney Monas, in his translation of *Crime and Punishment*, explains the allegorical meaning behind the characters' names in his preface. This information may also be provided in footnotes.

Foreign words. The history of colonization of eastern Europe has produced a mingling and layering of languages throughout the region. For example, in modern Hungarian, "there are words used in agriculture that have been taken from Turkish and Slavic peoples, religious words taken from Italian and Slavic missionaries, and trade and commerce terms borrowed from the German" (Gatto 677). The same is true of Russia, which, since the fifteenth century, when Ivan IV defeated the Mongols at the Battle of Kazan and assumed the title of tsar, has been a multiethnic, multilingual empire. At the same time, Peter's policy of westernization made German and French, and to a lesser extent English and Italian, into prestige languages among the educated elite. In fact, many well-born Russians in the eighteenth and nineteenth centuries grew up speaking French at home and learned Russian as a second language.

This knowledge of foreign languages made interlingual word play possible, which poses particular problems in translations destined for a largely monolingual English-speaking audience. For example, in Mikhail Lermontov's novel *A Hero of Our Time* (1840), the narrator notes that a certain mountain named Krestovaia was "called by the scholar Gamba le Mont St. Christophe." Krestovaia, however, means "of the cross" and so has nothing to do with St.

Christopher. Understanding Gamba's error allows the English-language reader to consider how translation is implicated in the political and cultural project of imperialism, which consequently makes available another level of irony: Lermontov offers no native "original," only a French (mis)translation of what may be a Russian mistranslation—given its Christian imagery—of the name attributed to the mountain by the local people. Moreover, the theme of colonization as mistranslation is elaborated in the passage that immediately follows: "So there we were going down Mount Gud into Chertova Valley.... What a romantic name! You derive Chertova from *chort* [devil] and visualize, at once, the aerie of the Evil Spirit among forbidding cliffs, but this is not the case at all; the name of the valley comes from the word *cherta* [border] and not *chort,* for here once lay the boundary of Georgia" (Lermontov 41). And if that weren't enough, the narrator concludes the paragraph by comparing the newly colonized landscape—"packed with snowdrifts"—to "Saratov, Tambov, and other good old places in our fatherland" (41). Here the cultural appropriation of the foreign landscape is complete, although Lermontov's irony is unrelenting: the valley looks like Saratov and Tambov only when it is completely covered in snow.

The combination of Russian imperial expansion, on the one hand, and of European (and, in particular, French) cultural imperialism, on the other, produced a complicated linguistic landscape that is reflected in the striking presence in Russian literature of foreign words and, as witnessed above, of translation as theme. And while "foreign words and foreign languages," as Shierry Weber Nicholsen maintains, "are in one sense the quintessence of the Other of and within language" (84), we should be careful not to homogenize that Other. Even a cursory glance at the foreign words that appear in Russian literary texts suggests at least two different kinds of otherness. The languages of the colonized peoples of the Russian empire that are included in Russian literary texts appear typically as isolated nouns, stressing the untranslatability, the essential otherness—and restrictedness—of the local reality. However, the prestige languages of French, German, and English, spoken by Russia's elite, appear much more frequently in the form of phrases, often with little semantic content, and even entire sentences that serve to signify the cosmopolitan identity of the speaker. Among such phrases appearing in *Crime and Punishment* are *ich danke, nihil humanum, pour vous plaire, tout court, en toutes letters,* and *cher ami,* among many others. Marian Schwartz, in her translation of *A Hero of Our Time,* segregates the two language groups in her appendices, placing words from the languages of the colonized peoples of the Russian empire in a glossary, while explaining the phrases and sentences from western European languages in explanatory notes.

In addition to the foreign words inserted into the text by the source text author, another category of foreign words often appears in translation: Russian words retained by the translator. Most typically these Russian words function like the words from the languages of the colonized peoples of the Russian empire, in that they are most frequently nouns and typically serve to signify the specificity of the local culture. For example, Graham Hettlinger, in his translation of Ivan Bunin's nostalgic short story "The Scent of Apples," retains the Russian names for the apples mentioned, "*antonovkas, plodovitkas, borovinkas,* and *belle barynyas,*" and for the traditional drink "*kvass,*" in order to underscore the specificity or localness of the landscape and culture described (Bunin 232). However, the overuse of the strategy of preserving Russian words in the target text, especially when those words are italicized, can place undue emphasis on the individual words, suggesting a thematic importance they do not always have. For example, Hettlinger preserves the Russian word *sych,* "a small forest owl," in his translation, prompting the reader to interpret it as a symbol, which it turns out not to be: sometimes a *sych* is just an owl.

Foreign words can be used in a variety of ways. In *Crime and Punishment,* for example, Dostoevsky uses French to paraphrase the heartless philosophy of social Darwinism—"Crevez, chiens, si vous n'êtes pas contents" (Die, dogs, if you're not happy). By metonymically associating this philosophy with France, and by extension the West, he intimates that it is foreign, inimical to traditional Russian values. Or consider the highly charged use of German words in the poetry of the post–World War II Polish poet Tadeusz Rozewicz. Of course, one of the most sustained and complex examples of the use of foreign words occurs in Tolstoy's monumental novel *War and Peace* (1869), in which French appears not only in isolated words and phrases, but in quite lengthy passages. The presence of French—and other western European languages—supports the novel's central theme: the birth of nationalism among Russia's French-speaking elite, a birth that was forcibly induced by the invasion of Russia by the French emperor, Napoleon. As Richard Pevear notes: "Tolstoy used French for a reason, or for several reasons: to give the tone of the period; to play on the ironies of a French-speaking Russian aristocracy suddenly finding itself thrown into war with France; to suggest a certain frivolity and uprootedness in characters like Prince Vassily and the witty Bilibin" (Remnick 109).

With its code-switching and borrowing, the two opening paragraphs of the novel expose the dynamic nature of culture, underscoring the notion that culture is never the stable, unified, coherent identity that traditional nationalists would have us believe, and preparing the reader for a complex narrative that plots not the defense of an already established national identity against an outside intruder but rather the creation of a historically new identity in battle with its own cosmopolitan roots. Self-conscious about its "belated" entry onto the European political and cultural scene and its attendant reliance on Western models and prototypes, Russian and eastern European "identity" is not available a priori for translation; it is an identity very much marked by translation, torn between cosmopolitan aspirations and nostalgia for a prelapsarian cultural unity before Peter's reforms or colonization by the West. The unique perspective Russian and eastern European literature offers on translation—as crucial to identity formation as it is threatening to the stability of that identity—is something no one teaching this literature *in translation* should ignore. Considered together with the cultural opposition *svoi/chuzhoi,* the theme of translation points to a central tension, even contradiction, in Russian and eastern European culture(s), pulled between the foreign and the familiar, or, as Andrei Sinyavsky put it, oscillating "between xenophobia and universal compassion" (261).

NOTES

1. Robert B. Pynsent and S. I. Kanikova, in their *Reader's Encyclopedia of Eastern European Literature,* take a broad view of the region and include Armenian, Finnish, Georgian, Greek, and Sorbian literatures, while excluding literatures written in the "imperial languages" of Russian and German. In this way, they make the experience of political and cultural domination constitutive of eastern European identity, which corresponds to Kundera's description of eastern Europe as composed of "small nations" (2007, 28).

2. Romania is, of course, one of the most glaring exceptions, "tugged toward the West by the Orthodox Church, toward the West by its Romance language" (Kundera 2007, 32).

3. When scholars define eastern Europe by its experience of colonial oppression, they necessarily repress eastern Europe's own history of colonial oppression (i.e., the Commonwealth of Poland and Lithuania).

4. Of course, one of the major reasons for the relative obscurity of Russian poets in English translation is the fact that Russian is an inflected language and Russian

poetry remains today largely metered and rhymed, which presents particular challenges when translating into an uninflected language like English, in which free verse is the norm.

5. As evidence of how defunct this distinction is in English, Graham Hettlinger, in his translation of the Ivan Bunin story "Tanya," actually gets it wrong, presenting "thou" as the formal form of address: "Well dressed for the city, she walked behind the stationmaster, who addressed her formally as 'thou' as he carried her two large sacks of good" (138).

6. Common nouns also take expressive suffixes, the most common one being -ka. However, the expressive meaning of common nouns with diminutive suffixes is typically rendered by the adjectives "dear" or "little," or even "dear little," which tends to express affection for the object thus modified rather than intimacy or closeness with the speaker, as the Russian expressive forms often do.

WORKS CITED

Akunin, Boris. *Death of Achilles.* Translated by Andrew Bromfield. New York: Random House, 2006.

Bunin, Ivan. *The Elagin Affair and Other Stories.* Translated by Graham Hettlinger. Chicago: Ivan R. Dee, 2005.

Gorky, Maxim. "Down and Out." Translated by George Rapall Noyes and Alexander Kaun. In *Masterpieces of the Russian Drama,* edited by George Rapall Noyes, 2:625–89. New York: Dover Publications, 1961.

Kundera, Milan. "The Tragedy of Central Europe." *New York Review of Books* 26 (1984): 33–38.

———. "Die Weltliteratur. How We Read One Another." *New Yorker,* January 8, 2007, 28–35.

Lermontov, Mikhail. *A Hero of Our Time.* Translated by Vladimir Nabokov and Dmitri Nabokov. New York: Everyman's Library, 1992.

May, Rachel. "Russian: Literary Translation into English." In *Encyclopedia of Literary Translation into English,* edited by Olive Classe, 1204–9. London: FitzroyDearborn, 2000.

———. *The Translator in the Text: On Reading Russian Literature in English.* Studies in Russian Literature and Theory. Evanston, IL: Northwestern University Press, 1994.

Monas, Sydney. "Translator's Preface." In *Crime and Punishment,* by Fyodor Dostoevsky, translated by Sydney Monas, v–ix. New York: Signet Classic, 1999.

Nicholsen, Shierry Weber. *Exact Imagination, Late Work: On Adorno's Aesthetics.* Cambridge, MA: MIT Press, 1997.

Peterson, Dale E. "Justifying the Margin: The Construction of 'Soul' in Russian and African-American Texts." *Slavic Review* 51 (1992): 749–57.

Pshenitsyn, Sergei. "Cultural Models and the Meaning of a Translated Work." In *Translation and Meaning,* edited by Marcel Thelen and Barbara Lewandowska-Tomoszczyk, 357–64. Maastricht: Maastricht School of Translation and Interpreting, 2001.

Pynsent, Robert B., and S. I. Kanikova, eds. *Reader's Encyclopedia of Eastern European Literature.* New York: HarperCollins, 1993.

Remnick, David. "The Translation Wars." *New Yorker,* November 7, 2005, 98–109.

Sinyavsky, Andrei. *Soviet Civilization: A Cultural History.* Translated by Joanne Turnbull. New York: Arcade Publishing, 1988.

Wierzbicka, Anna. *Semantics, Culture, and Cognition: Universal Human Concepts in Culture-Specific Configurations.* New York: Oxford University Press, 1992.

Wolff, Larry. *Inventing Eastern Europe: The Map of Civilization on the Mind of the Enlightenment.* Stanford, CA: Stanford University Press, 1994.

Zaitseva, Valentina. "National, Cultural, and Gender Identity in the Russian Language." In *Gender and National Identity in Twentieth-Century Russian Culture,* edited by Helena Goscilo and Andrea Lanoux, 30–54. DeKalb: Northern Illinois University Press, 2006.

Translation of Modern and Contemporary Literature in Arabic

Allen Hibbard

In a foreword to the English translation of Elias Khoury's novel *Little Mountain,* published in 1989, Edward Said wrote that "of all the major literatures and languages, Arabic is by far the least known and most grudgingly regarded by Europeans and Americans, a huge irony given that all Arabs regard the immense literary and cultural worth of their language as one of their principal contributions to the world" (ix). Just a year later, in a piece entitled "Embargoed Literature," published in *The Nation,* Said commented more specifically on the lamentable quality and quantity of works of Arabic literature available in English translation, speculated on some reasons for that state of affairs, and championed recently translated works by the great modern Arab poet Adonis (*An Introduction to Arab Poetics*), the Coptic Egyptian writer Edwar al-Kharrat (*City of Saffron*), and the widely acclaimed Lebanese writer Hanan al-Shaykh (*Women of Sand and Myrrh*).

Said's reflections came just after Egyptian novelist Naguib Mahfouz was awarded the Nobel Prize in Literature in 1988, an event that elevated the stature of Arabic literature and propelled a wave of translation activity. For a long time, *Midaq Alley,* in Trevor le Gassick's translation published in 1966, was virtually the only work by Mahfouz available in English; along with Denys Johnson-Davies's translation of Tayeb Salih's marvelous novel *Season of Migration to the North,* published in 1969, it occupied a very lonely space on the shelf devoted to contemporary Arabic novels available in English translation. At that time there were fairly limited opportunities for those with no knowledge of Arabic to become acquainted with this rich literary heritage. Fortunately, the scene has changed over the couple of decades since Said made his statements. While Arabic literature remains, to a large extent, ghettoized, translation activity picked up in the 1980s and has flourished in the past twenty years. My aim in these pages is to point to the array of materials available, present some of the specific translation issues Arabic poses, highlight the work of several authors, and suggest ways works of literature translated from Arabic can be incorporated into a variety of courses.

We now have access to sufficient literary material in translation to appreciate the vast scope and heterogeneity of modern and contemporary literature in Arabic, though many important, unrecognized works still await translators and publishers. The range of publishers willing to publish works translated from Arabic has expanded beyond pioneers such as the American University of Cairo Press, Three Continents, and Saqi, to include Random House, Doubleday, and Penguin, as well as a number of university presses (particularly Syracuse University Press, University of Arkansas Press, and Columbia University Press). Readers and publishers have shown a keen interest in works by contemporary Arab women writers. And while Egyptian writers, for understandable reasons, continue to be well-represented (with established, well-known writers such as Yusuf Idris, Yahya Haqqi, Nawal al-Saddawi, Sonallah Ibrahim, Radwa Ashour, Ibrahim Abdel Meguid, and many others, as well as Mahfouz), more and more writing from other Arab countries has been translated. For instance, from Yemen we have Zayd Mutee' Dammaj's *The Hostage,* translated by May Jayyusi and Christopher Tingley (Interlink, 1994) and Mohammad Abdul-Wali's *They Die Strangers,* translated by Abubaker Bagader and Deborah Aker (University of Texas Press, 2002). From Libya we have *The Bleeding of the Stone,* a short novel by Ibrahim al-Koni, translated by May Jayyusi and Christopher Tingley (Interlink, 2002), and another novel by al-Koni, *Anubis: A Desert Novel,* translated by William M. Hutchins (AUC Press, 2005). From Iraq we have *Scattered Crumbs,* a novella by Muhsin Al-Ramli, ably translated by Yasmeen S. Hanoosh (University of Arkansas Press, 2003), and *Basrayatha: The Story of a City,* translated by William M. Hutchins (Verso, 2008). From Syria comes *Just Like a River,* a short novel by Muhammad Kamil-al-Khatib, translated by Michelle Hartman and Maher Barakat (Interlink, 2003); from Algeria, *Memory in the Flesh* by Ahlam Mosteghanemi, translated by Baria Ahar and Peter Clark (AUC Press, 2003); and from Morocco, *The Last Chapter,* by Leila Abouzeid, translated by the author and John Liechety (AUC Press, 2003).

What is more, the speed of translation from Arabic has increased. For instance, *The Yacoubian Building,* the very popular Egyptian novel by Alaa Al Aswany originally published in Arabic in 2002 (*Omarat Yaqubian*), came out in an English translation (by Humphrey T. Davies, AUC Press) two years later, in 2004. (A film based on the novel came out in 2006.) And Marilyn Booth's translation of Hamdi Abu Golayyel's novel *Lusus mutaqa'idun*, originally published in 2002, was brought out by Syracuse University Press in 2006 under the title *Thieves in Retirement*.

Over the past two decades five important anthologies devoted exclusively to modern Arabic literature have been published: *Modern Arabic Poetry: An Anthology*, edited by Salma Khadra Jayyusi, published by Columbia University Press in 1987 (nearly 500 pages); *Literature of Modern Arabia: An Anthology*, edited by Salma Khadra Jayyusi and published by Columbia University Press in 1988 (around 500 pages); *Anthology of Modern Palestinian Literature*, edited by Salma Khadra Jayussi and published by Columbia University Press in 1992 (750 pages); *Modern Arabic Drama: An Anthology*, edited by Salma Khadra Jayyusi and Roger Allen, published by Indiana University Press in 1995; *Short Arabic Plays: An Anthology*, edited by Salma Khadra Jayussi and published by Interlink in 2003 (about 350 pages); and *Modern Arabic Fiction: An Anthology*, edited by Salma Khadra Jayyusi and published by Columbia University Press in 2005 (more than 1,000 pages). The publication of these volumes, supported by the Project of Translation from Arabic, is a sign of growing recognition of the value and importance of this literary tradition. These volumes are valuable resources for those of us who wish to learn more about modern Arabic literature and incorporate it into our teaching.[1]

Arabic presents a number of unique challenges for the translator, publisher, and reader, many related to the distance between western European languages and cultures and those of the Arab world. Denys Johnson-Davies, a widely respected pioneer in translating Arabic literary texts into English, has noted that "these sorts of difficulties exist particularly when languages concerned relate to such totally different social and cultural background, i.e., are more prevalent in translating Arabic into English than say from French into English" (276). These challenges might be divided between those that are linguistic in nature and those that involve culturally embedded meanings, though of course the two categories are very often intertwined and inseparable.

Arabic is a verbal language that relies heavily on cumulative patterns, with the prevalent use of the letter *wa*, a coordinating conjunction meaning "and." The very structure of the language places demands on the translator to create syntactical arrangements that do justice to the original and at the same time flow smoothly in English. Translating idiomatic expressions can also be particularly challenging for the translator. Sometimes glossaries or spare footnotes can be used to provide explanations, or readers might be left to fend for themselves.

One of the chief characteristics of Arabic is its diglossic or "semi-bilingual" condition. The difference between the classical Arabic of the Koran or the Modern Standard Arabic used in news broadcasts ([al-]fuṣḥa) and the spoken language ([al-]ʿammiyya) is great enough almost to think of the two as distinct languages. There are also significant dialectical differences between Arabic-speaking countries, such that it can often be difficult for speakers of one dialect to understand another dialect. An Egyptian, for instance, may have difficulty understanding someone speaking in Moroccan dialect, though the Moroccan likely will understand the Egyptian because of the wide circulation of Egyptian films, television shows, and popular music.[2] There is considerable debate among writers and the general public concerning how to negotiate this diglossic scene. More traditional positions (sometimes associated with pan-Arabist or pan-Islamic ideologies) reject the use of colloquial speech in literature, claiming that it is degenerate and vulgar and that it works against common understanding across the Arab world. More practical, liberal positions see at least some justification for using ʿammiya, particularly in drama, where dialogue in fuṣḥa would seem stilted and unrealistic. The use of dialect and different registers helps distinguish and define characters, often identifying their class, region and generation. Dialect is especially critical in comedy.

Many writers have employed styles that combine literary and conversational styles, or that involve code-switching and code-mixing. Traces of Egyptian colloquial speech can be felt, for instance, in some of Mahfouz's work, though he writes in formal Arabic. Sonallah Ibrahim's novel Zaat, as Mohammad Albakry notes, "mixes the literary narrative style punctuated by Egyptian colloquialisms with a collage of newspaper excerpts (news items, headlines, and advertisements). . . . The translation captures very well this multiplicity of registers and styles. The press clippings that appear in every other chapter of the novel document the major changes and upheavals and cultural economic turmoil in Egypt in the last five decades since Nasser's regime."[3] In her introduction to Thieves in Retirement, Marilyn Booth describes similarly how the novel deploys "Nasserist vocabulary" and "offers a send-up of the diction of religiously sanctioned authority and of the languages of traditional conventional literary expression, best represented in poetry."[4]

Translators of Arabic must also determine how to handle cultural references (place names, items of dress or food, historical events, religious practices, literary allusions and forms, etc.) that may not be familiar to western readers.[5] Marilyn Booth has noted that "translators from Arabic are expected to add more context than probably translators from any other region."[6] Translators of Adonis's poetry, for instance, have often used glossaries to provide information on terms and references that would be commonly understood in the original context. Similarly, *A Banquet for Seaweed,* a novel by Syrian writer Haidar Haidar that I am presently translating with Osama Isber, is set against the backdrop of political events in Iraq in the fifties and sixties and Algeria in the seventies and eighties, which will be less familiar to Western readers than to Arab readers. The novel also contains a number of references to Shiite rituals, beliefs, and practices that may at first perplex readers with no knowledge of Shiite traditions.

One of the key issues in translation practice and theory related to both linguistic and cultural issues concerns the extent to which translators "domesticate" a text, reducing key elements of its original character to make it more familiar or palatable to audiences in the target language. Lawrence Venuti is perhaps the best-known theorist who describes and critiques this phenomenon. Certainly the tendency to domesticate a text in the process of translation can often be felt in translations from Arabic to English. Sometimes translations can also exoticize a text, especially translations from non-Western languages. Ovidi Carbonell outlines both of these tendencies in "Exoticism, Identity and Representation in Western Translation from Arabic": "*Foreignising,* that is importing alien elements to the target culture which are supposed to belong to the source culture (for example, by means of loanwords, calques, the discursive structure of the original), is opposed to *familiarising,* a process by which alien elements and their references, that may cause a stranging effect, are reduced to familiar references so that the information of the original is easily understood in terms of the target culture" (Faiq 27). Translators of Arabic (as well as readers of translated texts) need to be aware of these phenomena as well as their ideological implications, which Venuti, Carbonell and others elaborate.

Arabic literature is embedded within the political and cultural tensions that have developed between the Arab world and the West. Sometimes those tensions—such as in Abdel Rahman Munif's marvelous epic work, *Cities of Salt,* which chronicles the effects of oil production and the influx of American engineers on traditional life in the Gulf region—are inscribed within the narrative. In "Embargoed Literature," Edward Said notes that Arabic literature "remains relatively unknown and unread in the West" and that "there almost seems to be a deliberate policy of maintaining a kind of monolithic reductionism where the Arabs and Islam are concerned" (278). He then asserts: "It is impossible not to believe that one reason for this odd state of affairs is the longstanding prejudice against Arabs and Islam that remains entrenched in Western and especially American culture" (278).

It might be argued that today, given the extent of our involvement in the Arab and Islamic world after the first Gulf War and now in Afghanistan and Iraq, there is a heightened interest in seeking out knowledge of those regions and their cultures, through literature as well as historical and political analyses. Still, as much as we might like to think that the activity of translation is uncontaminated by political factors, there can be unconscious or conscious forces at work as we approach Arabic literature, expecting confirmation of stereotypes, seeking representations of the exotic other, or wishing material to conform to preexisting ideas of what we think Arabic literature should be. As Said Faiq writes in "The Cultural Encounter in Translating from Arabic," "Arab culture and Islam, distanced by time, space and language(s), are usually carried over—into a Western tradition as an originary moment and image within a master narrative of western discourses full of ready-made stereotypes and clichés" (Faiq 8).

We know that the reputation of a work in the target language can be determined to a great extent by the quality of the translation. Generally, contemporary Arabic literature has been well-served by its translators. Among those trained translators actively committed to the collective project of bringing Arabic literature to English readers are Marilyn Booth, Peter Clark, Denys Johnson-Davies, Aida Bamia, Khalid Mattawa, Roger Allen, Catherine Cobham, William M. Hutchins, and William Granara. In terms of both quantity and quality, fiction has been better served by translators than poetry has. The choices of works to be translated have depended on a variety of factors: personal tastes of translators; what is deemed of significance, culturally or literarily; what publishers think will sell; what is known and readily recognized; the degree of difficulty of the text; perceptions of how easily the work will move from one cultural or linguistic scene to another; and the extent to which works fit within preconceived notions of the Middle East.

It is extremely difficult to select just a small handful of texts to discuss, given the hundreds now available in translation.[7] Any survey or assessment of modern and contemporary Arabic literature would have to include the towering figure of Naguib Mahfouz, whose output was prodigious and highly innovative. A noted Egyptian writer is reported as saying, "Just as you cannot picture Egypt without the pyramids, you cannot conceive of Arabic literature without Naguib Mahfouz" (Altoma 21). Mahfouz's development as a novelist might be seen as encapsulating, in compressed form, the history of the development of the novel in the West, from Balzac, say, through Faulkner and beyond, from his early novels drawing on the Pharaonic past to later works such as *Wedding Song* and *The Journey of Ibn Fattouma*, which experiment with point of view and challenge strict categorization.

Rather like Thomas Mann in *Buddenbrooks*, in *The Cairo Trilogy* Mahfouz focuses on the narrative of one family, that of al-Sayyid Ahmed Abd al-Jawad, and tells a story not only of the three generations family but of Egypt from the end of World War I up through World War II. The first and longest novel, named after the street on which the Abd al-Jawad family lives in Islamic Cairo, *Palace Walk* (1956, 1990), deals with the shortest amount of time, ending with the death of Fahmy in a demonstration against British occupation in 1919. The second novel, named after the street on which Abd al-Jawad's oldest son Yasin now lives, *Palace of Desire* (1957, 1991), is somewhat shorter and deals with a longer chunk of time, taking us up to the death of Egyptian nationalist hero Saad Zagloul in 1927. The last and shortest novel of the set carries on the story of the family from 1935 to 1944; its title, *Sugar Street* (1957, 1992), refers to the street on which Abd al-Jawad's daughter Khadiga and her children live.

These three novels, as well as *Midaq Alley*—a short novel that traces the lives of a handful of characters in a neighborhood of Old Cairo—serve as good introductions to Mahfouz's work and to life in modern Egypt. Other subsequent novels respond to historical developments and display various forms of literary innovation. In *Miramar* (1967, 1978), named after a hotel in Alexandria that serves as the hub of the novel's action, Mahfouz employs four different narrators to provide different angles on the same story. Each of the narrators brings a different political perspective to Nasser's socialist project.[8] In his epic novel *The Harafish* ("riff-raff" or "rabble" would be a rough translation of the term), Mahfouz chronicles the story of Ashur al-Nagi, a foundling who rises to become the neighborhood clan chief, and his descendants, covering a span of ten generations (1977, 1995). With no specific temporal markers, the novel has a timeless, archetypal quality, revealing the very pattern and rhythm of history and the quotidian lives in an Islamic society. *The Journey of Ibn Fattouma* (1983,1992) offers a kind of Swiftian satire in the form of a fictitious travelogue in which the traveler visits a number of types of societies, each flawed in its own way.

Because Mahfouz has received considerable attention (all justly deserved), I would like here to spotlight works by three other contemporary Arab writers: Tayeb Salih, Alifa Rifaat, and Adonis. *Season of Migration to the North* by Sudanese writer Tayeb Salih, brilliantly translated by Denys Johnson-Davies, remains one of the most popular modern Arab novels, especially in its English version. (It has been reissued nine times since its first edition in 1969.) A kind of inversion of Joseph Conrad's *Heart of Darkness* that employs fictional devices similar to those deployed by Conrad, the novel deals dramatically and compellingly with tensions between tradition and modernity, between the Arab/Muslim world and the West.[9] The unnamed narrator relates his story from a sleepy, rural Sudanese village along the banks of the Nile; thus, the land of the Thames becomes the heart of darkness, a site of barbarism. The enigmatic figure at the heart of the tale, the Kurtz, is a character named Mustafa Sa'eed. At an earlier time, Mustafa Sa'eed left Sudan and traveled via Cairo to London, where he studied economics and engaged in disturbing sexual exploits with English women (which can be seen as symbolic acts of revenge against colonialism) before returning to the Sudan. Much like Marlow in Conrad's narrative, the narrator becomes obsessed with Mustafa Sa'eed, searches for clues to explain his mysteries, and begins to identify himself with the story's haunting hero. In the final scene of the novel, the narrator enters the river and begins swimming "toward the northern shore." Then, "turning to left and right, I found I was half-way between north and south. I was unable to continue, unable to return" (166, 167). The novel does not provide a satisfactory resolution to the psychological turmoil produced by trying to reconcile East and West. While the resonating refrain in *Heart of Darkness* is "The horror! The horror!" in Salih's novel it is "Help! Help!"

The lyrical beauty of its language, its taut and compelling narrative, and its poignant themes make *Season of Migration to the North* an excellent work to bring into the classroom. The novel complicates commonplace notions of modernity, particularly its geographical and temporal dimensions. It also raises issues related to the connection between modernism and the postcolonial. Furthermore, it provides a rare glimpse of Muslim life in a Sudanese village—its rhythm, pace, rituals, and customs. Students are often amazed at Salih's depiction of Sudanese women's casual, frank sexual banter, and shocked by the patterns of Mustafa Sa'eed's sexual violence.

"More convincingly than any other woman writing in Arabic today, Alifa Rifaat, an Egyptian in her early fifties, lifts the veil on what it means to be a woman living within a traditional Muslim society," Denys Johnson-Davies writes in the "Translator's Foreword" to a collection of Rifaat's short stories, *Distant View of a Minaret and Other Stories* (vii). Though works by a good many fine Arab women writers have been translated since this collection first appeared in English, Rifaat's stories remain among the finest available to us and serve as a great entrance to the lives of ordinary modern Egyptian women and to the Arabic short story. The stories display an impeccable sense of timing and economy as well as a clarity and sharp edge reminiscent of stories by Kate Chopin and Charlotte Perkins Gilman. Particularly striking is her candid depiction of women's sexual desires and men's insensitivities. The wife in the title story concentrates on a spider's web on the ceiling while her husband makes love to her. After the lovemaking, she gets up to perform her ablutions, as required, before praying. She later returns to find her husband dead. "She returned to the living room and poured out the coffee for herself. She was surprised at how calm she was" (4). The story is set in an apartment in Cairo with a view of the one of the two minarets of Sultan Hasan Mosque and "a thin slice of the Citadel" that "was all that was now left of the panoramic view she had once had of old Cairo" (3).

"Bahia's Eyes" takes the form of a mother's address to her daughter, with references to her childhood dreams, her blindness caused by *bilharzia,* the trauma of female circumcision, menstruation, and a life controlled by the men around her. "Daughter," she concludes, I'm not crying now because I'm fed up or regret that the Lord created me a woman. No, it's not that. It's just that I'm sad about my life and my youth that have come and gone without my knowing how to live them really and truly as a woman" (11). In another story, "Badriyya and Her Husband," Badriyya is the last in her neighborhood to learn that her husband prefers his own gender, a discovery that explains his lack of sexual interest in her.

While most of the stories in the volume are offered from women's perspectives, and most often display profound disillusionment with their lot, these women grudgingly accept their fates. Neither Rifaat nor her female protagonists, as Johnson-Davies writes in his introduction, are radical feminists. The practices and spirit of Islam are affirmed, and the pursuit of solutions outside traditional boundaries of marriage is rejected. Rather, Rifaat's stories point to human failings and a perversion of religious principles. The themes are universal, the stories straightforward and accessible; footnotes are used sparingly to define specific terms and practices.

Adonis (Ali Ahmad Said) is widely recognized as one of the greatest living Arab poets. "Through his own highly original poetry, as well as through critical and theoretical books and essays, [Adonis] is deemed the most provocative and successful innovator of Arabic verse in our time," Eric Ormsby recently wrote in the *Times Literary Supplement*. Though for the last decade or so his name has regularly appeared on the shortlist of candidates for the Nobel Prize in Literature, the poet still is relatively unknown to the English-speaking world. "His impact on the Arab literary world has been huge, if controversial," Orsmby writes, "yet while many of his works have been translated into French, and he is celebrated in France, he remains relatively unknown in the English-speaking world, largely for lack of good translations" (13).

Born and raised in a village in the coastal region of Syria, Adonis attended university in Damascus, spent some time in prison in Syria, and moved to Beirut, where he was closely associated with the Sh'ir movement of modern Arab poets. Then, during the Lebanese civil war, he moved to Paris, which has since remained his base. These places and patterns of movement are inscribed in his poetry, as are historical events and conditions. Exile is a major theme in his poetry. In "Neffari," an homage to the classical Arab poet, for instance, he writes:

Ask the sun how it made me an exile.

It scattered me on the road,
letter by letter,
and the languages of exile
are not the sun's languages.

I have thus become a wanderer.
To be an exile is my identity.[10]

Adonis's poetry derives its force from both its thematic content and its powerful use of the Arabic language, which is difficult to convey in English because of its surreal metaphors, intertextual allusions, and historical references. His poetry is infused with the vital strength and value poetry has enjoyed in Arab culture, as well as the linguistic power residing in the Koran. (He provocatively titled his recent three-volume work *Al Kitâb* [The Book], a denomination usually reserved for the Koran.) Both formally and thematically, Adonis registers the shock of the modern in ways similar to modernist antecedents T. S. Eliot and Ezra Pound, poets who influenced him and to whom he is often compared. Like Eliot, Adonis draws extensively from rich, inherited poetic traditions while creating fresh, vital poetic forms. His "New Poetry" (*al-sh'ir al-jajîd*) enacts a rupture from traditional, strict *qasîda* forms—a rupture even more dramatic than that felt among modern poets in the Western tradition.[11]

The poet's critique of the modern condition is tough and penetrating. He responds to the present plight of the Arab world, plagued as it is by despotic rule, poverty, civil war, prolonged conflict with Israel, the demise of educational systems, displacement of various groups of people, the rise of fundamentalist Islam, the legacy of colonialism, and the sustained imperialist presence in the Middle East. This mood of despair and alienation, particularly pervasive in the modern Middle East, finds powerful articulation in Adonis's poetry, e.g., in "An Introduction to the History of Petty Kings" and his powerful poem "The Time," which gives voice to violence, despair, loss of homeland, fractured identity, and madness: "our steps / are a line of killing / does your killing come from your god / or does your god come from your killing?"[12] Yet while he depicts malaise and tragedy, his stance is profoundly humanistic. As Nasser Rabbat writes, his is "a revolutionary poetry committed to the values of pluralism, freedom, enlightenment, and the inevitability of change" (xii).

Adonis's poetry adroitly and consciously draws upon the best of both Western and Arab poetic traditions, bridging the two. Indeed, it is arguably Adonis's reading of European modernist poets that led to his radical break from a strict, conventional tradition in Arabic poetry. Among the Arab poets he draws into the body of his work are al-Niffari, al-Mutannabi, and Abu Nuwas. From the West, he absorbs, incorporates, and responds to the poetry of Walt Whitman, Baudelaire, Mallarmé, T. S. Eliot, and Ezra Pound. In his famous, important poem "A Grave for New York," he explicitly evokes Whitman. In "A Desire Moving through the Maps of the Material," the poet attempts to reconcile and inscribe the traditions and landscape of his homeland—in particular the small town of Kassabin, where he grew up and now has built a home, in the foothills near the Syrian coast of the Mediterranean—and those of the West, particularly Paris, his place of exile. The places and their respective cultural traditions become displaced and blurred in the poem. Section 11, for instance, begins with the headings "the eiffel tower," "notre dame" and "the louvre" laid out across the top of the page. Then the line: "is it a dream—the eiffel tower is no longer in its place and here is the louvre heading toward the eastern shore of the mediterranean as if it too wants to follow the footsteps of alexander the great." What Adonis accomplishes, in the end, is a merging or fusion of the two traditions within the space of mind and poem.[13]

No fewer than twenty volumes of Adonis's poetry have been published in Arabic. The translation industry has yet to catch up with his magnificent, prodigious output; however, three recently published volumes—all of which concentrate on his earlier works, many reproducing material previously published—provide just a glimpse or sliver of Adonis's achievement.[14]

There are a variety of ways in which translations of contemporary litera-ture in Arabic can be incorporated into the curriculum. Certainly, the field is important enough to warrant courses devoted exclusively to the subject. Arabic literature can also be integrated within a variety of existing courses. Samia Serageldin's very accessible novel *Cairo House,* for instance, could be taught in a sophomore introduction to literature course.[15] The novel, a straightforward narrative following an upper-class Egyptian family's adjust-ment to change in modern Cairo, acquaints readers with Muslim rituals and holidays and provides an antidote to prevalent images in American news and popular culture of Arabs as radical terrorists.

Translated works from Arabic can also be woven into the fabric of courses devoted to particular periods or styles. A course in the modern novel, for instance, could include Tayib Salih's *Season of Migration to the North* to provoke discussions of traditional temporal demarcations of the modern and shift the focus of discussion to the so-called Third World. (It occurs to me that novels by Palestinian writer Jabra Ibrahim Jabra—*The Ship* and *In Search of Walid Masoud*—could also be taught in this context.) Works by Egyptian writers Gamal al-Ghitani (*Zayni Barakat*) and Ahmed Alaidy (*Being Abbas El Abd*) or Lebanese writer Elias Khoury (*The Journey of Little Gandhi, Little Mountain,* or *Kingdom of Strangers*) could be incorporated in a course in postmodern literature, while any number of works (such as *Season of Migration to the North,* Adhaf Soueif's *Maps of Love*—written originally in English—and *A Banquet for Seaweed*) could be productively used in courses in postcolonial literature.

A wide array of resources is available for use in courses on particular genres, in addition to the anthologies listed earlier in the essay. Mention has already been made of numerous novels that could be used in courses on the novel; there are many more. Denys Johnson-Davies's fine collection *Modern Arabic Short Stories*, the Banipal collection *Sardines and Oranges: Short Stories from North Africa*, *Oranges in the Sun: Short Stories from the Arabian Gulf* (Lynne Rienner, 2008), or *Contemporary Iraqi Fiction* (Syracuse University Press, 2008) could be used in classes in the short story, as could volumes of stories by individual writers such as Yahyia Taher Abdullah (Egypt), Alifa Rifaat (Egypt), Zakariyya Tamer (Syria), Ghassan Kanafani (Palestine), Salwa Bakr (Egypt), and Naguib Mahfouz (Egypt). Sometimes general short-story anthologies include stories by Arab writers. For instance, *Worlds of Fiction*, an anthology edited by Roberta Rubenstein and Charles R. Larson, includes stories by Hanan Al Shaykh, Ghassan Kanafani, and Naguib Mahfouz. The *Riverside Anthology of Short Fiction: Convention and Innovation*, edited by Dean Baldwin, includes Naguib Mahfouz's fine story "The Time and the Place," which displays the tension between modernity and tradition, contains allusions to Sufi mystical traditions, deploys several registers of Arabic (including an older Koranic style), and can be read as an allegory of political life in Egypt during the Nasser regime.

In addition to the fine, comprehensive *Modern Arabic Poetry: An Anthology*, there are a number of single-author volumes that could be used in poetry courses: *Victims of a Map* (bilingual edition featuring works by Samih al-Qasim, Mahmud Darwish, and Adonis, translated by Adullah al-Udhari), Muhammad al-Maghut's *Fan of Swords* (translated by May Jayyusi) and *Joy is Not My Profession* (translated by John Asfour and Alison Burch), Mahmoud Darwish's *The Music of Human Flesh* (translated by Denys Johnson-Davies) and *The Butterfly's Burden* (translated by Fady Joudah), Nizar Kabbani's *Arabian Love Poems* (bilingual edition, translated by Bassam Frangieh and Celmentina R. Brown), Hatif Janabi's *Questions and Their Retinue* (translated by Khaled Mattawa), Muhammad Afifi Matar's *Quartet of Joy* (bilingual edition, translated by Ferial Ghazoul and John Verlenden), Abdul Wahab Al-Bayati's *Love, Death & Exile* (bilingual edition, translated by Bassam K. Frangieh), and any volume of poems by Adonis.

Drama is the least-represented genre among works of Arabic literature available in English translation. Works by Tewfiq al-Hakim (*The Tree Climber*), Saddallah Wannous (*The King's the King*), Ali Salim (*The Comedy of Oedipus*), and Abd al-Sabur (*Night Traveler*), either found in the aforementioned anthologies or in individual volumes, certainly would broaden the scope of any course in Modern drama.

As mentioned above, over the past several decades there has been a growing interest in literature by Arab women writers. Courses could be developed that concentrate exclusively on Arab women writers, or works could be incorporated into existing courses in women's studies or twentieth-century women's writing. One good resource for such a course is *Arab Women Writers: An Anthology of Short Stories,* edited by Dalya Cohen-Mor and published by SUNY Press in 2005; another is *Opening the Gates: A Century of Arab Feminist Writing,* edited by Margot Badran and Miriam Cooke. The latter volume pulls together and contextualizes a wide variety of material (autobiographical, polemical, historical, fictional) related to women's issues in the modern Arab world. Among those exceedingly accomplished contemporary Arab women writers whose works have been translated into English and might be incorporated into classes are Alifa Rifaat (Egypt), Nawal al-Sadaawi (Egypt), Ghada Samman (Syria/Lebanon), Hanan al-Shaykh (Lebanon), Sahar Khalifa (Palestine), Ulfaat al-Idilbi (Syria), Liana Badr (Palestine/Lebanon), and Salwa Bakr (Egypt).

The teaching of literary works translated from Arabic can also be woven into interdisciplinary (or even discipline-specific) courses on the Middle East that incorporate examinations of music, architecture, religion, history, and other aspects of Middle Eastern culture. (Any of the *Cairo* trilogy novels, for instance, could be productively used in a modern Middle East history course.) Various comparative treatments of Arabic literature can also be rich, such as comparisons between Arabic and Asian or Latin American literary traditions. In addition, Arabic literature could certainly be taught comparatively with Israeli literature, including novels, short stories, and poems by a wide range of writers such as A. B. Yehoshua, Naguib Mahfouz, Adonis, Yehuda Amichai, Aharon Shabtai, Etgar Keret, Ghassan Khanifani, Yehudid Katzir, Hanan al-Shaykh, Savyon Liebrecht, Fadia Faqir, and others.

There is perhaps no better way to become acquainted with a people and its culture (short of extended sojourns in those places we wish to know better) than through its literary and artistic production. The Arab world, stretching from Morocco to Iraq, has a rich and diverse literary heritage—a good deal of which, as demonstrated here, is available in English translation. Recent tragic and ill-fated historical events in the Middle East may be pushing Arabic literature from the margins toward the center. As unfortunate as the reasons are, the attention itself is both long overdue and welcome.

NOTES

I would like to thank my colleague Mohammed Albakry for his insightful comments on an earlier draft of this paper, which I liberally drew from in my revisions. I am also grateful to Maysa Hayward, Maggie Nassif, Michelle Hartman, Marilyn Booth, Michael Beard, and Aida Bamia for conversations and communications that have flowed into this paper.

1. See also "Contemporary Syrian Literature," edited by Allen Hibbard and Osama Isber, special issue of *Cimarron Review* (July 1994), featuring works by Mohammad al-Maghut, Nizar Kabbani, Mahud as-Sayed, Abdel Salam al-Ujayli, Zakariyya Tamer, and Ibrahim Samuel.

2. There are no coordinated, efficient publishing distribution mechanisms spanning Arab countries (much less within particular countries), so material tends to circulate sporadically, often transported in travelers' suitcases across sometimes impermeable borders.

3. E-mail correspondence, Mohammed Albakry to Allen Hibbard, December 30, 2006.

4. Introduction, *Thieves in Retirement* (Syracuse, NY: Syracuse University Press, 2006), xv.

5. For a treatment of traditional genres, see Roger Allen, *The Arabic Literary Heritage: The Development of Its Genres and Criticism* (Cambridge, UK: Cambridge University Press, 1998). Albert Hourani's *History of the Arab Peoples* (New York: Warner, 1992) provides historical background, as does Ira Lapidus's *A History of Islamic Societies* (Cambridge, UK: Cambridge University Press, 2002). Fazlur Rahman's *Major Themes of the Qur'an* (Minneapolis: Bibliotheca Islamic, 1994) is a good source for basic principles of Islam.

6. E-mail correspondence, Marilyn Booth to Allen Hibbard, December 21, 2006.

7. For a comprehensive listing of works of Arabic literature available in English translation, see Salih J. Altoma's *Modern Arabic Literature in Translation: A Companion* (London: Saqi, 2005).

8. For a relevant discussion of *Miramar*, Wagi Ghali's *Beer in the Snooker Club*, and Gamal al-Ghitani's *Zayni Barakat*, see my essay "Cultural Upheaval and Fictional Form: Three Novelistic Responses to Nasser's Egypt," in *Liminal Postmodernisms:*

The Postmodern, the (Post-)Colonial, and the (Post-)Feminist, eds. Theo D'haen and Hans Bertens (Amsterdam: Rodopi, 1994), 317–27.

9. See Waïl S. Hassan, *Tayeb Salih: Ideology and the Craft of Fiction* (Syracuse, NY: Syracuse University Press, 2003) for a thorough critical treatment of the novel.

10. Adonis, "Neffari," in *Pages of Day and Night,* trans. Samuel Hazo (Evanston, IL: Northwestern University Press, 2000), 88.

11. Adonis's *An Introduction to Arab Poetics,* trans. Catherine Cobham (Austin: University of Texas Press, 1990) contains the poet's essential thoughts on Arab poetry, tradition, religion, and modernity, as does his untranslated dissertation *"al-Thabit wa al-mutahawwil: bahth fi al-ibda' wa al-ittiba' 'inda al-'Arab"* ("The static and the changing: a study of creativity and conformity among the Arabs").

12. "The Time," trans. Allen Hibbard and Osama Isber, *Grand Street* 59 (1996): 166–73.

13. "A Desire Moving through the Maps of the Material," trans. Allen Hibbard and Osama Isber, *Sulfur* 39 (1996): 75–102.

14. See *The Pages of Day and Night,* trans. Mirène Ghossein, Kamal Boullata, and Samuel Hazo (Marlboro, VT: Marlboro Press, 1994; reprint, Evanston, IL: Marlboro Press/Northwestern University Press, 2000); *A Time Between Ashes and Roses,* bilingual edition, trans. Shawkat M. Toorawa (Syracuse, NY: Syracuse University Press, 2004); *If Only the Sea Could Sleep: Love Poems,* translated by Kamal Boullata, Susan Einbinder, and Mirène Ghossein (Copenhagen and Los Angeles: Green Integer, 2003); and *Mihyar of Damascus: His Songs,* translated by Adnan Haydar and Michael Beard (Rochester, NY: BOA Editions, 2008). A forthcoming volume of Khaled Mattawa's translations of Adonis's poetry (Yale University Press) will provide a much-needed comprehensive selection of his work.

15. Serageldin's novel was written originally in English and thus belongs to an interesting subcategory of works by Anglophone Arab writers, which includes Wagi Ghali's *Beer in the Snooker Club,* Ramzi Salti's *The Native Informant: Six Tales of Defiance from the Arab World,* Adhaf Soueif's *Maps of Love,* and Laila Leilami's *Hope and Other Dangerous Pursuits,* a wonderful novel about a handful of Moroccans who have sought to cross the Straits of Gibraltar for a better life in Europe. Other related subcategories include works by Arab writers in Hebrew (e.g., Anton Shammas's *Arabesques* and Sayed Kashua's *Let It Be Morning*) and the very rich and extensive tradition of Arab francophone literature, primarily by North African writers (e.g., Tahar ben Jelloun and Assia Djebar).

WORKS CITED

Altoma, Salih J. *Modern Arabic Literature in Translation: A Companion.* London: Saqi, 2005.

Faiq, Said, ed. *Cultural Encounters in Translation from Arabic.* Clevedon, UK: Multilingual Matters Ltd., 2004.

Johnson-Davies, Denys. "On Translating Arabic Literature." In *The View from Within,* edited by Ferial J. Ghazoul and Barbara Harlow, 272–82. Cairo: American University of Cairo Press, 1994.

Ormsby, Eric. "Of Strangled Bells." *Times Literary Supplement,* April 14, 2006, 13.

Rifaat, Alifa. *Distant View of a Minaret and Other Stories.* Translated by Denys Johnson-Davies. London: Heinemann, 1985.

Said, Edward W. "Embargoed Literature." *The Nation,* September 17, 1990, 278–80.

———. "Foreword." In *Little Mountain,* by Elias Khoury, ix–xxi. Translated by Maia Tabet. Minneapolis: University of Minnesota Press, 1989.

Salih, Tayeb. *Season of Migration to the North.* Translated by Denys Johnson-Davies. London: Quartet, 1980.

Hebrew Poetry, Ancient and Contemporary, in Translation

Chana Bloch

The linguistic and cultural barriers that separate any two languages are palpable to the translator who works her way across them, although more often than not they are invisible to the reader who picks up a poem in translation, comfortably ensconced on his side of the border. But when the languages in question differ as fundamentally as Hebrew and English, the roadblocks and checkpoints must be identified if the reader is to experience the poem in all its demanding particularity.

Hebrew is an ancient language, and its historical strata are transparent to an educated speaker; thus, allusion and intertextuality are a common form of shorthand in conversation, and even more so in written texts. The earliest examples of this practice are found in the Hebrew Bible, an anthology of narratives, poetry, wisdom literature, law, prophecy, and apocalypse spanning a millennium, from the archaic Song of Deborah (ca. 1200 BC) to the book of Daniel (ca. 165 BC). The author of the Song of Songs, for example, is in dialogue with Genesis, the prophets, and the book of Psalms. The contemporary Hebrew poet Yehuda Amichai (1924–2000) is able to draw upon the whole history of the language—biblical, rabbinic, medieval, and modern—alluding to texts from earlier periods without any sense of strain and relying on his audience to recognize the allusions.

It is customary to speak about the "revival" of Hebrew at the end of the nineteenth century. In fact, even when the language ceased to be spoken, it continued to live as a medium of textual exchange, and its historical layers were accessible in the daily life of Jewish males. Thus, when Hebrew once again became a spoken language, even the simplest words remained charged with ancient, often sacred meanings. A common term like *davar,* which means "word" or "thing," can also refer to a prophetic vision; *makom,* "place," and *shem*, "name," are familiar designations for God. The theological connotations of biblical and rabbinic language are present everywhere in Amichai's poetry, often serving as grist for his irony.

Hebrew verbs and nouns are typically based on triconsonantal roots that embody some general idea. The root can generate a multiplicity of related meanings, a fertile source of nuances and associations that has no semantic equivalent in English. For example, the root *chatza* means "to cut, divide, or cross a dividing line." Among the biblical nouns derived from *chatza* are *chetzi*, "half" (that which has been cut in two), and *chutz*, "outside" (implying the divide between inner and outer). In modern Hebrew *la-chatsot et ha-gvul* means "to cross the border," and *chutz la-aretz* means "abroad." The rabbinic term *mechitza* is the partition that separates men from women in an Orthodox synagogue; the plural form of that word, *mechitzot*, may occur in the modern Hebrew phrase "linguistic and cultural barriers" with which I began. The Hebrew language today is very fluid; like the English of Shakespeare's day, it is open to new coinages, portmanteaus, and all forms of wordplay. A reader of Hebrew needs no special expertise to divine the meaning of an unknown word, because it is usually based on a familiar root, whereas a reader of English might have to call upon a knowledge of Latin or to look up the word's etymology.

Verbs and nouns in Hebrew are either masculine or feminine in form (there is no neuter); gender is readily apparent, and it exerts an insistent pressure. Hence the fact that the woman has most of the lines in the Song of Songs—remarkable indeed in a book of the Bible!—is much more obvious in Hebrew than in an English translation. When the lovers address one another, there is no doubt in the Hebrew about who is speaking to whom, because masculine and feminine are differentiated in the second person. (Some English translations resort to such devices as "The Shulamite Speaks," "The Bridegroom Speaks"; in the translation I did with Ariel Bloch, we used different typefaces—roman type for the man and italics for the woman.) Gendered nouns lend themselves easily to personification. For example, the common word for "moon" in biblical and modern Hebrew is the masculine *yare'ach*, from *yerach*, "month," while the poetic word, found most often in rabbinic texts, is the feminine *levana*, from *lavan*, "white." *Yare'ach* is often personified in Hebrew poetry as a man and *levana* as a woman.

A synthetic language, Hebrew does a lot of its semantic work with prefixes and suffixes rather than discrete lexemes. The compact phrase *bati le-gani*,

for example, requires six words in English: "I-have-come into-my-garden."
In Song of Songs 5:1, the quick succession of one-word verbs that follow the
same pattern—*bati, 'ariti, 'akhalti, shatiti* (I have come, I have gathered,
I have eaten, I have drunk)—reinforces the effect of energetic action. The
sinewy concision of biblical Hebrew, most pronounced in the poetic books
and a special delight in the Song, is often the first casualty in a translation.

The reader of a biblical text needs to know something about the vagaries
of transmission and the history of interpretation and translation. The Song
of Songs, which celebrates the sexual awakening of a young unmarried
woman and her lover, is the only love poem that has survived from ancient
Israel. Some of the individual lyrics of the Song may have circulated orally
for centuries, but judging from linguistic clues, the Song in its present form
appears to have been written down in the third century BC. The Hebrew
text that was copied by scribes for century after century had no chapter and
verse divisions, no vowels, no capital letters, no system of punctuation, no
line breaks for poetry, and in many ancient manuscripts, no spaces between
words. It is not hard to appreciate the potential for ambiguity: in English, for
example, "Godisnowhere" may mean "God is now here" or "God is nowhere."
Although a scribe would certainly have been vigilant in copying the sacred text,
he might inadvertently omit or repeat a letter or a word, misread one letter
as another, separate words incorrectly, or change the word order. During the
sixth through the tenth centuries AD, scholars known as the Masoretes ("Tra-
ditionalists") established an authoritative text, adding vowel signs—diacritical
marks above and below the consonants—to record the pronunciation as it
was handed down in the liturgical tradition. We have no way of knowing how
closely the Masoretic Text reflects the pronunciation of the original; vowel
lengths and syllabic stresses would be of particular significance in a poetic
text, especially because biblical poetic meter, as Benjamin Harshav has shown,
depends on syntactically natural stress patterns (typically a 3/3 line) and not
a superimposed metrical scheme.

The language of the Song is often obscure, with an unusually high propor-
tion of *hapax legomena* (words occurring only once) and an abundance of
rare words and constructions. Because the biblical corpus is small and there
is very little extrabiblical material available for comparison, the translator-as-
interpreter must look to the immediate context for clues, but even where these
are to be found, it is hard to establish the meaning of a *hapax*. Thus, a line
like "your *shelachim* [branches?] are an orchard" (4:13) must finally remain a

mystery. The parallelism of verses that characterizes most biblical poetry—in which one verset is echoed, inverted, or elaborated in the next—can be an aid to interpretation, but not when there is no parallel verse to offer a clue.

The Bible has been disseminated by means of translation, which has frequently resulted in ideological distortion. Because Bible translations have been instrumental in shaping our culture, this is hardly an academic matter. Let me offer two telling examples. In the opening chapter of Genesis, we read in the King James Version (KJV, 1611): "And God said, Let us make man in our image" (1:26). Together with the creation story in the second chapter of Genesis, this has been taken to assert the primacy of man over woman. Today it is commonly accepted that the word *'adam* is a generic term for human beings; many contemporary versions translate this word as "a human" or "humankind." Another example, no less momentous: the Hebrew of Isaiah 7:14 literally means "A young woman (*'almah*) is pregnant, and she will give birth to a son, and will call him Immanuel." In the Septuagint, the Greek version of the Hebrew Bible (250–100 BC), *'almah* is translated as *parthenos*, which can mean either "young unmarried woman" or "virgin"; the Latin Vulgate of St. Jerome (ca. 400 AD) has *virgo*; the KJV and most English translations before our own day have "virgin." Thus, by virtue of a semantic choice, a verse where Isaiah offers reassurance to King Ahaz in a particular historical situation becomes a prooftext about Jesus's divine origin. One could hardly find a better example of the impact of translation on human history.

The word *'almah* is found in 1:3 and 6:8 of the Song, and here too it does not mean "virgin," as the KJV would have it. Advances in biblical scholarship during the past four centuries have shown that many of the other readings of the KJV are in error as well, including some of the best-known verses, such as "Stay me with flagons, comfort me with apples" (2:5) or "terrible as an army with banners" (6:10). And its language is often dated, such as "I am sick of love" (2:5) or the unfortunate "My beloved put in his hand by the hole of the door, and my bowels were moved for him." The Song of Songs in the KJV is beloved for its rich textures and resounding cadences, but its formal, stately music—conceived for liturgical purposes and somewhat archaic even in the seventeenth century—does not convey the heat, the speed, the erotic intensity of the original. One would hardly know that this is a poem about young lovers.

In the Song, the young man often praises the Shulamite as an "enclosed garden" of earthly delights, an image that inevitably calls to mind the Eden of Adam and Eve, the first human couple:

Your branches are an orchard
of pomegranate trees heavy with fruit,
flowering henna and spikenard,
spikenard and saffron, cane and cinnamon,
with every tree of frankincense,
myrrh and aloes,
all the rare spices. (4:12–14)

In 4:12, the word *pardes* (orchard), a Persian loan word in Hebrew, is the origin of our word "paradise." In the Song of Songs, the emblem of divine perfection is embodied in a woman. The garden of the Song, with its abundance and variety, its textures and scents, its enticing ripeness, is by no means a spiritual site, as it was to become in the allegorical tradition, but rather the setting for distinctly physical pleasures. (The word *eden* in Hebrew means "sensual delight.")

The dialogue that comes after these verses about the garden highlights some of the distinctive features of the Song—the surprising boldness of the young woman, the reciprocity of the lovers' discourse, and the sexual freedom they celebrate:

Awake, north wind; O south wind, come,
breathe upon my garden,
let its spices stream out.
Let my lover come into his garden
and taste its delicious fruit.

I have come into my garden,
my sister, my bride,
I have gathered my myrrh and my spices,
I have eaten from the honeycomb,
I have drunk the milk and the wine.

Feast, friends, and drink
till you are drunk with love! (4:16–5:1)

The Shulamite's summons to the winds makes it clear that she is no ordinary woman. Elsewhere in the Bible it is God who commands the elements, his control of nature attesting to his power as Creator (Ps. 147:8, Jer. 10:13) and his role in history—ending the Deluge, parting the Red Sea, providing food in the desert (Gen. 8:1, Exod. 14:21, Num. 11:31). The Shulamite's forceful commands are followed by an invitation as restrained and delicate as it is voluptuous: "Let my lover come into his garden / and taste its delicious fruit" (4:16). This passage is characteristic both in what it so clearly suggests and what it leaves unexpressed. The subtlety and delicacy of her erotic language is possible not only because she speaks metaphorically, but also because her metaphors derive their evocative power from the story of Eden.

The young man's exultant reply makes it clear that their love has already been consummated. The verb "to come into" often has a patently sexual meaning in biblical Hebrew, and the metaphors of feasting suggest fulfillment. Furthermore, the perfective aspect of the verbs *bati, ariti, akhalti,* and *shatiti* (I have come, I have gathered, I have eaten, I have drunk) signifies a completed action—a grammatical fact that many translators and exegetes have chosen to ignore. (The KJV translates this correctly.) This lyric concludes with the young man's address to a group of friends. Some scholars believe that 5:1 may have originated in a drinking song; in any case, it is a convincingly masculine expression of exuberance.

Many readers have seen in the Song of Songs a response to the Genesis story of paradise lost: instead of God's prohibition on eating the fruit, there is the woman's invitation; instead of a punishment for the act of eating, there is joyous celebration. But the Shulamite's body is not only the Garden of Eden. The honey and milk that are "under [her] tongue" (4:11) recall a familiar epithet for the Promised Land, "flowing with milk and honey." Thus, her body is identified with the two major biblical sites for bounty and fulfillment in primeval and national history.

If one were to read this book apart from its biblical context, one might surmise that women had great sexual freedom in ancient Israel and that equality of the sexes was the norm. In fact, the Bible was written for the most part from a male point of view, and women are by definition the second sex. History is traced through the line of the fathers, as in the priestly genealogies ("And Enoch begat Methuselah"); the typical formulas for sexual relations ("he knew her," "he came in unto her," "he lay with her") make the women characters seem passive and acted upon. In the Song, however, where the lovers take turns inviting one another, desire is entirely reciprocal. Both are described in images that suggest tenderness (lilies, doves, and gazelles) as well as strength and stateliness (pillars and towers). In this book of the Bible, the woman is clearly the equal of the man.

What's more, the young lovers are unmarried. Now, sex is no sin in the Hebrew Bible. But because its purpose is procreation, sex is sanctioned only in marriage; on this point the Old Testament laws are unequivocal. Outside the pale of marriage there are only sexual crimes and their punishments, catalogued in exhaustive detail. There are some intimations in the Song of the barriers that exist in the real world: the young man appears "on the other side / of our wall" (2:9); the "watchmen of the walls" brutally beat the Shulamite (5:7); her brothers exhort her to be a "wall" and not a "door" (8:9). But the two young lovers fulfill their passion in the world of nature, a world that is confidently open, expansive, and free of societal constraints.

How did the Song, with its surprisingly powerful female voice and its un-abashed celebration of unmarried love, ever find its way into the Bible? The allegorical interpretation of the Song was probably a decisive factor for the rabbis who shaped the canon. While the Song was in all likelihood composed as a poem about erotic love, the rabbis read it as an allegory about the love of God and the people of Israel; this interpretation, along with the attribution to King Solomon in 1:1, helped it to survive the final cut of the canon-makers. The Church Fathers in turn read the Song as a dialogue between Christ and his Bride, the Church. Once it became part of the Holy Scriptures, the Song demanded exegesis befitting its holiness, and religious interpretations of one kind or another prevailed. Some of the more extravagant "findings" of the exegetes now seem very curious: the Shulamite's two breasts, for example, were said to signify Moses and Aaron or the Old and New Testaments.

Two millennia of translations and interpretations for the sake of propriety presented the young lovers as yearning for one another from a respectable distance, though such interpretations ignored the plain sense of the Hebrew. The translators and interpreters also toned down the spirited presence of the Shulamite, imagining her as a sweet young thing, chaste and demure and properly bridal. In most translations (the KJV is a notable exception), the young woman wears a veil, a reading not supported by the Hebrew. That incongruous veil, like the fig leaf of Renaissance painting and sculpture, is a sign of the discomfort of the exegetes. When we lift the veil from her face, the Shulamite is revealed as a passionate young woman, as active and assertive as Juliet. She is the one who teaches that love must not be roused carelessly:

Daughters of Jerusalem, swear to me now
by the gazelles, by the deer in the field,
that you will never awaken love
until it is ripe. (2:7, 3:5, 8:4)

And she is the one, finally, who pronounces the great truths about love:

For love is as fierce as death,
its jealousy bitter as the grave.
Even its sparks are a raging fire,
a devouring flame. (8:6)

In modern Hebrew poetry, the Song of Songs became the model for a boldly secular eroticism, explicitly challenging the allegorical interpretations. The work of Yehuda Amichai, acclaimed as Israel's national poet, is a notable example. Among the most widely read poets in the canon of contemporary poetry, Amichai is considered one of the great poets of our time. His work has been translated into some thirty-seven languages, including Catalan, Estonian, Korean, Serbo-Croatian, and Vietnamese. Born in Germany in 1924, Amichai grew up in an Orthodox Jewish home. After Hitler's rise to power, his family emigrated to Palestine, and for most of his adult life he lived in the secular world of modern Israel. The tension between cultures—male and female, Orthodox and secular, Jewish and Arab—was always a fertile source of poetry for him.

Amichai's magnum opus, *Open Closed Open,* was composed in the last decade of his life; it was published in Hebrew in 1998 and in English translation shortly before his death in 2000. Like the Song of Songs, this book is a series of lyrics woven together by theme, language, and point of view rather than by a coherent, linear narrative, and it asks to be read as a single, unified work. And here too, as in the Song, women are the bearers of a special wisdom about love.

In a particularly telling example, Amichai writes that he learned about love in the Orthodox synagogue of his childhood, with its strict separation of the sexes and subordination of women, by studying the women "on the other side" of the partition (*mechitza*):

I studied love in my childhood in my childhood synagogue
in the women's section with the help of the women behind the partition

that locked up my mother with all the other women and girls.
But the partition that locked them up locked me up
on the other side. They were free in their love while I remained
locked up with all the men and boys in my love, my longing.
I wanted to be there with them and to know their secrets
and say with them, "Blessed be He who has made me
according to his will." And the partition—
a lace curtain white and soft as summer dresses, swaying
on its rings and loops of wish and would,
lu-lu loops, lullings of love in the locked room.
And the faces of women like the face of the moon behind the clouds
or the full moon when the curtain parts: an enchanted
cosmic order. At night we said the blessing
over the moon outside, and I
thought about the women.

Amichai is known as a love poet, so it is not at all surprising that there are
frequent allusions to the Song in his work. Certainly the image of the women's
faces as "an enchanted cosmic order" owes something to the hyperbolic
praise of the Shulamite:

Who is that rising like the morning star,
clear as the moon,
bright as the blazing sun,
daunting as the stars in their courses!

Amichai chooses *levanah,* the feminine word for "moon" in Song 6:10, rather
than the masculine *yare'ach,* not only for the sake of the personification but
also because it is the word used in the rabbinic blessing on the moon (*birkat
ha-levanah*). That blessing is recited outdoors between the third and fourteenth days of the lunar month, from the time when the crescent moon is first
visible until mid-month, when the moon is full. "Outside" (*chutz,* from the
root *chatza*) in line 16 refers not only to the location of the moon but also to
that of the worshippers, who leave behind the walls of the synagogue with its
established male hierarchy—symbolized by the *mechitza*—and go out into the
world of nature with its female moon. This is one of the rare occasions indeed
on which an Orthodox Jew may be said to commune with nature.

"I Studied Love" is part of a sequence called "Gods Change, Prayers Are Here to Stay," in which Amichai boldly takes the measure of the Orthodox Jewish practices he grew up with. As I have suggested, some knowledge of Jewish liturgy is necessary for an informed reading of this poem. Particularly crucial is the blessing in lines eight and nine, "Blessed be He who has made me according to His will," which is part of the morning prayers recited by women. A reader who does not know this will probably find the lines unambiguously pious, not recognizing just how iconoclastic they are—first, because Amichai wishes to say the woman's blessing instead of the man's, and second, because the man's blessing happens to be "Blessed be He who has not made me a woman." In our notes to the poem, Chana Kronfeld and I quote the man's blessing, though we are aware that a footnote cannot begin to express how information of this kind can radically alter the reading of a poem. More often than not, a note points to a problem rather than resolving it. It signals to the reader: "The following bit of culture-stuff, which we will now define in a few words, is something that cannot be defined in a few words."

A translation should provide annotations for cultural references that are not common knowledge. In "opening" what may be "closed" to the reader of English, we identify references to the Bible (most often the Psalms and Ecclesiastes, as well as figures from the historical narratives like Balaam, Korah, Gideon, and King David, and the prophets Isaiah, Jeremiah, and Ezekiel), Jewish liturgy (Sabbath hymns, prayers for the Day of Atonement, weddings, and funerals), ceremonial objects (prayer shawls, spice boxes, Torah pointers, Seder plates), and Jewish and Israeli history. It would take far more than a note, to be sure, to describe the vexed position of women in a society where the male-dominated military and the Orthodox rabbinate hold sway. Yet such information is essential if the reader is to understand the young boy's transgressive wish and the mature poet's critique of Israeli machismo.

The most salient aspects of Amichai's poetry are precisely those that resist translation: his linguistic and thematic dialogue with texts from all the historical layers of the Hebrew language. But his dialogue with the Bible, the Midrash, and the liturgy is only half the story. Amichai draws equally on vernacular Israeli culture: popular songs, Jewish jokes, nursery rhymes, doggerel, children's games, legal language, military slang. His poetry is noted for its playfulness and wit, and it moves easily from one register to another, often in the middle of a line or phrase.

All this presents a considerable challenge to the translator. In conveying biblical references, for example, one turns first to the KJV, counting on its heightened diction to alert the reader to the allusion. But biblical expressions that sound perfectly natural in colloquial Hebrew may seem stilted or academic in an English poem. A translator can suggest some of the semantic effects possible in Hebrew, for example by juxtaposing words of Germanic or Latinate origin, though it would be jarring to introduce a bit of Old English or Middle English into a twentieth-century poem that is colloquial in diction and rhythm. Moreover, the norms of English tend to resist rapid shifts in register, so a translation that attempts to reproduce every nuance of Amichai's complex and variegated Hebrew will very likely seem muddled.

The barrier between English and Hebrew poses more difficulties for a reader than that between English and a European language. Readers of Hebrew literature in translation can be assumed to have some knowledge of the Bible, one of the foundations of Western civilization, though probably less than an educated Israeli, who will have studied it in school. The KJV is an indispensable resource, given its influence on English literature, but the reader should compare it with contemporary translations such as the New Revised Standard Version. The reader should also consult some of the many linguistic and literary commentaries. Marvin Pope's commentary includes an comprehensive history of exegesis, and Ariel Bloch's presents the Hebrew of the Masoretic Text, a phonetic transliteration, a literal prose translation, and a detailed analysis of the verse. Robert Alter, in *The Art of Biblical Poetry* and other books, approaches the Bible from a literary rather than a theological or philological perspective. As for Amichai's poetry, readers of English in our day share a common culture, to a certain extent, with Hebrew writers. But for any depth of comprehension, they will need to have some familiarity with the Bible and liturgy, Jewish religious practices, the history of the Jewish people, and Israeli society. A good starting place would be the complete works of the poet—along with the daily newspaper.

The biblical Song of Songs and Yehuda Amichai's *Open Closed Open,* written more than two millennia apart, are nothing less than astonishing when read in the context of traditional Jewish culture, ancient and contemporary, in which women have been—and still are—accorded a subordinate role. It is not surprising to discover parallels between these works, because cultural attitudes toward women's place in society have evolved far less than one would have imagined. In the Song, the brothers who rebuke and threaten the Shulamite about her sexual behavior and the "watchmen of the walls" who assault her represent, in symbolic form, the social strictures that mark the woman as "other." In "I Studied Love," the partition in the Orthodox synagogue serves much the same function.

The evocative image of the partition lends itself to a variety of interpretations. Amichai's poem presents the specific tensions between Orthodox and secular, man and woman, and beyond that, the encompassing question of self and other. Some essential knowledge about "the other side" is "locked up" behind that partition, the poem tells us, and yet, with effort and imagination, it can be retrieved. The same is true of the knowledge of other ages, other cultures, that is locked up behind the barriers of language—knowledge that we need in order to be fully human and that we may grasp in the imaginative act of understanding called translation.

NOTE

Many of the formulations in this essay draw upon my collaborative work with Professor Chana Kronfeld of the Department of Comparative Literature, University of California, Berkeley. The essay as a whole benefitted immeasurably from her critical eye.

SELECTED BIBLIOGRAPHY

Alter, Robert. *The Art of Biblical Poetry.* New York: Basic Books, 1985.

———. *The Five Books of Moses: A Translation With Commentary.* New York: W.W. Norton, 2004.

———, and Frank Kermode, eds. *The Literary Guide to the Bible.* Cambridge, MA: Harvard University Press, 1987.

Amichai, Yehuda. *Open Closed Open.* Translated by Chana Bloch and Chana Kronfeld. New York: Harcourt, 2000.

———. *The Selected Poetry.* Translated by Chana Bloch and Stephen Mitchell. Berkeley: University of California Press, 1996.

Bloch, Chana, and Ariel Bloch. *The Song of Songs: A New Translation with an Introduction and Commentary.* New York: Modern Library Classic, 2006.

Bloch, Chana, and Chana Kronfeld. "On Translating Amichai's *Open Closed Open.*" *American Poetry Review* 29 (2000): 15–19.

————. "Amichai's Counter-Theology: Opening *Open Closed Open.*" *Judaism* 49 (2000): 153–67.

Fox, Michael. *The Song of Songs and Ancient Egyptian Love Songs.* Madison: University of Wisconsin Press, 1985.

Harshav (Hrushovski), Benjamin. "Prosody, Hebrew." In *Encyclopaedia Judaica,* 3:1200–1202. New York: Macmillan, 1971.

Kronfeld, Chana. "'The Wisdom of Camouflage': Between Rhetoric and Philosophy in Amichai's Poetic System." *Prooftexts* 10 (3): 469–91.

————. *On the Margins of Modernism: Decentering Literary Dynamics.* Berkeley: University of California Press, 1996.

The New Oxford Annotated Bible, New Revised Standard Version. Bruce M. Metzger and Roland E. Murphy, eds. New York: Oxford University Press, 1991.

Pope, Marvin H. "Song of Songs: A New Translation with Introduction and Commentary." *The Anchor Bible.* Vol. 7. Garden City, NY: Doubleday, 1977.

Seidman, Naomi. *Faithful Renderings: Jewish-Christian Difference and the Politics of Translation.* Chicago: University of Chicago Press, 2006.

Notes on Contributors

Tomoko Aoyama is senior lecturer in the School of Languages and Comparative Cultural Studies, University of Queensland. Her most recent publications include *Reading Food in Modern Japanese Literature* (University of Hawaii, 2008) and a special issue of *Asian Studies Review* (32, no. 3 [2008]) on "The Girl, the Body, and the Nation in Japan and the Pacific Rim," which she guest-edited. Her "Appropriating Bush Tucker: Food in Inoue Hisashi's *Yellow Rats*," *Journal of Australian Studies* 87 (2006), was awarded the inaugural Inoue Yasushi Award for Outstanding Research in Japanese Literature in Australia.

Rosemary Arrojo is professor of comparative literature at Binghamton University, where she directed the Translation Research and Instruction Program from 2003 to 2007 and helped implement the first Ph.D. in Translation Studies in the United States. Before that, she taught translation studies in Brazil for almost twenty years. Her work has focused on the interface between translation studies and contemporary thought (deconstruction, psychoanalysis, and postcolonial and gender studies). She has published extensively on the topic both in Portuguese and in English.

Brian James Baer is professor of Russian language, literature, and translation studies at Kent State University. He is founding editor of the journal *Translation and Interpreting Studies* and author of *Other Russias: Homosexuality and the Crisis of Post-Soviet Identity*. He is presently editing a volume on the role of literary translation in Eastern Europe and Russia.

PAUL F. BANDIA is professor of francophone and translation studies in the Department of French at Concordia University, Montréal, Canada. His interests lie in postcolonial theory, sociolinguistics, discourse analysis and pragmatics, cultural theory, and history. He has published widely in the fields of translation studies and postcolonial literatures and cultures. He is the author of *Translation as Reparation: Writing and Translation in Postcolonial Africa* (Manchester, UK: St. Jerome Publishing, 2008), coeditor of *Charting the Future of Translation History* (Ottawa: University of Ottawa Press, 2006), and coeditor of *Agents of Translation* (Amsterdam: John Benjamins, 2009).

CHANA BLOCH is a poet, translator, and literary critic. Her poetry collections are *The Secrets of the Tribe, The Past Keeps Changing, Mrs. Dumpty* (winner of the Felix Pollak Prize), and *Blood Honey* (winner of the Di Castagnola Award of the Poetry Society of America). She is cotranslator of the biblical *Song of Songs,* now a Modern Library Classic; *The Selected Poetry of Yehuda Amichai* and his *Open Closed Open* (winner of the PEN Award for Poetry in Translation); and *Hovering at a Low Altitude: The Collected Poetry of Dahlia Ravikovitch.* She also is the author of a critical study, *Spelling the Word: George Herbert and the Bible.* Among her awards are fellowships from the National Endowment for the Arts, the National Endowment for the Humanities, and the Rockefeller Foundation. Bloch is professor emerita of English literature at Mills College, where she taught for many years and directed the Creative Writing Program.

RONALD CHRIST taught English literature and classical rhetoric at Rutgers University. Currently he is the publisher of Lumen Books and does translations, especially of works from Latin America and Spain.

ISABEL GARAYTA is professor of English at the University of Puerto Rico at Cayey, where she has served as department chair and associate dean of academic affairs. She has taught translation theory and worked with colleagues to promote a better understanding of translation, help make teachers and students more informed and sophisticated readers of translations, and make translation more visible in the curriculum. In *Womanhandling the Text: Feminism, Rewriting and Translation,* she explored the the intersection of feminist theory and translation.

ALLEN HIBBARD received his B.A. in international studies from American University in Washington, DC, and his Ph.D. in English from the University of Washington. His teaching and research interests have been in the areas of twentieth-century American literature, literary theory, Middle Eastern literatures, and transnational and comparative literature. He taught at the American University of Cairo (1985–89) and at Damascus University as a Fulbright lecturer in American literature (1992–94). He is the author of *Paul Bowles: A Study of the Short Fiction* (Twayne, 1993), *Paul Bowles, Magic & Morocco* (Cadmus Editions, 2004), and *Crossing to Abbassiya and Other Stories* (in Arabic, Damascus: Dar al Mustaqbal, 1994). He also is the editor of *Conversations with William S. Burroughs* (University Press of Mississippi, 1999). His reviews, essays, stories, and translations have appeared in numerous journals, including *Partisan Review, The Review of Contemporary Fiction, The Centennial Review, Tennessee Folklore Society Bulletin, Grand Street, Edebiyat, Digest of Middle East Studies,* and *Middle East Studies Bulletin.* Among his current projects are a biography of Alfred Chester, a translation (with Osama Isber) of *A Banquet for Seaweed* by Syrian novelist Haidar Haidar, and a volume on the great modern poet Adonis (University of California Press). Presently he is professor of English and Director of the Middle East Center at Middle Tennessee State University.

YUNTE HUANG is professor of English at the University of California, Santa Barbara. He is the author of *Shi* (1997), *Transpacific Displacement* (2002), *Cribs* (2005), and *Transpacific Imaginations* (2008). He is also the translator into Chinese of Ezra Pound's *Pisan Cantos.*

NIELS INGWERSEN was a native of Denmark and taught at the University of Wisconsin–Madison from 1965 (and as Torger Thompson Professor since 1999) until his death in 2009. He wrote extensively on Scandinavian literature, Scandinavian folklore, and on literary criticism; served as coeditor of the journal *Scandinavian Studies;* and taught a distance-learning television course on the tales of Hans Christian Andersen. His *The Scandinavian Magic Tale and Narrative Folklore* was published in 2008.

CAROL MAIER is professor of Spanish at Kent State University, where she is affiliated with the Institute for Applied Linguistics and the NEOMFA program in creative writing. Her research interests include translation

theory, practice, and pedagogy. Among her current projects are transla-
tions of work by Octavio Armand, Rosa Chacel, and Nuria Amat. Her most
recent publications are translations of Severo Sarduy's *Beach Birds* (with
Suzanne Jill Levine) and Nivaria Tejera's *The Ravine*. Her translation of
Rosa Chacel's *Dream of Reason* was published in 2009 by the University of
Nebraska Press.

FRANÇOISE MASSARDIER-KENNEY is professor of French and director of
the Institute for Applied Linguistics at Kent State University. She is the editor
of the American Translators Association Scholarly Series and coeditor of the
journal *George Sand Studies*. Her publications include *Gender in the Fiction
of George Sand* (2001) and translations of Sand's *Valvèdre* (2007), Antoine
Berman's *Toward a Translation Criticism: John Donne (2009)*, and *Translating
Slavery* (vols. 1 and 2), both of which she coedited with Doris Y. Kadish.

CHRISTI A. MERRILL is associate professor of South Asian literature and
postcolonial studies at the University of Michigan. Her translations from
Hindi, French, and Rajasthani and her essays on translation have appeared
in journals such as *Genre, Studies in Twentieth Century Literature, The Iowa
Review, Modern Poetry in Translation, Parabola, Poetry Review, Exchanges: A
Journal of Translation*, and *Indian Literature: Sahitya Akademi's Bimonthly
Journal*. In addition to translating a collection of Vijay Dan Detha's stories, she
is the author of a book on the theory and practice of translation, titled *Riddles
of Belonging: India in Translation and Other Tales of Possession (2009)*.

KATHLEEN ROSS, formerly a member of the faculty at New York University,
is now a psychotherapist practicing in Philadelphia. She is the translator of
numerous works of Spanish American literature, including D. F. Sarmiento's
Facundo: Civilization and Barbarism (University of California Press, 2003)
and Jesús Díaz's *The Initials of the Earth* (Duke University Press, 2006).

SERGIO WAISMAN is associate professor of Spanish at George Washington
University. He received his Ph.D. from the University of California, Berkeley,
and an M.A. in creative writing from the University of Colorado at Boulder.
He is the author of the novel *Leaving* and of *Borges and Translation: The
Irreverence of the Periphery*. He has translated six books of Latin American
literature, including *The Absent City* by Ricardo Piglia, for which he received

an NEA Translation Fellowship Award in 2000. Sergio Waisman's most recent translation is *The Underdogs: A Novel of the Mexican Revolution*, published by Penguin Classics in 2008.

JUDY WAKABAYASHI is professor of Japanese translation at Kent State University. She is a coeditor, with Eva Hung, of *Asian Translation Traditions* (St. Jerome Publishing, 2005), and with Rita Kothari, of *Decentering Translation Studies: India and Beyond* (John Benjamins, 2009) and the co-organizer of a series of conferences on Asian translation traditions. She has published extensively on translation theory, history, and pedagogy, particularly in the Japanese context, and she has translated seven nonfiction books in the sciences and religious studies. Current projects include a history of translation in Japan.

KELLY WASHBOURNE is a translator from Spanish and Portuguese, and he teaches Spanish translation at Kent State University. His translation publications include the Brazilian epic poem "Cobra Norato" by Raul Bopp in *Brasil/Brazil,* short fiction by the late Cuban exile Antonio Benítez-Rojo in *The Literary Review,* and *An Anthology of Spanish American Modernismo* for the Modern Language Associaton's Texts and Translation series. He is currently translating the short fiction of Miguel Angel Asturias and a collection of poetry of resistance from the Americas. His *Manual of Spanish-English Translation,* a translator training textbook, was published in 2009 with Prentice-Hall.

MICHELLE YEH is professor of Chinese literature at the University of California, Davis. Her research interests include Chinese poetry, comparative poetics, and modernism. Among her major publications are: *Modern Chinese Poetry: Theory and Practice Since 1917; Anthology of Modern Chinese Poetry; No Trace of the Gardener: Poems of Yang Mu; Frontier Taiwan: An Anthology of Modern Chinese Poetry;* and several collections of critical essays in Chinese.

Index

Fictional characters alphabetized by first name.